D0084635

The 1984
Olympic Scientific
Congress
Proceedings
Volume 3

# Sport
# and
# Elite
# Performers

## Series Editors:

Jan Broekhoff, PhD
Michael J. Ellis, PhD
Dan G. Tripps, PhD

*University of Oregon*
*Eugene, Oregon*

The 1984
Olympic Scientific
Congress
Proceedings
Volume 3

# Sport and Elite Performers

Daniel M. Landers
Editor

Human Kinetics Publishers, Inc.
Champaign, Illinois

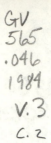

**Library of Congress Cataloging-in-Publication Data**

Olympic Scientific Congress (1984 : Eugene, Or.)
    Sport and elite performers.

(1984 Olympic Scientific Congress proceedings; v.3)
Bibliography: p.
1. Sports--Psychological aspects--Congresses.
2. Sports--Physiological aspects--Congresses. 3.
Physical education and training--Congresses. I.
Landers, Daniel M., 1942-        . II. Title. III.
Series: Olympic Scientific Congress (1984: Eugene,
Or.). 1984 Olympic Scientific Congress proceed-
ings; v.3.
GV565.046    1984 vol. 3    796 s      85-18115
[GV706.4]      [796'.01]
ISBN 0-87322-015-3

Managing Editor: Susan Wilmoth, PhD
Developmental Editor: Gwen Steigelman, PhD
Production Director: Sara Chilton
Copy Editor: Kristen LaDuke-Gallup
Typesetter: Theresa Bear
Text Layout: Cyndy Barnes
Cover Design and Layout: Jack Davis
Printed By: Braun-Brumfield, Inc.

ISBN: 0-87322-006-4   (10 Volume Set)
ISBN: 0-87322-015-3

Copyright © 1986 by Human Kinetics Publishers, Inc.

All rights reserved. Except for use in review, the reproduction
or utilization of this work in any form or by any electronic,
mechanical, or other means, now known or hereafter invented, including
xerography, photocopying and recording, and in any information retrieval
system, is forbidden without the written permission of the publisher.

Printed in the United States of America

10  9  8  7  6  5  4  3  2  1

Human Kinetics Publishers, Inc.
Box 5076, Champaign, IL 61820

# Contents

629413

# Series Acknowledgments

The Congress organizers realize that an event as large and complex as the 1984 Olympic Scientific Congress could not have come to fruition without the help of literally hundreds of organizations and individuals. Under the patronage of UNESCO, the Congress united in sponsorship and cooperation no fewer than 64 national and international associations and organizations. Some 50 representatives of associations helped with the organization of the scientific and associative programs by coordinating individual sessions. The cities of Eugene and Springfield yielded more than 400 volunteers who donated their time to make certain that the multitude of Congress functions would progress without major mishaps. To all these organizations and individuals, the organizers express their gratitude.

A special word of thanks must also be directed to the major sponsors of the Congress: the International Council of Sport Science and Physical Education (ICSSPE), the United States Olympic Committee (USOC), the International Council on Health, Physical Education and Recreation (ICHPER), and the American Alliance for Health, Physical Education, Recreation and Dance (AAHPERD). Last but not least, the organizers wish to acknowledge the invaluable assistance of the International Olympic Committee (IOC) and its president, Honorable Juan Antonio Samaranch. President Samaranch made Congress history by his official opening address in Eugene on July 19, 1984. The IOC durther helped the Congress with a generous donation toward the publication of the Congress papers. Without this donation it would have been impossible to make the proceedings available in this form.

Finally, the series editors wish to express their thanks to the volume editors who selected and edited the papers from each program of the Congress. Special thanks go to Caroline G. Shell of The University of Oregon for her work on this volume.

Jan Broekhoff,
Michael J. Ellis, and
Dan G. Tripps

Series Editors

# Series Preface

*Sport and Elite Performers* contains selected proceedings from this inter-disciplinary program of the 1984 Olympic Scientific Congress, which was held at the University of Oregon in Eugene, Oregon, preceding the Olympic Games in Los Angeles. The Congress was organized by the College of Human Development and Performance of the University of Oregon in collaboration with the cities of Eugene and Springfield. This was the first time in the history of the Congress that the event was organized by a group of private individuals, unaided by a federal government. The fact that the Congress was attended by more than 2,200 participants from more than 100 different nations is but one indication of its success.

The Congress program focused on the theme of Sport, Health, and Well-Being and was organized in three parts. The mornings of the eight-day event were devoted to disciplinary sessions, which brought together specialists in various subdisciplines of sport science such as sport medicine, biomechanics, sport psychology, sport sociology, and sport philosophy. For the first time in the Congress' history, these disciplinary sessions were sponsored by the national and international organizations representing the various subdisciplines. In the afternoons, the emphasis shifted toward interdisciplinary themes in which scholars and researchers from the subdisciplines attempted to contribute to crossdisciplinary understanding. In addition, three evenings were devoted to keynote addresses and presentations, broadly related to the theme of Sport, Health, and Well-Being.

In addition to the scientific programs, the Congress also featured a number of associative programs with topics determined by their sponsoring organizations. Well over 1,200 papers were presented in the various sessions of the Congress at large. It stands to reason, therefore, that publishing the proceedings of the event presented a major problem to the organizers. It was decided to limit proceedings initially to interdisciplinary sessions which drew substantial interest from Congress participants and attracted a critical number of high-quality presentations. Human Kinetics Publishers, Inc. of Champaign, Illinois, was selected to produce these proceedings. After considerable deliberation, the following interdisciplinary themes were selected for publication: Competitive Sport for Children and Youths; Human Genetics and Sport; Sport and Aging; Sport and Disabled Individuals; Sport and Elite Performers; Sport, Health, and Nutrition; and Sport and Politics. The 10-volume set published by Human Kinetics Publishers is rounded out by the disciplinary proceedings of Kinanthropometry, Sport Pedagogy, and the associative program on the Scientific Aspects of Dance.

Jan Broekhoff,
Michael J. Ellis, and
Dan G. Tripps

Series Editors

# *Preface*

Mention the words *Olympic Games* and images of elite athletes and elite performances come to mind. These athletes, their successes and failures, and their efforts and perseverance are what the Olympics are all about. For this reason, it is especially relevant that the 1984 Olympic Scientific Congress features sport and elite athletes as one of its themes.

Athletes are seldom alone, however, in their quest for better performance. Coaches, trainers, managers, and sport scientists contribute greatly in the continuous improvement of elite performances. Sport scientists are instrumental in the preparation and development phases because they provide elite athletes with pertinent information concerning techniques, training, and psychological preparation. These exercise physiologists, biomechanists, and sport psychologists are actively engaged in research that probes the physical, mechanical, and emotional characteristics symbolic of elite performers and performances. The results of such research comprise the contents of this volume of the 1984 Olympic Scientific Congress proceedings.

The 20 chapters of this volume were selected from the 50 papers presented at the Congress. The chapters include research conducted on a wide array of sportsmen and sportswomen, including runners, speedskaters, ice hockey players, squash players, rowers, gymnasts, and pistol shooters. In chapter 1, Alain, Sarrazin, and Lacombe begin by reporting the influence of probability and time pressures on the cognitive strategies guiding squash players in their choice of preparation state. Strategies of another sort, that is, visio-manual strategies that experienced pistol shooters use when transporting the weapon from target to target are Ripoll's topic in chapter 16.

Athletes' response to training is the subject matter of chapters 2 and 3. In chapter 2, Bannister and co-researchers propose a method for enhancing the training process. Training is monitored quantitatively and its effects are modeled on actual performance and related physiological responses. Then in chapter 3, Butts, Pein, and Stevenson compare physiological responses of men and women collegiate swimmers who trained in an identical 8-week training program.

Although many physiological profiles have recently been conducted on athletes, the diversity of sporting events and the lack of adequate information concerning elite female athletes has prompted additional research in this area. Thus, in chapter 19, Greek athletes who competed in 19 Olympic sports are featured. Then in chapter 6, Daniels and his co-workers identify some discriminating characteristics between elite and subelite female middle- and long-distance runners. In chapter 14, Montgomery and Dallaire discuss the physiological profile they developed after studying professional ice hockey players throughout two consecutive years. Two other chapters focus on $\dot{V}O_2$ max and runners' performance time. In chapter 12, Léger, Mercier, and Gauvin reexamine the link between $\%\dot{V}O_2$ max and running performance time by analyzing predictive regression equations. Next in chapter 13, Martin, May, and Pilbeam question whether ventilation systems may be a limiting factor of optimal performance during maximum intensity performance.

Several chapters in this volume are based on research conducted with elite speedskaters. Topics of these investigations include training intensity and menstrual irregularities (chapter 4); age and gender as factors affecting psychological training responses (chapter 10); perceived vulnerability to illness and injury (chapter 11); and comparisons of body composition and cardiorespiratory response to maximum exercise of men and women (chapter 15).

Biomechanical applications to sport are represented in three chapters. In chapter 8, Fukunaga, Yamamoto, and Asami discuss mechanical efficiency in rowing. The topic of chapter 5 is on starting techniques for sprinters in which the Chen start, using a thrust-and-pull concept, is compared to a conventional two-leg thrust start. Similarly, in chapter 18 Shin and Groppel compare the effectiveness of the tract start and the grab start for competitive swimmers.

Psychological parameters impinging on elite performance are discussed from several perspectives. In chapter 7, Durtschi and Weiss draw interesting parallels and digressions as they outline the preparation differences, psychological characteristics, and cognitive strategies employed by elite and nonelite marathon runners. Israeli athletes were the performers in Furst and Tenebaum's report in chapter 9 on the relationships among worry, emotionality, and sport performance in six different sports. The volume concludes with chapter 20 in which Wrisberg and his co-researchers attempt to determine the generalizability of Butt's theory when applied to elite athletes of various ages and competitive sports. This theory deals with the psychological and sociological motivation of athletes.

The 1984
Olympic Scientific
Congress
Proceedings
Volume 3

# Sport and Elite Performers

# 1

# The Use of Subjective Expected Values in Decision-Making in Sport

*Claude Alain, Claude Sarrazin, and Daniel Lacombe*
UNIVERSITY OF MONTREAL
MONTREAL, QUEBEC, CANADA

In the sports context the performer faces many situations in which he or she must quickly react to the outcome of one of several possible environmental stimuli. In such situations, both the speed and the accuracy of the information processing taking place after the stimulus has occurred are influenced by the preparation state the performer had decided upon prior to stimulus onset.

Individuals appear capable of consciously deciding whether or not they should bias their preparation in favor of one event and, if so, to what extent this should be done. This is substantiated by several choice reaction time (CRT) experiments which have investigated the effect of predicted outcome (e.g., Bernstein & Reese, 1965), subjects' confidence in their predicted outcomes (e.g., Geller, 1975), stimulus probability (cf. Welford, 1980, for a review) and time deadlines within which to react (e.g., Yellott, 1971).

Despite the fact that the notion of preparation has received much experimental attention (e.g., Requin, 1980), relatively little is known about the cognitive strategy guiding subjects in their choices of preparation states. Recently, Alain, Lalonde, and Sarrazin (1983) and Sarrazin, Lacombe, Alain, and Joly (1983) addressed this question in the context of the applied environment of racquet sports. They portrayed the defending player (D) as a decision-maker whose task is to choose among three categories of preparation—total preparation for one particular event, partial preparation in favor of one event, and absence of biased preparation. According to their model, D would organize all of the available information into two main parameters: (a) a subjective probability

This research was supported by funds from F.C.A.C. Gouvernement du Québec, grant # EQ 1350.

(Ps) assigned to each of the possible shots the attacking player could use, and (b) a perceived outcome (Po) resulting from the choice of one of the preparation states and the execution of one of the shots. In this particular instance, Po refers to D's estimate of reaching the ball and playing a return shot within the time deadline. The performer would then combine the values Ps and Po according to a decision rule based on an expected value maximization principle (cf. Coombs, Dawes, & Tversky, 1970). This principle states that the decision rule the player would use involves the computation of the expected value of each alternative and, subsequently, the selection of the alternative with the higher value. The expected value of a preparation state with Po values of $Po_1 \ldots Po_n$ and Ps values of $Ps_1 \ldots Ps_n$ is given by $\Sigma_{i=1}^{n} Ps_i(Po_i)$.

The purpose of this study is twofold. First, it aims at verifying if, as suggested by the above model, the performer's choice of preparation state is the result of a conjoined consideration of both probability and time pressure. Second, it aims to verify whether the decision rule governing the choice of the preparation state is the expected value maximization principle.

## Methods and Procedures

### Subjects

Eight expert squash players, 4 women and 4 men, (Class A of the Quebec Squash Federation) volunteered to participate in the experiment. All subjects were tested under each of the experimental conditions described below.

### Task

The experimental setting was a squash court. On each trial the subject had a squash racquet in hand and stood in a position judged to be most conducive to quick lateral displacements. From this starting position, the subject faced a screen located 4 ft from the front wall of the court. Both feet were positioned on separate sensitive plates fixed on the floor. Behind the screen, a ball-throwing device could shoot the ball off the front wall in such a way that its trajectory was either that of a lob or a smash. The lob and the smash constituted a relatively low and a relatively high time pressure situation, respectively. On each trial the screen was used to inform subjects of the objective probability assigned to the shots (either .8 or .2) and of the area on the court where each shot was aimed (i.e., either to the right or to the left of the subject). After this information had been presented, the activation of a light fixed to the screen informed the subject that the ball had been fired via the ball-throwing device. Once the ball had been fired, the subject was to move to the right or to the left in order to reach the ball and drive it to a target located on the front wall. Appropriate clock counters and timers were set up to enable the measurement of *processing time*. That is, the time interval between the onset of the light and the moment the subject moved a foot to engage in a specific direction.

Prior to the actual testing trials, each subject was allowed a large number of practice trials, permitting a clear perception of the levels of time pressure and probability used in this study.

## Experimental Conditions

In two of the four experimental conditions, LOB .2/LOB .8 and SMASH .2/SMASH .8, the time pressure accompanying each of the two possible events was the same, but the .8 probability assigned to each event differed. In the other two conditions, both the probability and the time pressure covaried— SMASH .8/LOB .2 and SMASH .2/LOB .8. Each subject participated in 20 trials for each of the four experimental conditions. In half of the trials the .8 probability was presented to the right of the subject, and in the remaining half of the trials the .8 probability was to the subject's left. The order of presentation of the 80 test trials was randomized, and the frequency of execution of each possible shot corresponded to the objective probability.

## Verbal Reports

Immediately after each trial, every subject was asked to indicate which of the following preparation states he or she had adopted to solve the situation presented on that particular trial: (a) Total preparation (TP), in which the performer determines in advance the response to be produced; (b) Partial preparation (PP), in which the performer primes one response without excluding the possibility that an alternate response could be required; and (c) equal preparation (EP), in which the performer's degree of preparation is the same for each of the possible events. It is noteworthy to mention that, for TP and PP, the preparation can be biased in favor of either one of the two events. Therefore, subjects could choose from five categories of preparation states: TP left, TP right, PP left, PP right, and EP. The subject was also asked to indicate the probability that he or she had subjectively assigned to the respective events on that particular trial.

## Perceived Outcomes (Po)

After the 80 experimental trials had been completed, an attempt was made to obtain subjects' perceived outcomes (Po). Po was defined as the performer's estimate of the percent chance of reaching and hitting the ball given that one event has occurred and that one preparation state had been adopted. Since five preparation states and two events were possible for each subject, 10 Po values existed for each of the four experimental conditions, yielding a total of 40 Po values.

In order to gain subjects' Po, subjects were shown a graphic representation of each of the four experimental situations used in this study. For each situation, subjects were instructed to assume one of the five preparation states and try to estimate their percent chances of reaching the ball, first, if the ball had been fired to the right, and second, if it had been projected to the left. The process was repeated four more times, one for each of the remaining preparation states. The order of presentation of the 40 graphic representations was randomized. Twelve of the 40 graphics were also presented twice to each subject in order to verify the consistency of evaluating the Po values. In none of the cases did the difference between the two Pos assigned to a same graphic representation exceed 5%.


## Results and Discussion

### Combined Effect of Probability and Time Pressure

One of the purposes of this study was to test whether or not a performer's choice of preparation state was the result of a conjoined consideration of both probability and time pressure. To answer this question a MANOVA with repeated measures on the four experimental conditions was computed on the scores obtained from two dependent variables: (a) processing time and (b) subject's choice of preparation state. For the purpose of the analysis, the latter was numerically described in the following way. The choices of total or partial preparation in favor of the most probable event were assigned scores of +2 and +1, respectively. Alternately, scores of −2 and −1 were attributed to the choices of total and partial preparation, respectively, in favor of the least probable event. A score of 0 was given when an equal preparation state was opted for. Results revealed only one significant difference between conditions SMASH .2/LOB .8 and SMASH .8/LOB .2 for the subject's choice of preparation state ($p < .01$). Table 1 shows the mean values of processing times and subjects' choices of preparation states for each of the four experimental conditions.

An examination of Table 1 reveals that, for conditions LOB .8/ LOB .2 and SMASH .8/SMASH .2, subjects generally engaged in partial preparation as evidenced by the scores of 1.05 and 1.20 obtained for the choice of preparation state. The biased preparation observed in each of these two conditions can only be attributed to the difference in the probability assigned to the events since this was the only factor varying in each condition. This is in line with several CRT experiments which have shown that expecting a stimulus more than any other can lead subjects to bias their preparation states in favor of that event (e.g., Bernstein & Reese, 1965; Geller, 1975).

Also, the absence of a statistical difference between conditions LOB .8/LOB .2 and SMASH .8/SMASH .2 showed that by equally increasing the time pressure accompanying both events, the choice of preparation state was not al-

**Table 1.** Mean values of processing time and subjects' choice of preparation state for the four experimental conditions

| | Experimental Conditions | | | |
| | LOB.8/LOB.2 | SMASH.8/SMASH.2 | SMASH.2/LOB.8 | SMASH.8/LOB.2 |
| --- | --- | --- | --- | --- |
| Processing time (ms) | .572 | .520 | .569 | .485 |
| Preparation | 1.05 | 1.20 | − .73 | 1.56 |

tered. Perhaps the difference in time pressure was not large enough to lead subjects to engage in what Yellott (1971) has termed *fast guessing*. Nevertheless, these results are in line with a recent CRT study in which both probability and time pressure were the factors of interest (Proteau & Alain, 1983). These authors found no interaction between probability and time pressure when, for each given probability condition, time pressure was gradually increased.

With respect to the statistical difference observed between conditions SMASH .8/LOB .2 and SMASH .2/LOB .8, examination of Table 1 reveals that, when the two events within a condition convey unequal time pressure, the bias in a subject's preparation is reversed in favor of the less probable event when this event bears the highest time pressure. Thus, the performer's choice of preparation state appears to be the result of a conjoined consideration of probability and time pressure accompanying each of the possible events.

The absence of statistical difference between the means of the four processing times (Table 1) may be attributable to the biased preparations adopted by the subjects within each experimental condition. These biased preparations would all be of the partial preparation type since no significant differences were found between conditions LOB .8/LOB .2, SMASH .8/SMASH .2 and SMASH .8/LOB .2 (Table 1: 1.05, 1.20, and 1.56). Furthermore, for condition SMASH .2/LOB .8, subjects also opted for a partial preparation but for the least probable event.

### The Cognitive Strategy Underlying the Choice of Preparation

The second purpose of this study was to verify the Sarrazin et al. (1983) contention that the performer will select the preparation state to which he or she has allotted the highest subjective expected value. The subjective expected value of a preparation state is given by $\Sigma_i \underset{=}{\underline{n}}_i Ps_i(Po_i)$ where Ps represents the probability of one event and Po stands for the subject's perceived outcome.

The Ps values were given on each trial. Po values of each subject had been obtained via the previously described procedure. Thus for each trial it was possible to use the formula to compute the expected value of each of the five preparation states and to identify which one would be chosen if subjects had operated on the basis of an expected value maximization principle. This computation was done in two ways. First, the Ps values used in the formula were the objective probabilities. That is, the ones the experimenter had assigned to the two events (.8 and .2). Second, the Ps values used were the subjective probabilities as they were perceived by the subjects on each trial.

In either case the percent correspondence between the "predicted" preparation states and the ones subjects reported using ranged from 10% to 50%, depending on which subject and which experimental condition was examined. The average correspondence was 23.4%, which approximates chance expectations. Such results cast serious doubt on the possibility that the choice of preparation results from the application of the expected value maximization principle. Note that, in applying the expected value maximization principle, the performer has to go through two successive component processes, each of which could potentially result in information overload. The first one is the combination process, which leads to the computation of the expected values and is based on multiplication and addition operations ($\Sigma Ps_i(Po_i)$). The second process is the comparison of the expected values respectively assigned to the different decision alternatives in order that the one with the highest value be chosen. It could well be that the amount of information-processing required exceeds the capacity of the cognitive-information-processing system if an expected value maximization principle is applied.

# References

Alain, C., Lalonde, C., & Sarrazin, C. (1983). Decision-making and information-processing in squash competition. In H. Reider, K. Bos, H. Mechling, & K. Reischle (Eds.), *Motorik und bewvegungs forschung* [Motor learning and movement behavior] (pp. 196-202). Schorndoef, Germany: Karl Hofman.

Bernstein, I.H., & Reese, C. (1965). Behavioral hypotheses and choice reaction time. *Psychonomic Science*, **3**, 259-260.

Coombs, C.H., Dawes, R.M., & Tversky, A. (1970). *Mathematical psychology*. Englewood Cliffs, NJ: Prentice-Hall.

Geller, E.S. (1975). Prediction outcome and choice reaction time: Inhibition versus facilitation effects. *Acta Psychologica*, **39**, 69-82.

Proteau, L., & Alain, C. (1983). Stratégie de décision en fonction de l'incertitude de l'événement: 1. Latence de la décision. *Journal Canadien des Sciences Appliqueées au Sport*, **8**(1), 63-71.

Requin, J. (1980). Toward a psychobiology of preparation for action. In G. Stelmach & J. Requin (Eds.), *Tutorials in motor behavior* (pp. 373-391). Amsterdam: North Holland.

Sarrazin, C., Lacombe, D., Alain, C., & Joly, J. (1983). Simulation study of a decision-making model of squash competition, phase one: The analysis of the protocol. *Human Movement Science*, **2**, 279-306.

Welford, A.T. (Ed.). (1980). *Reaction times*. London: Academic Press.

Yellott, J.I. (1971). Correlation for fast guessing and the speed-accuracy tradeoff in choice reaction time. *Journal of Mathematical Psychology*, **8**, 159-199.

# 2

# Modeling the Training Response in Athletes

*Eric W. Banister, Pat Good, Geoffrey Holman,*
*and Cindy L. Hamilton*
INSTITUTE FOR HUMAN PERFORMANCE
SIMON FRASER UNIVERSITY
BURNABY, BRITISH COLUMBIA, CANADA

Training a team or an individual is a complex process. An increasingly sophisticated approach to it is evident in every sport and in every country. A systems model of the training process is shown in Figure 1 in which several fundamental processes such as general physical preparation, skills and tactical training, mental conditioning, and everyday lifestyle patterns are included.

Even in this simple model, the complexity of the positive or negative feedback mechanisms as they summate to effect the output (performance), is quite evident. An obvious problem posed by such a model is how to measure all of the variables within the system. How does one really measure training or skill acquisition quantitatively? How much of each is transmitted to an individual as a result of participating in a given training session?

It would be useful for any coach or selection committee to have concise, continuous information on the physical and mental status of an athlete. This status would be especially important to know in the lead-up phase immediately prior to major competitive events. If such data were to be gathered over 1-, 2-, 3-, or 4-year periods, a coherent assessment of the efficacy of different training procedures and the responsiveness of an individual to the training stimulus might be attained. Additionally, the physiological and psychological factors important to the trained state and to competitive success would be better understood.

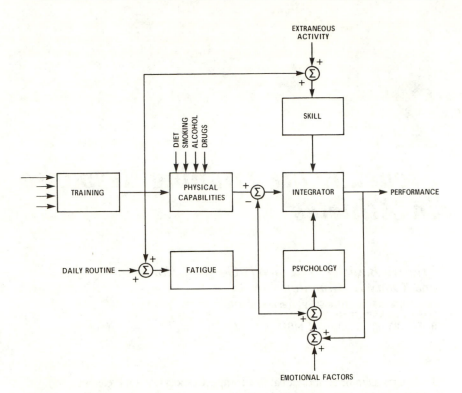

**Figure 1.** An overall systems model of performance showing the complex interaction of several factors as they contribute to the realization of optimal athletic performance. They range from the influences of common daily life to direct intervention in the organism with training manipulations. The factors also include intangibles such as the psychological effect of good or bad execution of the performance itself in competition, or even during training. From "Monitoring Training" by E.W. Banister and H.A. Wenger. In J.D. MacDougall, H.A. Wenger, and H.J. Green (Eds.) *Physiological Testing of the Elite Athlete* (p. 164), 1982, Ottawa: Canadian Association of Sport Sciences. Copyright 1982 by the Canadian Association of Sport Sciences. Reprinted by permission.

## The Fundamental Effects of Training

Being a good athlete requires cardiorespiratory fitness, strength, and power. These attributes are a fundamental base upon which skill, strategy, mental toughness, and overall success either flourish or flounder.

## Physiological Systems: Dimensions and Function

The model in Figure 2 (Holmgren, 1967) illustrates the importance of both the dimensions and the functional capacity of a system for performance. Similar considerations apply to every other physiological system in the body. Judicious, optimal training of the young, growing organism will first induce changes in all systems necessary to attain the endowed (inherited) dimensions of each system component as shown in Figure 2.

A moment's reflection will indicate, however, that the sheer dimensions of the system do not necessarily ensure elite athletic performance. Rather, the functional capacity (probably better termed *functional power*) of the system is a better indicator of athletic success. Thus, it is not sufficient to have merely a large lung capacity (i.e., vital capacity), but it is vital to be able to inhale and exhale large quantities of air per minute. It is this time factor which is critical in producing athletic superiority. Maximum oxygen uptake ability, the physiological variable most often chosen by sport scientists as representing the quality that is characteristic of good athletes, is measured as the maximum amount of oxygen per minute that an individual can extract from the air in the surrounding atmosphere. Oxygen is transported to working muscles or other tissues via the circulatory system, and the tissues use it to generate the energy required for work. Everyone is able to do this, of course. The hallmark of superiority, however, is the ability to deliver more per minute than one's adversary. The training processes that induce the best change in the various subsystems contributing to the overall effect of the performance model shown in Figure 1 are those which warrant wide implementation.

As indicated, the underpinnings of excellent athletic performance include such basic components as cardiorespiratory fitness, strength/power, and flexibility. Of course motor coordination, specific skills, strategic appreciation, and mental toughness build upon the basics. The latter qualities may even be-

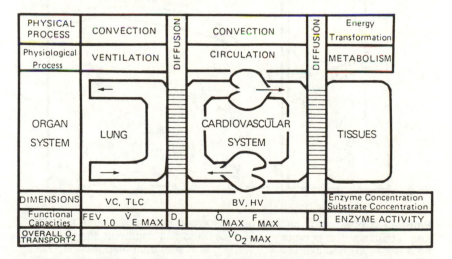

**Figure 2.** Schematic illustration of the oxygen-transport system showing respresentative dimensions and functional power of the individual links in the system. From "Cardiorespiratory Determinants of Cardiovascular Fitness" by A. Holmgren, 1967, *Canadian Medical Association Journal*, **96**, p. 697. Copyright 1967 by Canadian Medical Association. Adapted by permission.

come dominant as typified in the sage, wily campaigner saving tired, old limbs by judicious appreciation of the game's future pattern of action.

## Typical Patterns of Training Response in Physiological Systems: The Time Constant Concept

### Cardiorespiratory Training

Cardiorespiratory fitness is induced by training that includes components of intensity, frequency, and duration (Davies & Knibbs, 1971; Shephard, 1969). The less fit the beginning trainee is, the lower the intensity of the initial training sessions are (measured as that proportion of the maximum heart rate that the training generates in an individual). The duration typically is 1 h and is usually carried out at least four to five times per week to be effective.

Figure 3 shows changes in peak $\dot{V}O_2$ induced by detraining followed by retraining (Åstrand, 1975). The pattern of increase in $\dot{V}O_2$ during retraining describes a particular path; many other physical attributes change with training a similar way, that is, they follow a typical growth curve. The decrease in $\dot{V}O_2$ in the absence of continuous training also follows a typical pattern called a decay curve.

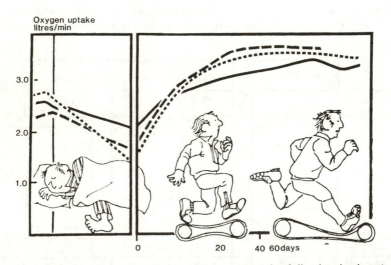

**Figure 3.** Showing the fall and rise of oxygen uptake following bed rest and retraining. The contour of the decay and rise segments may be fitted by a decay exponential, $Y = Y_{ss} \cdot e^{-t/\tau}$, and saturation exponential, $Y = Y_{ss}(1 \cdot e^{-t/\tau})$, respectively. Both t and the time constant ($\tau$) of each curve are measured in days, and $Y_{ss}$ is the steady state (asymptote) value of $\dot{V}O_2$. From *Health and Fitness* (p. 19) by P.-O. Åstrand (drawing by Claes Folcker), 1978, Stockholm, Sweden: Skandia Insurance Co. Ltd. and the Swedish Information Service. Copyright 1978 by the Skandia Insurance Co. Ltd. and the Swedish Information Service. Reprinted by permission.

### Strength Training

Muscle strength increases by repetitive exercise of a particular muscle group against resistance, either of the body itself or of free weight in the form of barbells or pulley weights. Figure 4 shows how strength gains are made in response to almost any sort of weight-training program (Banister, 1979). The path of change in strength acquisition is again along a typical growth curve no matter what form the training task takes, that is, isometric training, barbell lifting, or nautilus exercises. Each of the curves of Figures 3 and 4 may be described by a characteristic value called the time constant, $\tau$ (either a time constant of growth or a time constant of decay). $\tau$ is the Greek symbol tau. It represents the time it takes for the gain in a particular attribute ($\dot{V}O_2$ or strength) to reach two thirds of the steady state (asymptote) value appropriate to the size of the training stimulus causing the change. Thus, separate $\tau$ values may be expressed for $\dot{V}O_2$ increases, for natural strength gain directly attributable to the growth process itself, and for the growth in strength due to natural growth supplemented by weight training.

The time constant described in these examples turns out to be an important value in evaluating training since not only does any type of performance—not just $\dot{V}O_2$ or strength—grow in response to training, but performance also

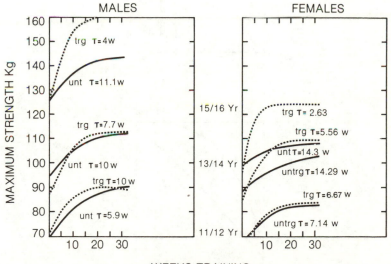

WEEKS TRAINING

**Figure 4.** Showing strength changes in boys and girls as they occur naturally during normal growth and as they are induced by regular weight training. These curves may be fitted with saturation exponentials of the form shown in Figure 3. Different time constant values characterize the shape of each curve. From "Strength Gains from Muscle Training" by E.W. Banister, 1980, *National Strength Coaches Association Journal*, **2**(1), p. 28. Copyright 1980 by NSCA. Reprinted with permission. NSCA, P.O. Box 81410, Lincoln, NE 68501.

declines in a precise way with bed rest as shown in the $\dot{V}O_2$ curve. This decay is described by the decay time constant. A typical decay time constant indicates the time it would take for a performance attained by training to decline to two thirds of its current value if training suddenly ceased entirely. Figure 5 shows how tissue components (in this case an enzyme in the muscle, cytochrome c, that helps the muscle use oxygen delivered to it) grow in a prescribed way with a typical time constant that varies according to the type of training undertaken (Booth, 1977). If we need even more convincing of the predetermined fashion in which human attributes change in response to training stimuli, then the growth in the mile world record shown in Figure

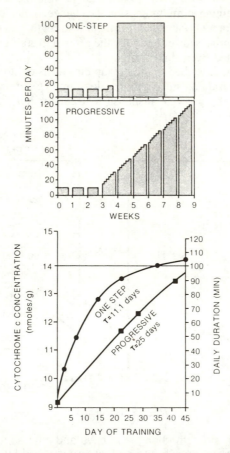

**Figure 5.** Exponential changes in cytochrome c in rat skeletal muscle due to step and ramp (progressive) changes in training, respectively. From "Effects of Endurance Exercise on Cytochrome C Turnover in Skeletal Muscle" by F. Booth, 1977, *Annals of the New York Academy of Science,* **301**, p. 435. Copyright 1977 by New York Academy of Science. Adapted by permission. Frank Booth, Dept. of Physiology, School of Medicine, University of Texas Health Science Center, Houston, Texas, 77025.

6 should serve our purpose (Banister & Calvert, 1979). Growth occurs in two well-defined phases, each with a separate time constant. The break in the curve could very well be explained by advances in equipment design, running surfaces, or changes in training methods.

If performance grows in a predetermined fashion in response to a training stimulus, and the growth responds positively or negatively to increases or decreases in the training stimulus, then we have the very tools with which to fashion a rational picture of the training process, to quantify the training dose accumulating during each training session, and to build a model of the effects of training to predict long-term performance ability.

## Quantity of Training

The quantity of daily training may be calculated and expressed as a single score or training impulse, (TRIMP) expressed in arbitrary training units (ATU). Very

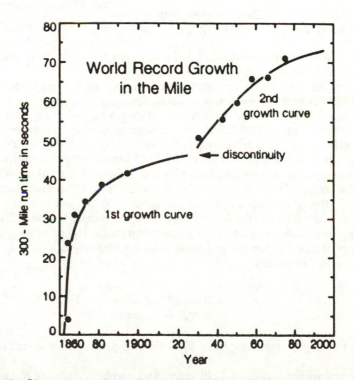

**Figure 6.** Changes in mile world records display the typical growth curve (saturation exponential) form. After the first stage, growth seems to plateau, then a second steady growth period occurs. Each growth curve may be characterized by its own time constant. From "Training the Competitive Female Athlete" by E.W. Banister, In A. Popma (Ed.), *The Female Athlete,* 1980, Burnaby, Canada: Simon Fraser University, Institute for Human Performance. Copyright 1980 by the Institute for Human Performance. Reprinted by permission.

simply, a TRIMP is calculated from an individual's maximum heart rate (taken from a maximum treadmill test or an all-out 400 m run), basal heart rate (taken before rising in the morning), average heart rate during training, and duration of exercise (in minutes). A basic principle considered in calculating the size of the training stimulus is that training is impulsive in nature, absorbed in discrete quanta which contribute to the development of both fitness and fatigue, thus

$$\text{Training Impulse} = \text{Stress} \times \text{Strain}$$
$$\text{(in arbitrary units)}$$

in which stress defines any type of training demand (usually measured by the duration of the activity in minutes and strain defines the individual reaction to that demand (usually and most conveniently measured as a heart rate response).

$$\underset{\text{(in arbitrary units)}}{\text{TRIMP Score}} = \underset{\text{(minutes)}}{\text{Duration of Activity}} \times \frac{\text{Exercise(HR)} - \text{Basal(HR)}}{\text{Maximum(HR)} - \text{Basal(HR)}}$$

Scores from several training sessions per day may be combined to determine a single representative daily TRIMP score.

As a guard against too disproportionate an importance being given to long duration activity at low heart rate levels compared with intense but short duration activity, the fractional heart rate elevation is weighted in a manner which reflects the intensity of the effort. As a greater proportion of maximum oxygen uptake is reached, a multiplying factor, based upon the classically described increase in blood lactate in trained male and female subjects, respectively, weights the heart rate proportionally higher the higher its elevation during the exercise period. This factor serves to equate the TRIMP scores of activities in which stress is prolonged and heart rate elevation is low with activities where heart rates are high and the activity cannot be maintained for long. The multiplying factors are built into a computer program developed to model training responses; the factors are generated from the following equations for males and females, respectively:

$$y = 0.64e^{1.92x} \text{ (male)}$$
$$y = 0.86e^{1.67x} \text{ (female)}$$

where $y$ = multiplying factor and $x$ = fractional heart rate elevation in exercise.

Besides providing a compact, objective, and graphic display of training for an extended period, this method of quantifying an activity allocates a numerical score to training which may be used to elaborate a theory of athletic performance.

## Predicting Fitness, Fatigue and Performance from Training

Training is undertaken so that performance capacity grows under the influence of its repeated stimulus; with each training impulse an individual's ability to perform should improve. However, it is known (Matveyev, 1981; Zauner & Reese, 1972), that unremittingly hard training decreases the ability to perform, and that rest or light training is needed before improvement may be noticed. Theoretically therefore the training impulse (I) generated during a training session contributes to developing both fitness and fatigue. This concept may be used to infer the quality of future performance based upon the training impulses sustained at each session over any given period of time. If the initial training impulse is I, its effect upon both fitness and fatigue persists but decays as shown in Figure 7 (Banister & Calvert, 1979) in the interval between training sessions.

The time constants of decay of fitness ($\tau_{Fit}$) and fatigue ($\tau_{Fat}$) are judged to be different ($\tau_{Fat} < t_{Fit}$) as shown by the faster decay of fatigue in Figure 7. The training impulse I is judged to contribute a greater fatiguing effect than training effect. The size of the fatigue impulse shown in Figure 7 is $K_2I$, and the size of the fitness impulse is $K_1I$ ($K_1$ and $K_2$ are multiplying factors). In the interval between training, fatigue and fitness decay according to the generalized equations, where Fit(t) and Fat(t) are the residuals of fitness and fatigue remaining from the previous day's training.

$$Fit(t) = K_1 \cdot I \cdot e^{-t/\tau_{Fit}}$$
$$Fat(t) = K_2 \cdot I \cdot e^{-t/\tau_{Fat}}$$

Each new impulse of training on successive days contributes to the growth of fitness and fatigue by adding impulsively to the residual (decay) level of

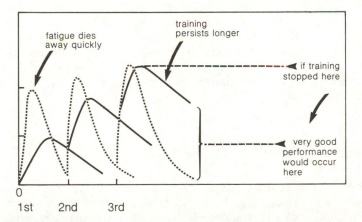

**Figure 7.** Contribution of a TRIMP score to fatigue growth and fitness or training growth. A TRIMP score shown here contributes twice as much to fatigue generation as to fitness growth. Fatigue also declines more rapidly ($\tau_{Fat}$ shorter) than does fitness, which persists ($\tau_{Fit}$ longer). The ability to perform is always measured as the difference between accumulated fatigue and fitness. From "Planning for Future Performance: Implications for Long Term Training" by E.W. Banister, 1980, *Canadian Journal of Applied Sport Science,* **5**(3) p. 172. Copyright 1980 by Canadian Journal of Applied Sport Science. Adapted by permission.

each previous day's accumulation before decaying again according to the respective time constants of fitness and fatigue.

A measure of Performance P(t) at any time t may be taken as the simple difference existing between the residual levels of fitness and fatigue at the time t:

$$P(t) = Fit(t) - Fat(t)$$

As each successive day's training impulse is added to the residual fitness and fatigue from the previous day's decay, both fitness and fatigue slowly grow. Performance which is their difference, will either grow as P(t) is positive or decline as P(t) is negative, depending on which effect predominates (e.g., fitness during peaking or fatigue during heavy training).

Thus a cumulative picture of developing fitness, fatigue, and the ability to perform may be drawn from a single measure of training load (the TRIMP score). The hypothesized values for decay constants ($\tau_{Fit}$, $\tau_{Fat}$) and the weighting factors $K_1$ and $K_2$ may be replaced by individual-specific values when a hypothetical predicted performance curve is modeled, by successive computer iteration, to match the pattern of real performance measures (criterion points) attained by the athlete throughout the monitored training period.

### Criterion Performances

Real performances for the athletes, called criterion performances, are measured as frequently as possible with the cooperation of each athlete and coach. Performance times (in seconds) for any standard distance are expressed as a score on a point scale ranging up to 1,000, on the basis that 110% of the world record time for any distance gained 1,000 points. It is the points gained in this manner, labeled "criterion points," against which the arbitrary performance scores P(t) derived from training impulses are iteratively modeled (patterned) in order to obtain the least squares best fit of predicted to real performance and thus determine the specific constant $\tau_{Fit}$, $\tau_{Fat}$, $K_1$, and $K_2$ for each individual.

## Results

Figure 8 (Banister & Wenger, 1982) shows a year's TRIMP scores calculated retrospectively from the "log" book records of several runners. Although these runners "felt" they were training adequately, their training demonstrates no coherent, optimal pattern of training and "peaking" (relative rest before competition), and no dramatic improvement in any actual performance was attained. Performances at the end of the year were not much better, sometimes even worse, than at the beginning of the year.

These records may be contrasted with those of Figure 9. Figure 9 shows the result of successfully manipulating training to produce an optimal real performance at a critical (competition) time in a male swimmer. "Crit points" for coincident days have been positioned on the predicted performance curve (bottom panel). Notice that the pattern of predicted performance mirrored real performance (criterion points) closely since the parameters $\tau_{Fit}$, $\tau_{Fat}$, $K_1$, and $K_2$, discussed previously, were iteratively modeled until the best least square's fit of the predicted curve to the real curve of criterion performance was obtained. Here the coach could assess the athlete's training immediately prior to competition because the athlete's individual responsiveness to training had been well modeled in the months previous to the final preparation.

Figure 10 shows several graphs of the pattern of variation of training with criterion performances (an anaerobic endurance run 8 mph, 20% grade) and physiological indices of physical performance for a soccer team member as his physical attributes were peaked for area, district, and championship tournament games extending over a 3-week period. During this period the coach contrived to manipulate the physical training aspect of his team's preparation to ensure that each individual was approaching peak physical condition prior to the championship games.

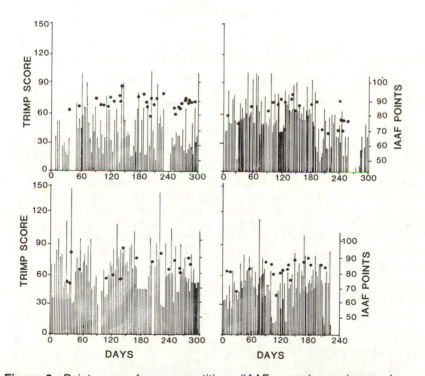

**Figure 8.** Point scores from competitions (IAAF scores) superimposed upon TRIMP units from training for several male runners. Their training and results over the year showed little change and little coherent pattern. From "Monitoring Training" by E.W. Banister and H. Wenger. In J.D. MacDougall, H.A. Wenger, and H.J. Green (Eds.), *Physiological Testing of the Elite Athlete* (p.166), 1982, Ottawa: Canadian Association of Sport Sciences. Copyright 1982 by the Canadian Association of Sport Sciences. Reprinted by permission.

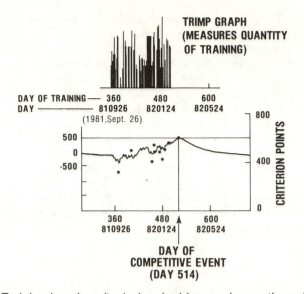

**Figure 9.** Training impulses (top) absorbed by a swimmer throughout a 120-day swim season leading to championships on Day 514. The lower panel shows performance (the thick line) predicted to accrue from the training according to the impulse theory of fitness and fatigue described in the text. The units of performance are of course the arbitrary units measuring the training impulse from which the curve is derived. The accumulated units (the difference between fitness and fatigue) are shown on the left axis. Superimposed on the predicted curve are real performances made by the swimmer throughout the measured training period as a proportion of the world record plus 10% which is accorded 1,000 points (criterion points right axis). The variables defining the predicted curve for the indivdiual could be changed quite sensitively to make prediction coincide quite well with reality. Predictions of performance from future training undertaken by this "modeled" athlete may now be made. From *"Trimp Training Program"* (p.6) by E.W. Banister and G. Holman, 1983, Vancouver, Canada: BHP Consultants. Copyright 1978 by BHP Consultants. Reprinted with permission.

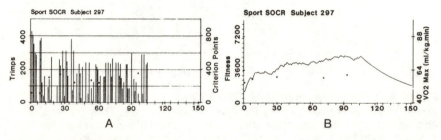

**Figure 10.** cont.

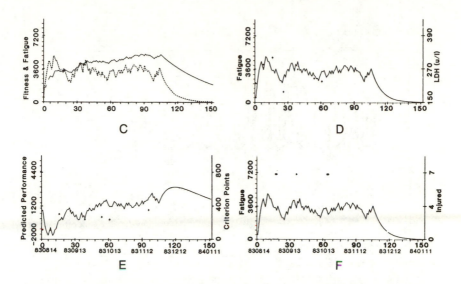

**Figure 10.** Management of physical training for a typical player (ID 297) on a soccer team. Graph A shows the training undertaken by the player up to and including the championship rounds for the NAIA Championship. Each bar represents the quantity of training undertaken on the day. The last five bars indicate the week of the championship rounds. Full circles superimposed on the training scores (TRIMPS) are criterion performances (in this case measured by anaerobic run times on the treadmill). Performance ability (graph E) at any time is the difference between accumulated fitness and fatigue. Training intensity was modified in the days leading up to the championship rounds (enclosed by the vertical solid lines) so that predicted physical performance was on an upswing. Playing four games in 1 week diminished predicted performance slightly, but by and large each player played the championship rounds at or near his personal physical best. A computer-generated measure of performance (thin line, graph E) derived from training is modeled (by a least squares fit) to the real anaerobic run criterion performances (full circles). This is achieved by changing the variables that influence fitness (thin line, graph C) and fatigue (thick line, graph C) built up throughout training. It may be observed that fitness after an initial rise at the beginning of training remains fairly constant and that fatigue is quite sensitive to the degree of training undertaken.

In graphs B, D, and F, measures of $\dot{V}O_2$max vary closely with fitness; after an initial rise they remain fairly constant. Logically this is because training intensity could not be held high enough for a long enough period of time (except in training camp in the beginning 2-week period) to make large gains in $\dot{V}O_2$max because players had to be ready to play one or two times per week. Very striking agreement may be observed between serum LDH levels and the fatigue line (shown in graph D). Serum LDH indicates stressed muscle cells. Two occasions when injury (graph F) occurred, serum LDH was considerably elevated above its normal pattern in this athlete. During recovery from injury LDH falls to its normal level.

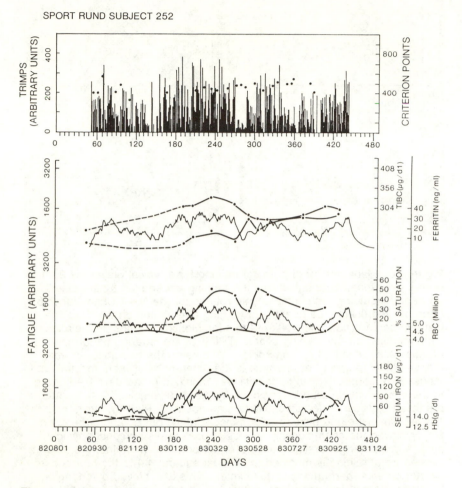

**Figure 11.** Actual performances (top, closed circles) superimposed on daily TRIMP scores for Subject 252. The lower three panels show measures of iron status and hematological variables patterned against an objective measure of a fatigue score in arbitrary units derived from modeling training against real performances for the individual as shown in the middle and lower panels of Figure 1. In the lower three panels the fatigue score is plotted as a thin continuous line. The pattern of variation of the physiological variables plotted as closed circles is shown against the pattern of variation in fatigue accumulation. Each physiological value has been joined by a free-drawn line to emphasize its pattern of variation. The sensitivity of iron status variables TIBC (early in training) and percent saturation, and serum iron (throughout training) to changes in training intensity reflected by fatigue accumulation are clearly apparent. These measures appear to vary in phase with fatigue, that is, being high when fatigue is high and low when fatigue diminishes. Ferritin remains low throughout, rising after Day 360 as percent saturation and SI decrease. From "Variations

**Figure 11.** cont.
in Iron Status with Fatigue Modelled from Training in Female Distance
Runners" by E.W. Banister and C. Hamilton, 1985. *European Journal of
Applied Physiology*, **54**, p.19. Copyright 1985 by the European Journal of
Applied Physiology. Reprinted with permission.

When patterns of training responses are compared in an objective manner
to the training producing them, fundamental factors influencing performance
may be revealed. Thus in Figure 11 (Banister & Hamilton, 1985) which shows
the varying iron status of a female distance runner with training, it may be
observed that when fatigue patterns (calculated from modeling training against
actual performances) are compared to variations in iron status monitored
throughout the training period, then transferrin, a molecule that transports iron
to and from iron depots in the body, is always saturated with iron. This is
reflected in the high percent saturation values shown. At this time ferritin levels are low in the blood, indicating low iron stores. When fatigue decreases,
percent saturation decreases and ferritin stores rise. Thus a perplexing feature
of so-called "sport anemia" (i.e., hemoglobin levels of athletes in hard training continue to be low despite iron supplementaton in the diet) may be explained by the fact that transferrin is fully saturated and cannot function in
absorbing iron from the gut. Thus a slow loss of iron from feces, sweat, and
menstruation (in the case of females) ensues, and iron deficiency anemia de-
velops. Such a hypothesis would be impossible to advance if a quantitative
measure of training and a conceptualized model of the training response was
not formulated so that patterns of training and the physiological response
produced by the training could be compared objectively.

## Fatigue and Serum Enzyme Elevation

Figure 12 shows variations in the pattern of serum enzyme elevation with
training impulse. Enzyme elevation is high when fatigue, modeled from training and actual performances, is high. If the object of training is to extend the
trainee to the limit of his or her ability, then responses to training must first
be understood, and goals to be achieved in training must be set in the long
term. The goals of training are set by the level of performance needed on a
future competition day at the particular level of competition desired. The model
of training response described in this paper allows performances, which follow from particular patterns and intensity of training, to be predicted. Thus
goals of training may be set. Whether they may be achieved by an athlete
without breakdown is another matter. If fatigue patterns calculated from training
do indeed reflect real measures of the fatigue (breakdown) process (as measured by serum enzyme elevation), then sensible patterns of training may be
set once the individual athlete's responsiveness to training has been modeled.
This can be done so that fatigue patterns calculated from the "long-term" pattern set for the athlete are just below or at the level that previously caused
critical (breakdown) levels of serum enzymes. In this way the true potential
of an athlete may be safely exploited.

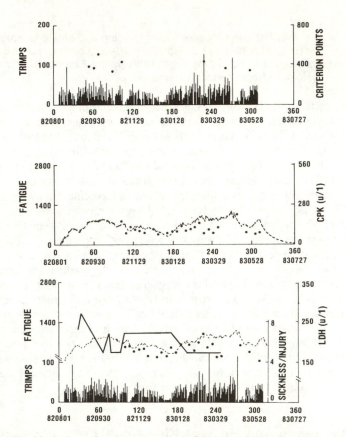

**Figure 12.** Variation of serum enzymes CPK and LDH with fatigue (dashed line) defined from the training model proposed in the text and calculated from modeling training impulses against real performances (bars and full circles, respectively, in the top panel). Both enzyme concentrations track the calculated fatigue curve quite accurately, rise with intense training, and decrease with relative rest. Their coincidence with an arbitrarily scored injury index (bottom) shows that high enzyme levels and high fatigue derived from training scores show a similar pattern to the sickness and injury line (5 = sore, 7 = pain, 9 = injury, 10 = sick and injured).

## Conclusions

In this paper a quantity of training, termed the *training impulse* (TRIMP), has been defined as the product of the duration of a training session and the average fractional elevation of the heart rate accompanying it. This numerical evaluation of training has been used to elaborate a model of an athlete's physiological and performance response to training. The model proposes that actual performance at any time is the result of the balance obtained at the time between accumulated fitness and fatigue levels that accrue from successive training impulses throughout a period of training.

It is suggested that by monitoring training quantitatively and modeling its effects upon overt actual performance as well as upon related physiological subsystems, fundamental insight into the training process may be gained so that the absolute potential of young, aspiring, elite athletes may be safely and optimally developed.

## References

Åstrand, P.O. (1975). *Health and fitness* (p. 48). Ottawa: Information Canada.

Banister, E.W. (1979). Strength gains from muscle training: Preparation for competition. *National Strength Coaches Association Journal*, **2**, 27-31.

Banister, E.W., & Calvert, T.W. (1979). Planning for future performance: Implications for long term training. *Canadian Journal of Applied Sports Sciences*, **5**, 170-176.

Banister, E.W., & Wenger, H. (1982). Monitoring training. In J.D. MacDougall, H.A. Wenger, & H.J. Green (Eds.), *Physiological testing of the elite athlete* (pp. 163-170). Ottawa: Canadian Association of Sport Sciences.

Banister, E.W., & Hamilton, C. (1985). Variations in iron status with fatigue modelled from training in female distance runners. *European Journal of Applied Physiology*, **54**, 16-23.

Banister, E.W., & Holman, G. (1983). *TRIMP training program*. Vancouver, B.C., Canada: BHP Consultants.

Booth, F. (1977). Effects of endurance exercise on cytochrome c turnover in stretched muscle. In P. Milvy (Ed.), *The marathon* (pp. 431-439). New York: Annals of the New York Academy of Science.

Davies, C.T.M., & Knibbs, A.V. (1971). The training stimulus. The effects of intensity, duration and frequency of effort on maximum aerobic power output. *International Zeitschrift Agnew Physiologie*, **29**, 299-305.

Holmgren, A. (1967). Cardiorespiratory determinants of cardiovascular fitness. *Canadian Medical Association Journal*, **96**, 697-702.

Matveyev, L. (1981). *Fundamentals of sports training*. Moscow: Progress Publishers.

Shephard, R.J. (1969). Intensity, duration and frequency of exercise as determinants of the response to a training regime. *International Zeitschrift Agnew Physiologie*, **26**, 272-278.

Zauner, C.W., & Reese, E.C. (1972). Specific training, taper and fatigue. *Track Technique*, **49**, 1546-1550.

# 3

# Male and Female Responses to Similar Swim Training Programs

*Nancy Kay Butts, Richard Pein, and Maura Stevenson*
UNIVERSITY OF WISCONSIN—LA CROSSE
LA CROSSE, WISCONSIN, USA

In 1980 Sparling presented a comprehensive overview of studies comparing the physiological responses of males and females to various exercise modalities and attempted to synthesize the results through the technique of meta-analysis. When aerobic power was expressed in absolute terms ($L \cdot min^{-1}$) males had the higher values. Although these differences tended to be diminished when the $\dot{V}O_2$ max was expressed relative to body weight ($ml \cdot kg \cdot min^{-1}$ and $ml \cdot kgFFW \cdot min^{-1}$), it was not completely negated. In addition, it has been postulated that females respond to training in a similar manner as males; however, in some studies women have shown relatively larger gains than those often obtained by men. This greater improvement has been attributed to the lower initial fitness levels generally found in females rather than to a true biological sex difference (Burke, 1977; Ekblom, 1969; Roswell, 1974). Although numerous studies contrast the acute responses of males and females to exercise, a paucity of research directly compares the effects of similar training programs between the sexes. The purpose of the present investigation was to compare the responses of male and female intercollegiate swimmers to an identical 8-week swim training program.

## Method

Subjects were members of the men's and women's intercollegiate swim teams (NCAA Division III) who had previous competitive swimming experience ranging from 4 to 10 years. Prior to any practice or testing sessions, all subjects received medical clearances and signed informed consent forms. The majority of the subjects were familiar with the testing apparatus and procedures.

Percent body fat was estimated from the density obtained from hydrostatic weighing. Residual volume was obtained by the oxygen dilution technique (Wilmore, 1969) in a seated position outside the weighing tank. The underwater weighing procedure was performed 6 to 10 times until three similar readings to the nearest 25 g were obtained (Katch, 1968). The resulting density was converted to percent body fat according to the formula of Brozek, Grande, Anderson, and Keys (1963).

For determination of power, the rope of a tethered swimming apparatus (Seabreeze Enterprises) was secured to a belt at the waist of the swimmer. The swimmer was instructed to push off the wall and swim the front crawl as fast and hard as possible. When the rope was taut and the weight left its base, time was started. The time stopped when the weight was lifted to a designated mark on the pole and the swimmer was signaled at this point to stop. This procedure was repeated with additional weights being added until the swimmer failed to completely extend the rope and/or a leveling off or decrease in power output occurred. Power in kilogram•meter/second (kgm•sec$^{-1}$) was calculated according to the following formula:

$$\text{Power (kgm•sec}^{-1}) = \frac{(\text{Weight}) \ (\text{Distance})}{(\text{Seconds})}$$

The tethered swim device was modified into a direct pull system for administering a continuous, progressive swimming test using the front crawl to determine $\dot{V}O_2$ max. Workloads were increased each minute based upon preliminary work with that swimmer. When the swimmer could no longer support the resistance with ease, a red card was placed directly under the swimmer to signal him or her to go all out. The test was terminated when the swimmer could no longer support this weight or when he or she reached voluntary exhaustion. During the posttest each individual duplicated his or her pretest weight sequence. Standard open-circuit, expired air procedures were used for the determination of oxygen uptake each minute throughout the test.

The pretest was conducted during the first week of the regular season prior to any formal practice, and the posttest was completed after a full 8 weeks of formal practice. The swimmers' workouts during this time lasted approximately 90 min per day, 5 days per week. Prior to each daily workout the coaches met to coordinate their teams' workouts for that day in order to make them as equal as possible. All swimmers were instructed in the proper method of taking their pulses for 10 s at the carotid artery using a large pacing clock that was easily visible to all swimmers. Individual intensities were based on the percentage of each individual's maximal heart rate determined during his or her $\dot{V}O_2$ max test. Swimming speeds were adjusted to produce approximately 60% maximal during the first 2 weeks and increased to approximately 80-85% during the last 6 weeks. The actual swim times at the designated heart rates were equalized between the groups as much as possible.

Standard descriptive statistics were calculated for all variables. An independent $t$ test was used to discern any significant differences in selected physical characteristics between the sexes at the start of the training. A two-way analysis of variance with repeated measures was employed to determine the effects of training between the sexes.

## Results

Due to various factors such as injury, loss of interest, dropping from the team, and incomplete test data, only 14 males and 14 females of the original 38 subjects completed all aspects of the study.

The general descriptive characteristics of the subjects are presented in Table 1. No significant ($p > .05$) difference was apparent in the ages of the males and females. As expected, the males were significantly ($p < .05$) taller and heavier than the females. In addition, the males had a significantly ($p < .05$) lower body fat and higher fat free weight than the females. Over the weeks both groups slightly decreased their total body weights by .9 and .5 kg for the males and females respectively, but these changes were not significant ($p > .05$).

The results of the $\dot{V}O_2$ max and power tests are presented in Table 2. In response to the $\dot{V}O_2$ max swim tests, the males had significantly ($p < .01$) higher maxVE and $\dot{V}O_2$ max values when expressed in both absolute terms (L•min$^{-1}$) and relative to total body weight (ml•kg•min$^{-1}$) than the females. No significant ($p > .05$) differences were found between the sexes for maximal heart rates and respiratory exchange ratios.

With training, both sexes demonstrated significant ($p < .01$) increases in absolute and relative $\dot{V}O_2$ max, but no significant ($p > .05$) changes occurred in maxVE, RER, and heart rate responses. Furthermore, no significant ($p > .05$) interaction existed between the test and sex for any of these variables.

**Table 1.** Means and standard deviations of physical characteristics of male and female swimmers during pretest

|  | Males ($n = 14$) | Females ($n = 14$) |
| --- | --- | --- |
| Age (yr) | 20.3[a] | 20.8 |
|  | 1.8[b] | 1.6 |
| Weight (kg) | 75.4 | 64.1* |
|  | 8.00 | 9.16 |
| Height (cm) | 179.3 | 166.9* |
|  | 7.26 | 8.84 |
| Fat free weight (kg) | 65.0 | 48.6* |
|  | 6.79 | 5.69 |
| Percent body fat (%) | 13.7 | 23.4* |
|  | 4.58 | 5.16 |

[a]Mean. [b]Standard deviation.
*$p < .05$.

**Table 2.** Means and standard deviations of physiological responses to $\dot{V}O_2$ max and power tests in male ($n=14$) and female ($n=14$) swimmers

| Variable | Males Pre | Post | Females Pre | Post |
|---|---|---|---|---|
| $\dot{V}O_2$ max (L•min⁻¹) | 3.792[a] | 4.091 | 2.825 | 3.072 |
| | .401[b] | .392 | .343 | .427 |
| $\dot{V}O_2$ max (ml•kg•min⁻¹) | 49.9 | 55.0 | 44.5 | 48.8 |
| | 4.24 | 3.05 | 5.56 | 7.63 |
| Heart rate (bpm) | 182.1 | 182.6 | 183.4 | 182.7 |
| | 8.21 | 5.72 | 10.54 | 10.31 |
| maxVE (L•min⁻¹) | 137.5 | 141.4 | 98.1 | 101.3 |
| | 14.92 | 16.19 | 16.60 | 14.48 |
| RER | 1.03 | 1.07 | 1.01 | 1.02 |
| | .065 | .083 | .076 | .082 |
| Power (kgm•sec⁻¹) | 7.63 | 8.01 | 3.51 | 3.98 |
| | 2.141 | 2.086 | 1.076 | 1.018 |

[a]Mean. [b]Standard deviation.

The responses to the power test also indicated a significant ($p<.01$) difference between the males and females during both the pre- and posttests. Both groups significantly ($p<.01$) increased their power outputs over the training period, but the statistical analysis indicated that these improvements were similar ($p>.05$) between the sexes.

## Discussion

It is often assumed that swimmers have higher percent body fats than many other athletes. One of the most frequently cited values of 26.3% for intercollegiate female swimmers was indirectly determined by skinfolds (Conger & Macnab, 1967). Wilmore, Brown, and Davis (1977) hydrostatically weighed a team of female intercollegiate swimmers including sprint ($n=4$), middle distance ($n=7$), and distance swimmers ($n=4$) and reported percent body fats of 14.6%, 24.1%, and 17.1%, respectively. As a team these swimmers had an average of 19.7%, which is very similar to the 19.5% found for a group of 41 elite female swimmers (events not specified) by Fleck and Hagerman (1980). The 23.8% ascertained in the present study is higher than these values as well as those values reported for many other female athletes (Wilmore et al., 1977).

Although the 13.7% body fat for the male swimmers in the present study is higher than the 8.5% Sprynarova and Parizkova (1971) and the 5.0% Novak, Hyatt, and Alexander (1968) reported for male swimmers, it is similar to the 12.4% determined on 39 elite swimmers (Fleck & Hagerman, 1980).

The percent body fats of these swimmers are similar to those values of 15% and 25% often cited as representative of average males and females, respectively (Fox & Mathews, 1981). The subjects in the present study were not national caliber or elite swimmers but rather typical of a Division III, nonscholarship school. In addition, body fat determinations were obtained during the week prior to the actual start of the swimmers' fall training programs. Although both of these factors may have influenced the body composition of these swimmers, it also appears to support the assumption that swimmers do have a higher percent body fat than other athletes.

As expected, the males' maxVE was significantly higher throughout the pre- and posttests than the females' due to the significant differences in stature. The maxVE slightly increased in both groups with the training; however, these increases were not significant. These results support the findings of Houston, Wilson, Green, Thomason, and Ranney (1981); Lavoie and Thibault (1981); and Lavoie, Taylor, and Montpetit (1981) that maxVE does not increase in response to swim training. McArdle, Magel, Delio, Toner, and Chase (1978) found significant increases in maxVE responses to both swimming and running after run training. As a result of training, maxVE is thought to increase (Fox & Mathews, 1981), but this generalization is based predominately upon the results of running or cycling programs. The maxVE responses to swim training may be more restricted due to the limitations imposed by exercising in water.

No significant differences existed in heart rates or respiratory exchange ratios in response to the maximal swim tests between the sexes or with training. These values and lack of significant changes are similar to those results previously reported in response to swim testing/training (Houston et al., 1981; Lavoie, Taylor, & Montpetit, 1981; McArdle et al., 1978).

The initial $\dot{V}O_2$ max levels for both the male and female swimmers were higher than values previously reported for recreational swimmers (Lavoie & Thibault, 1981; Lavoie, Taylor, & Montpetit, 1980; McArdle et al., 1978), but lower than values reported for elite swimmers (Holmer, Lundin, & Eriksson, 1974; Lavoie, Taylor, & Montpetit, 1981). Specific comparisons are somewhat difficult since the majority of the aforementioned studies only reported values in $L \cdot min^{-1}$ which were quite dependent upon the physical size of the individual.

When $\dot{V}O_2$ max was expressed in absolute values ($L \cdot min^{-1}$) the male swimmers attained approximately a 34.2% greater value than the female swimmers. This difference was considerably reduced to 12.1% when expressed relative to body weight ($ml \cdot kg \cdot min^{-1}$). Recently Sparling (1980) analyzed the research literature dealing with $\dot{V}O_2$ max of males and females. When the $\dot{V}O_2$ max was expressed in absolute terms he found the average difference to be 56% (range: 28-70%) greater for males compared to females. The value in the present study falls at the lower end of this range. Sparling also found that the difference in $\dot{V}O_2$ max between the sexes was reduced to 28% (range: 16-46%) when expressed relative to bodyweight. The 12.1% difference in the present study was outside this range. Swimmers were not included in Sparling's (1980) analysis.

Over the 8 weeks of training both the males and females significantly increased the $\dot{V}O_2$ max ($L \cdot min^{-1}$) by 7.9% and 8.7%, respectively, and their $ml \cdot kg \cdot min^{-1}$ by 10.2% and 9.7%. Although larger improvements in $\dot{V}O_2$ max have been reported as a result of running programs for both sexes (Burke, 1977), the increases found in the present study are comparable to those previously found in response to swim training. Lavoie and Thibault (1981) reported a 4.2% and 7.1% increase as a result of an 8-week training program in male and female recreational swimmers. In contrast, Houston et al. (1981) did not find a significant increase after 6.5 weeks of training in their elite swimmers.

The statistical analysis revealed that there were no differences in the magnitude of improvements between the males' and females' $\dot{V}O_2$ max with the training, thus both sexes responded to the training in an analogous manner. These results support the findings of Burke (1977) for running. He compared improvements in the $\dot{V}O_2$ max of untrained college males and females after 8 weeks of training and concluded that both sexes significantly improved their $\dot{V}O_2$ max in a similar manner. Another study (Massicotte, Avon, & Corriveau, 1979) compared an older group of subjects to a 20-week aerobic type training program and reported no significant differences in the magnitude of cardiorespiratory improvements between the sexes. In a study of recreational swimmers, Lavoie and Thibault (1981) also reported no sex differences in response to swim training. Another study by Lavoie, Taylor, & Montpetit, (1981) reported significant increases of 8% and 7% in elite male and female swimmers' $L \cdot min^{-1}$ after 6 months of training. Although these authors did not indicate whether or not these increases were significantly different between the sexes, they would not appear to be.

As with the $\dot{V}O_2$ max, the males were able to generate significantly higher peak powers than the females. The females' peak powers were only 46% and 50% of the males' pre- and posttest values, respectively. These differences were a result of the males' ability to carry heavier weights rather than their ability to go faster during the test. Over the training period both the males and females significantly increased their peak powers by approximately 4.6% and 13.5%, respectively. The greater relative improvement in the females may have been a result of their lower initial power which would inflate the improvement when expressed as a percentage. Although the females increased their peak power to a relatively greater extent than the males, there was no significant interaction between the sexes in these increases. Again this indicated that both sexes responded in a similar manner to the equivalent training programs. Although there have been few studies reporting the effect of training on power changes between the sexes, these results would be in support of Wilmore (1974) who reported equal relative improvements in strength by males and females as a result of standard weight-training programs.

Based on numerous cross-sectional studies it has been established that males have a greater physiological work capacity than females. The results of this study support that concept, but they also support the theory that, when exposed to equivalent training, men and women do not show sex-related differences in the rate or magnitude of their physiological adaptations to such training.

# References

Brozek, J., Grande, G., Anderson, J., & Keys A. (1963). Densitometric analysis of body composition: Revisions of some quantitative assumptions. *Annals of the New York Academy of Science*, **110**, 113-140.

Burke, E. (1977). Physiological effects of similar training programs in males and females. *Research Quarterly*, **48**, 510-517.

Conger, P., & Macnab, R. (1967). Strength, body composition, and work capacity of participants and nonparticipants in women's intercollegiate sports. *Research Quarterly*, **38**, 184-192.

Ekblom, B. (1969). Effect of physical training on oxygen transport system in man. *Acta Physiologia Scandinavica* (Suppl. 328), 1-45.

Fleck, S., & Hagerman, G. (1980, July). Athlete's body-fat charts show interesting trends. *The Olympian*, pp. 14-17.

Fox, E., & Mathews, D. (1981). *The physiological basis of physical education and athletics*. New York: Saunders.

Holmer, I., Lundin, A., & Eriksson, B. (1974). Maximum oxygen uptake during swimming and running by elite swimmers. *Journal of Applied Physiology*, **36**, 711-714.

Houston, M., Wilson, D., Green, H., Thomason, J., & Ranney, D. (1981). Physiological and muscle enzyme adaptations to two different intensities of swim training. *European Journal of Applied Physiology*, **46**, 281-291.

Katch, F. (1968). Apparent body density and variability during underwater weighing. *Research Quarterly*, **39**, 993-999.

Lavoie, J., & Thibault, G. (1981). Specificity of swim training on maximal oxygen uptake: An inter-sex comparison. In J. Borms, M. Hebbelinck, & A. Venerando (Eds.), *Women and sport* (pp. 112-118). Basel, Switzerland: S. Karger AG.

Lavoie, J., Taylor, A., & Montpetit, R. (1980). Skeletal muscle fibre size adaptation to an eight-week swimming programme. *European Journal of Applied Physiology*, **44**, 161-165.

Lavoie, J., Taylor, A., & Montpetit, R. (1981). Physiological effects of training in elite swimmers as measured by a free swimming test. *Journal of Sports Medicine and Physical Fitness*, **21**, 38-42.

Massicotte, D., Avon, G., & Corriveau, G. (1979). Comparative effects of aerobic training on men and women. *Journal of Sports Medicine and Physical Fitness*, **19**, 23-32.

McArdle, W., Magel, J., Delio, D., Toner, M., & Chase, J. (1978). Specificity of run training on $VO_2$ max and heart rate changes during running and swimming. *Medicine and Science in Sports*, **10**, 16-20.

Novak, L., Hyatt, R., & Alexander, J. (1968). Body composition and physiologic function of athletes. *Journal of American Medical Association*, **205**, 764-770.

Roswell, L. (1974). Human cardiovascular adjustments to exercise and thermal stress. *Physiology Review*, **54**, 75-159.

Sparling, P. (1980). A meta-analysis of studies comparing maximal oxygen uptake in men and women. *Research Quarterly for Exercise and Sport*, **51**, 542-552.

Sprynarova, S., & Parizkova, J. (1971). Functional capacity and body composition in top weight lifters, swimmers, runners and skiers. *International Zeitschrift Agnew Physiologie*, **29**, 184-194.

Wilmore, J. (1969). A simplified method for determination of residual lung volume. *Journal of Applied Physiology*, **27**, 96-100.

Wilmore, J. (1974). Alterations in strength, body composition and anthropometric measurements consequent to a 10-week weight training program. *Medicine and Science in Sports*, **6**, 133-138.

Wilmore, J., Brown, C., & Davis, J. (1977). Body physique and composition of the female distance runner. *Annals of New York Academy of Science*, **301**, 764-776.

# 4

# Effect of the Onset and Intensity of Training on Menarchal Age and Menstrual Irregularity Among Elite Speedskaters

*Murray Joseph Casey, Ethelene C. Jones, Carl Foster, and Michael L. Pollock*
UNIVERSITY OF WISCONSIN AND MOUNT SINAI MEDICAL CENTER
MILWAUKEE, WISCONSIN, USA

*Jeffrey A. DuBois*
SMITH-KLINE CLINICAL LABORATORIES
SCHAUMBURG, ILLINOIS, USA

Delayed menarche and menstrual dysfunction among women engaged in strenuous exercise and athletic endeavors have been abundantly reported and the mechanisms which may be reponsible for these deviations are still the matter of considerable clinical endocrinologic research. The effect of body fat composition and variations in the serum levels of several hormones intimately involved in regulation of the menstrual cycle have been implicated by a number of authors. The current status of etiologic theorizing is little more than speculation based on data generated from observations on relatively small numbers of athletes and control subjects (Baker, 1981).

An elaborate program to medically and physiologically evaluate members of the 1983-84 U.S. Speedskating Team at the U.S. Olympic Committee Sports Medicine Research Site at Mount Sinai Medical Center in Milwaukee gave us an opportunity to gather data from the female members of that team. The data might be useful in further elucidating what effects the onset of training and training habits may have on menstrual function in these young women.

## Material and Methods

Female members of the U.S. Speedskating Team ($n = 17$) were evaluated. Their average age was 20.6 years (range 15 to 27). Team members were seen over 3-day periods at the beginning of team training in September and just prior to competition in December 1983. Thirteen skaters were seen in both September and December, two were seen only in September, and two others were seen only in December.

On both occasions, all skaters were meticulously interviewed by a gynecologist as to their lifelong training habits, competitive athletic experience, and menstrual histories. Details regarding past illnesses, medications, and methods of menstrual hygiene were recorded.

Percent body fat by the underwater weighing method and physiologic studies (Pollock, Wilmore, & Fox, 1984) were performed on all members of the team and are the subjects of another report (Pollock, Foster, Pels, & Holum, 1986). Complete physical examinations were offered to all skaters, and nine of the females elected to have pelvic examinations, but these findings will not be reported in this paper.

Sera for all biochemical tests were drawn in the morning with subjects in the resting, fasting state before interviews or physiologic tests were undertaken. During the first visit in September, sera were obtained from all subjects for determinations of androstenedione (A), dehydroepiandrosterone sulfate (DHEA-S), testosterone (T), esterone ($E_1$) and prolactin (PL). Sera were collected from 14 of 15 female skaters who were seen in December, and levels were determined for DHEA-S, dehydroepiandrosterone (DHEA), follicle stimulating hormone (FSH), luteinizing hormone (LH), $E_1$, estradiol ($E_2$) and estriol ($E_3$). Biochemical tests were performed in the Smith-Kline Clinical Laboratories, Inc., Schaumburg, IL.

Data gained from the interviews were correlated with determinations of percent body fat composition and the results of biochemical testing. A computer-assisted multivariant analysis was used, $r$-test values were determined for all correlations, and $t$ tests were conducted to determine differences in subgroup means. One of the skaters began using oral contraceptives in 1981; hormonal determinations from this subject were excluded from group means and correlations.

## Results

Tables 1 and 2 present a summary of the data which were gathered during the present project. Obviously, many interesting correlations may be drawn through a computer-assisted analysis of such a large number of variables in this small number of subjects. Therefore, this communication will be confined to the presentation of data which showed important trends and significant mean differences between subgroups and significant correlations that appeared as though they may be associated with delayed menarche and later tendencies to oligomenorrhea.

**Table 1.** Summary of data from menstrual and training histories of 17 elite female speed skaters in 1983

| Subject number | Age of menarche (years)* | Age began training (years)* | Current age (years)* | Longest interval periods (months) | Critical** level of training (hrs/wk) | Current level of training (hrs/wk) | Age at which training reached | | |
|---|---|---|---|---|---|---|---|---|---|
| | | | | | | | 8 hrs/wk (years)* | 16 hrs/wk (years)* | 24 hrs/wk (years)* |
| 8441† | 10 | 10 | 22 | 28 | 30 | 30 | 10 | 21 | 21 |
| 8426 | 12 | 16 | 19 | 28 | NE | 36 | 16 | 16 | 16 |
| 8401 | 12 | 6 | 16 | 30 | 35 | 35 | 6 | 6 | 11 |
| 8430 | 12 | 13 | 15 | 45 | 25 | 30 | 14 | 14 | 14 |
| 8429 | 12 | 8 | 27 | 365 | NE | 30 | 13 | 13 | 13 |
| 8402 | 13 | 14 | 18 | 180 | 28 | 18 | 14 | 14 | 18 |
| 8407 | 14 | 12 | 20 | 30 | NE | 42 | 16 | 16 | 17 |
| 8417 | 14 | 15 | 20 | 60 | NE | 24 | 15 | 15 | 18 |
| 8433 | 14.5 | 9 | 17 | 28 | NE | 24 | 9 | 9 | 17 |
| 8436 | 15 | 8 | 17 | 90 | NE | 30 | 8 | 9 | 12 |
| 8414 | 15 | 8 | 19 | 60 | 28 | 35, | 8 | 12 | 15 |
| 8415 | 15 | 9 | 17 | 240 | 18 | 30 | 14 | 19 | 19 |
| 8434 | 15 | 9 | 17 | 999≠ | 9 | 24 | 10 | 10 | 17 |
| 8423 | 17 | 12 | 22 | 150 | 12 | 26 | 12 | 16 | 16 |
| 8431 | 18 | 15 | 22 | 180 | NE | 36 | 16 | 16 | 16 |
| 8403 | 18 | 12 | 22 | 365 | 24 | 24 | 12 | 21 | 21 |
| 8437 | 18 | 14 | 21 | 365 | 6 | 24 | 14 | 21 | 21 |

*Note.* NE = No effect of training noted on menstrual function.

* Rounded to nearest years recalled by subject.

** Level of training at which irregular cycle or scantier menses was noted.

†Subject started oral contraceptives 1981.

≠ Subject had one menstrual period between menarche and September, 1983.

**Table 2.** Summary of body fat composition and serum hormone determinations of 17 elite female speed skaters in 1983

| Subject number | Body fat composition (percent) | Esterone Sept* (pg/ml) | Esterone Dec (pg/ml) | Estradiol Dec (pg/ml) | Estriol Dec (pg/ml) | Total estrogen Dec (pg/ml) | LH Dec (miu/ml) | FSH Dec (miu/ml) | T Sept ng/dl) | A Sept (ng/dl) | DHEA Dec (ng/dl) | DHEA-S Sept (ng/ml) | DHEA-S Dec (ng/ml) | PL Sept (ng/ml) |
|---|---|---|---|---|---|---|---|---|---|---|---|---|---|---|
| 8441 | 11 | 230 | 224 | 11 | 92 | 327 | 10 | 4 | 43 | 209 | 1690 | 3222 | 3515 | 13 |
| 8426 | 13 | 172 | 252 | 299 | 105 | 656 | 9 | 2 | 67 | 233 | 714 | 1928 | 2355 | 7 |
| 8401 | 17 | 200 | 241 | 87 | 89 | 417 | 7 | 2 | 54 | 103 | 1322 | 1921 | 2943 | 8 |
| 8430 | 21 | ND | 198 | 26 | 63 | 287 | 4 | 2 | ND | ND | 960 | ND | 1561 | ND |
| 8429 | 18 | 203 | ND | ND | ND | ND | ND | ND | 50 | 151 | ND | 1705 | ND | 9 |
| 8402 | 14 | 358 | 248 | 74 | 70 | 392 | 8 | 2 | 86 | 248 | 944 | 2195 | 3156 | 16 |
| 8407 | 19 | ND | 222 | 137 | 69 | 428 | 16 | 2 | ND | ND | 643 | ND | 2987 | ND |
| 8417 | 17 | 221 | 223 | 114 | 78 | 415 | 14 | 2 | 65 | 248 | 940 | 1895 | 2545 | 11 |
| 8433 | 13 | 205 | 204 | 37 | 97 | 338 | 11 | 5 | 81 | 257 | 1267 | 2160 | 2929 | 8 |
| 8436 | 19 | 280 | ND | ND | ND | ND | ND | ND | 64 | 367 | ND | 3609 | ND | 20 |
| 8414 | 22 | 263 | 222 | 5 | 55 | 282 | 7 | 2 | 69 | 242 | 1038 | 1932 | 2950 | 7 |
| 8415 | 15 | 244 | 226 | 82 | 79 | 387 | 11 | 2 | 96 | 158 | 788 | 1270 | 1874 | 6 |
| 8434 | 13 | 279 | 265 | 43 | 107 | 415 | 30 | 5 | 84 | 333 | 1656 | 3336 | 4247 | 11 |
| 8423 | 26 | 321 | 434 | 552 | 124 | 1110 | 26 | 2 | 83 | 187 | 1316 | 2716 | 3391 | 11 |
| 8431 | 21 | 291 | 259 | 39 | 98 | 396 | 7 | 2 | 72 | 291 | 2500 | 2238 | 2905 | 7 |
| 8403 | 12 | 260 | 217 | 16 | 91 | 324 | 16 | 7 | 88 | 287 | 1118 | 3908 | 3921 | 14 |
| 8437 | 17 | 276 | ND | ND | ND | ND | ND | ND | 67 | 282 | ND | 3289 | ND | 5 |

*Note.* ND = Not determined.
*Month determination was mode.

Although two of the 15 skaters who were seen in September at the beginning of team training had not had a menstrual period for over 90 days (8431, 8434), both of these young women reported at least one period before they were seen a second time in December. During the 3-month course of team training, which individually ranged from 18 to 42 h per week, only one athlete failed to menstruate (8415).

Skaters were divided into two groups depending upon whether they began training for competitive sports before or after menarche. A significant difference existed in the mean menarchal age of 15.3 years for those who began training prior to menarche compared with 12.2 years for those who began training after menarche (Table 3).

The 12 skaters who began training before menarche also appeared to be more prone to oligomenorrhea, as measured by the mean of the longest interval between periods. Eight of the 12 skaters who began to train for competition before menarche experienced prolonged intervals of 90 days or more between menstrual periods compared with only one of five skaters who began their training after menarche (Table 4). Moreover, the mean "critical level" of training hours per week at which some skaters noted prolongation of menstrual cycles and/or scantier menses was lower in the group of 12 skaters who began training before menarche compared with the five skaters who began to train after menarche (Table 3). Individually, seven of those who trained premenarchally and three of those who began training after menarche reported changes in their cycles or menstrual flow with training. The average critical level of training at which changes were noted by those who experienced disturbances in the group training before menarche was only 19 h per week compared with an average critical level of 28 h per week noted by those who delayed training until after menarche (Table 4).

When the 10 skaters who trained at least 8 h per week before menarche were compared with those who engaged in no premenarchal training, the difference in mean menarchal age reached an even higher level of statistical significant (Table 5). Again, the group that trained premenarchally reported greater

**Table 3.** Group mean differences in age of menarche and menstrual histories between skaters who began training prior to menarche compared with skaters who began training after menarche

| Variable | Some premenarchal training (12 subjects) | No premenarchal training (5 subjects) |
|---|---|---|
| Age competitive training began (years) | 10.2* | 13.6* |
| Age of menarche (years) | 15.3** | 12.2** |
| Longest interval between periods (days) | 241.8 | 68.2 |
| Critical level of training for menstrual change (hrs/wk) | 18.9 | 27.7 |

*$p < .05$.
**$p < .01$.

**Table 4.** Effect of onset and intensity of training on menarchal age and menstrual histories in 17 elite speedskaters

| Group | Age of menarche (range) | Longest interval between periods 90 days or more (no. with prolong periods/ no. in group) | Menstrual periods affected by training (no. noting changes/ no. in group) | Average critical level of training of subjects noting changes (hrs/wk) |
|---|---|---|---|---|
| No premenarchal training | 10-14 Yrs | 1/5 | 3/5 | 28 |
| Some premenarchal training | 12-18 Yrs | 8/12 | 7/12 | 19 |
| Trained < 8 hrs/wk before menarche | 12-14 Yrs | 1/2 | 0/2 | none with change |
| Trained > 8 hrs/wk before menarche | 12-18 Yrs | 6/10 | 7/10 | 19 |
| Began > 8 hrs/wk training before age 10 yrs | 10-15 Yrs | 1/4 | 2/4 | 32 |
| Began > 8 hrs/wk training after age 10 yrs and before menarche | 15-18 Yrs | 6/6 | 5/6 | 14 |

intervals between their longest periods and lower critical levels of training at which menstrual disturbances were noted (Table 5).

Of the 10 skaters who began training more than 8 h per week before menarche, 6 reported prolonged intervals between menstrual periods of 90 days or more (Table 4). Among the 12 skaters who trained before menarche, 7 skaters within the group who trained more than 8 h per week experienced changes in their menstrual functions with training at average critical levels of 19 h per week. All but two of those who began to train before menarche reached an intensity of at least 8 h per week. Neither of the two skaters who trained less than 8 h per week before menarche reported noticing any association between their levels of training and menstrual disturbances; although one of these young women acknowledged an interval of oligomenorrhea lasting for 1 year (Table 4).

The subgroup of skaters who trained seriously more than 8 h per week before menarche were also examined, and significant mean differences were found between four skaters who started training prior to age 10 years and the six skaters who began training after 10 years of age (Table 6). Here the mean differences between both longest intervals and lower critical levels reached statistical significance.

All of the six young women who began training more than 8 hr a week after age 10 years but before menarche reported intervals of 90 or more days between menstrual periods, whereas prolonged intervals were reported by only one of the four subjects who began training 8 h per week before 10 years of age (Table 4). Five of the six athletes in the former group and two of the latter group reported that changes in their cycles were associated with training. The critical level at which these changes were noted was only 14 h per week in the group that began training after 10 years but before menarche. In contrast, critical levels of 28 and 35 h per week were reported by the two subjects who reached 8 h of training before age 10 years (Table 4).

Comparing the group of six skaters who began to train more than 8 h per week after age 10 but before menarche with those who engaged in no premenarchal training showed statistically significant differences in the mean age of

**Table 5.** Group mean differences in age of menarche and menstrual histories between skaters who began training 8 hrs/week or more prior to menarche compared with skaters who began training after menarche

| Variable | Group means | |
| | Premenarchal training > 8 hrs/wk (10 subjects) | No premenarchal training (5 subjects) |
| --- | --- | --- |
| Age competitive training began (years) | 10.2* | 13.6* |
| Age of menarche (years) | 15.8** | 12.2** |
| Longest interval between periods (days) | 250.7 | 68.2 |
| Critical level of training for menstrual change (hrs/wk) | 18.9** | 27.7** |

*$p < .05$.
**$p < .01$.

**Table 6.** Group mean differences in age of menarche and menstrual histories between skaters who began premenarchal training 8 hrs/week or more before age 10 years compared with skaters who began premenarchal training 8 hrs/week or more after age 10 years

| | Group means | |
| | Premenarchal training before age 10 yrs > 8 hrs/wk | Premenarchal training after age 10 yrs > 8 hrs/wk |
| Variable | (4 subjects) | (6 subjects) |
| --- | --- | --- |
| Age competitive training began (years) | 7.8** | 11.8** |
| Age of menarche (years) | 14.1* | 16.9* |
| Longest interval between periods (days) | 52.0* | 383.2* |
| Critical level of training for menstrual change (hrs/wk) | 31.5* | 13.8* |

*$p < .05$.
**$p < .01$.

menarche, longest intervals between periods, and critical levels of weekly training at which menstrual changes were noted. No significant differences existed in the mean menarchal age, longest interval, or critical level between the four young women who had started training before age 10 years and those who had no premenarchal training experience (Table 7).

In spite of the older menarchal ages and greater tendency to menstrual irregularities seen in skaters who began competitive training prior to menarche, especially if training exceeded 8 h per week and began after age 10 years, no significant differences were apparent between mean body fat composition or serum hormone levels of those groups compared with skaters who began training after menarche (Table 2).

Next we sought to elucidate possible physiologic mechanisms which may be responsible for the abnormalities that had been noted in those who undertook intensive competitive training shortly before their expected menarche. The mean data of nine subjects who reported longest intervals between periods of 90 days or more were compared with the mean data of eight subjects who had never experienced intervals as long as 90 days between periods (Table 8). Although there were significant differences in the mean menarchal age, the longest intervals between periods, and the critical levels when these two groups were compared; no other differences were found.

Correlation coefficients were calculated for 24 variables for all 17 skaters as well as for several subgroups of skaters. In the total group of skaters, the critical levels of training at which menstrual changes were noticed decreased as menarchal ages increased. Lower critical levels of training before menstrual changes, in turn, correlated with longer reported intervals between periods (Table 9). Furthermore, both lower critical levels and longest intervals correlated with levels of serum LH.

In the whole group of 17 female skaters, a high correlation existed between levels of DHEA-S in sera drawn during the first evaluation in September and DHEA-S levels in sera drawn 3 months later in December ($p < .001$). Serum

**Table 7.** Group mean differences in age of menarche and menstrual histories comparing skaters who began training after menarche with skaters who began premenarchal training 8 hrs/week or more before and after age 10 years

| Variable | No premenarchal training (5 subjects) | Premenarchal training > 8 hrs/wk before age 10 yrs (4 subjects) | Premenarchal training > 8 hrs/wk after age 10 yrs (6 subjects) |
|---|---|---|---|
| Age competitive training began (years) | 13.6* | 7.8* | 11.8* |
| Age of menarche (years) | 12.2* | 14.1 | 16.9* |
| Longest interval between periods (days) | 68.2** | 52.0 | 383.2** |
| Critical level of training for menstrual change (hrs/wk) | 27.7* | 31.5 | 13.8* |

*p < .05.
**p < .01.

**Table 8.** Group mean differences in age of menarche and menstrual histories comparing skaters who reported no oligomenorrhea with skaters who reported oligomenorrhea

| Variable | No oligomenorrhea longest interval < 90 days (8 subjects) | Oligomenorrhea longest interval 90 days or more (9 subjects) |
|---|---|---|
| Age competitive training began (years) | 11.1 | 11.2 |
| Age of menarche (years) | 12.9* | 15.7* |
| Longest interval between periods (days) | 38.6** | 326.0** |
| Critical level of training for menstrual change (hrs/wk) | 29.5* | 16.2* |

*$p < .05$.
**$p < .01$.

**Table 9.** Correlations of paired variables from menstrual histories and serum biochemical determinations in 17 elite female speedskaters

| Paired variables | | $r$ | $p$ |
|---|---|---|---|
| Age of menarche | Critical level | − .703 | <.05 |
| Longest interval | Critical level | − .664 | <.05 |
| Longest interval | LH | .701 | <.01 |
| Critical level | LH | − .865 | <.01 |
| DHEA-S[1] | DHEA-S[2] | .916 | <.01 |
| DHEA-S[1] | LH | .625 | <.05 |
| DHEA-S[2] | LH | .687 | <.01 |
| DHEA-S[1] | FSH | .793 | <.01 |
| DHEA-S[2] | FSH | .623 | <.05 |
| DHEA-S[1] | PL | .646 | <.05 |
| DHEA-S[2] | PL | .845 | <.01 |

[1]Determination in September.
[2]Determination in December.

levels of DHEA-S drawn in both September and December correlated with serum FSH and LH levels which were determined only in December. Serum PL determinations correlated with DHEA-S levels in September ($p < .05$) and also with serum levels of DHEA-S drawn in December ($p < .01$).

Data were segregated into several subgroups for correlation analysis. Subjects were divided into those whose longest intervals between menstrual periods equaled or exceeded 90 days and those whose longest intervals were shorter than this. A negative correlation was found between reported critical levels of training at which menstrual disturbances were noted and serum levels of LH ($p < .05$) in the group of young women with longer periods, but not among those with more normal cycles. In both groups, serum levels of DHEA-S drawn in September correlated with serum FSH levels.

Finally, mean variables of the young women who won the opportunity to compete in the 1984 Winter Olympic games were compared with those who did not participate. No significant differences existed between these two groups for mean age, age of menarche, longest intervals between periods, critical levels of training at which changes in menstrual cycles were noted, age at which athletic training began, level of athletic training at the time of these studies, or any serum hormone determinations. While there was no difference between the mean age at which the two groups reached training levels of 8 h per week, the mean age at which training reached 16 h per week was 17.3 years for those who participated in the Olympic games, compared with 12.7 years for those who did not ($p < .05$).

## Summary and Conclusions

We found that female members of the 1983-84 U.S. Speedskating Team who began competitive training before menarche tended to have older ages of menarche and were more likely to report one or more episodes of oligomenorrhea, defined here as intervals between menstrual periods of at least 90 days, than skaters who did not begin training until after menarche. Moreover, the mean critical level of training in hours per week at which those who trained premenarchally experienced menstrual disturbances was significantly lower than the level of training at which changes were reported by those whose competitive training began after menarche.

The latest menarchal ages and greatest disruption in menstrual function, as measured by oligomenorrhea and lowest critical levels, were found in a group of skaters who began intensive competitive training in late childhood or early adolescence. Those who began training in earlier childhood, even when training was intensive, had menarchal ages and critical levels similar to skaters who delayed training until after menarche.

As a group, we found that subjects who reported oligomenorrhea also noted that they experienced irregular and/or scanty menstrual periods at lower levels of training in hours per week than those who did not have oligomenorrhea. Although the mean ages at which athletic training began and the current hours per week of training did not differ significantly between skaters who reported oligomenorrhea and those who did not, the mean age of menarche was significantly older in the oligomenorrheic subjects.

During the period of team training when we examined the skaters in late 1983, there was considerable similarity in the intensity of their athletic training. All but one of the skaters trained more than 24 h per week (range 18 to 42 h, mean 30 hr). The level of training during this time equaled or exceeded the critical level at which eight skaters reported changes in their menstrual function; yet only one skater developed oligomenorrhea during the 3-month interval between our examinations.

In spite of the marked differences in menarchal age and menstrual function that were apparently associated with the time of onset and intensity of training in the various subgroups that are reported here, we could demonstrate no difference in body fat composition or levels of the several serum hormones that were determined. Furthermore, differences in body fat composition and serum hormones did not exist between subgroups or skaters who reported oligomenorrhea and those who did not.

Although the focus of this study has been on the long-range effects of intensive athletic training and no attempt was made to determine acute changes in serum hormone levels that may be brought on by exercise, we found that the lowest critical levels of training before menstrual disturbances and the longest intervals between periods correlated positively with serum LH levels. A correlation also existed, though lower, between prolonged menstrual periods and serum levels of DHEA-S. Serum DHEA-S levels, in turn, correlated with levels of LH, FSH, and PL. Additional investigations are needed to determine the significance of these findings before they can be related to menstrual and reproductive functions.

Our data suggest that the initiation of intensive training programs during the pubertal phase of development may have a disruptive effect on the establishment of menarche at the usual age and may lead to subsequent menstrual irregularities. Skaters who first began intensive training before menarche but after 10 years of age reported delayed menarchal ages, oligomenorrhea, and menstrual irregularities at relatively lower levels of training. On the other hand, normal menstrual histories were found in elite skaters who engaged in serious training before the perimenarchal period or after menarche. Further studies are necessary to confirm these observations.

# References

Baker, E.R. (1981). Menstrual dysfunction and hormonal status in athletic women: A review, *Fertility & Sterility*, **36**, 691-696.

Pollock, M.L., Foster, C., Pels, A.E., & Holum, D. (1986). Comparison of male and female speed skating candidates. In D. Landers (Ed.), *Sport and the elite performer* (pp. 143-152). Champaign, IL: Human Kinetics.

Pollock, M.L., Wilmore, J.H., & Fox, S.M. II (1984). *Exercise in health and disease*, Philadelphia: Saunders.

# 5

# *Biomechanical Study on a New Crouching Start (Chen's Start)*

*Chuan-Show Chen, Tetsuo Koyama, Norio Higuchi, Ching-Long Chen, and Hiroyuki Taki*
CHUKYO UNIVERSITY
TOYOTA CITY, AICHI PREFECTURE, JAPAN

A good start in sprint events can make a major contribution to performances (Luhtanen & Komi, 1979; Mascurier, 1974). Studies have employed biomechanical parameters to examine the mechanism of the sprint start, and most of these studies have been concerned mainly with the reaction at the start and the forces exerted by the thrusting of the sprinter's legs against the starting block when using different foot spaces (Kinbara, 1964; Luhtanen & Komi, 1979; Moore & Hutton, 1980). Many studies have stressed examination of the runner's starting reaction time and movement time following firing of the gun (Kinbara, 1964).

For this study, a new modified crouching start (Chen's start) was designed for the sprint events. The position of the rear leg differs in Chen's start from the conventional start. The new start follows the conventional one in placing both feet on the starting blocks, but in the "set" position the front leg thrusts while the rear leg pulls isometrically. In the conventional start, both legs push at the same time. The Chen's start allows the rear leg to be released vigorously at the sound of the gun.

---

The author thanks Mrs. Chi Cheng (former sprint world record holder and now a senator in the Legislative Yen of Taiwan, ROC) for her helpful and constructive advice during this study. Miss Annette Lord also helped so much to complete this manuscript.

## Method

### Equipment

The newly designed starting block is shown in Figure 1. The rear block stands out at right angles to the shank, and the arms of the rear block slide to adjust the height of the pulling leg. Adjustment of the foot space is made by moving both blocks. A roller covered with rubber is fixed on the rear block, allowing the back of the rear pulling foot to move out from it quickly and with tension.

### Subjects

Subjects were eight university decathlon athletes, 19 to 22 years of age. They had all trained regularly for several years and had already mastered the conventional start (Table 1). Measurements taken included EMGs, forces, angles, position, reaction time, movement time, and performance time for the 30 m dash.

### EMGs

The mechanism of muscle contraction during the "on your mark" and "set" position were studied by recording the action potential from the muscles of both legs. Muscles concerned were the rectus femoris, gluteus medialis, biceps femoris, tibialis anterior, and gastrocnemius in the lower extremities.

**Figure 1.** Chen's starting block.

**Table 1.** Characteristics of subjects

| Subject | Age (yr) | Ht (cm) | Wt (kg) | 100m time (s) | Front leg |
|---------|----------|---------|---------|---------------|-----------|
| 1 | 22 | 175.0 | 66.6 | 10.9 | Left |
| 2 | 21 | 179.0 | 73.0 | 11.2 | Left |
| 3 | 19 | 170.0 | 62.5 | 11.3 | Left |
| 4 | 22 | 174.0 | 68.5 | 10.7 | Left |
| 5 | 21 | 169.0 | 71.0 | 11.0 | Right |
| 6 | 22 | 171.5 | 61.0 | 11.4 | Right |
| 7 | 21 | 179.0 | 72.0 | 11.2 | Right |
| 8 | 21 | 173.0 | 69.5 | 11.2 | Right |
| *M* | 21.1 | 173.81 | 68.01 | 11.24 | |
| *SD* | 0.9 | 3.52 | 4.09 | 0.42 | |

## Forces

Forces exerted by the thrusting legs in the "set" position until the runner broke contact with the front block were measured by force platforms (KISTLER Type 9281B). The force platform placed on the track with specially devised aluminum covers on which the starting blocks were firmly fixed. Forces along the vertical and horizontal directions of both legs were measured.

## Performance

Reaction time, movement time, and performance time in the 30 m dash were measured by a time counter which was triggered automatically by the starting gun. It was stopped by a signal from the photocell located at the finish line (Figure 2).

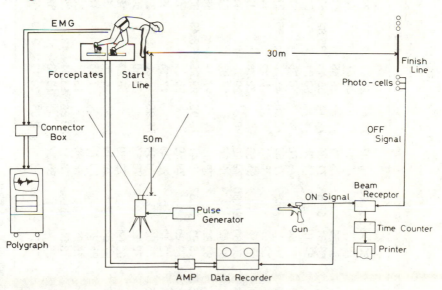

**Figure 2.** Scheme of the setup for start comparisons.

**Table 2.** Comparison of peak forces (kg) of two different starts

| | Conventional start | | | | Chen's start | | | |
|---|---|---|---|---|---|---|---|---|
| | Front leg | | Rear leg | | Front leg | | Rear leg | |
| Subject | Horizontal (backward) | Vertical | Horizontal (backward) | Vertical | Horizontal (backward) | Vertical | Horizontal (forward) | Vertical |
| 1 | 83.44 | 79.19 | 19.42 | 32.27 | 78.91 | 82.88 | 16.81 | 4.85 |
| | 80.04 (81.05) | 80.37 (79.45) | 20.14 (21.98) | 29.04 (34.59) | 92.07 (85.31) | 81.55 (82.88) | 19.47 (18.52) | 0.76 (2.37) |
| | 79.67 | 78.80 | 36.37 | 42.46 | 84.94 | 84.21 | 19.29 | 1.50 |
| 2 | 53.59 | 73.71 | 38.48 | 61.65 | 78.91 | 74.46 | 13.78 | 0.33 |
| | 63.81 (60.53) | 71.35 (72.14) | 35.16 (35.82) | 59.44 (60.86) | 79.46 (77.09) | 78.01 (76.38) | 15.06 (14.30) | 0.73 (0.85) |
| | 64.19 | 71.35 | 33.81 | 61.48 | 72.89 | 76.68 | 14.05 | 1.50 |
| 3 | 78.54 | 78.80 | 6.35 | 17.49 | 77.82 | 82.44 | 15.15 | 0.70 |
| | 76.25 (75.89) | 77.63 (78.28) | 11.15 (7.95) | 27.17 (20.32) | 76.72 (75.44) | 80.22 (77.53) | 13.41 (13.90) | 0.90 (1.45) |
| | 72.87 | 78.41 | 6.35 | 16.30 | 71.79 | 69.93 | 13.13 | 2.76 |
| 4 | 81.18 | 81.55 | 22.78 | 37.19 | 94.81 | 89.53 | 9.92 | 7.91 |
| | 80.80 (80.80) | 79.19 (80.24) | 29.73 (26.69) | 61.65 (53.61) | 84.94 (89.69) | 84.21 (84.51) | 16.35 (14.05) | 5.52 (4.70) |
| | 80.42 | 79.98 | 27.57 | 61.99 | 89.33 | 79.78 | 15.89 | 0.66 |
| 5 | 83.82 | 79.19 | 27.69 | 58.01 | 103.57 | 89.97 | 22.50 | 2.19 |
| | 78.91 (80.67) | 78.41 (79.06) | 29.25 (28.49) | 60.12 (59.36) | 97.00 (99.74) | 85.54 (85.69) | 20.21 (21.34) | 0 (0.73) |
| | 79.29 | 79.59 | 28.53 | 59.95 | 98.64 | 81.55 | 21.31 | 0 |
| 6 | 72.12 | 78.40 | 17.14 | 38.55 | 77.82 | 70.92 | 21.68 | 0 |
| | 75.89 (73.38) | 76.84 (77.36) | 17.98 (19.54) | 37.70 (42.40) | 71.79 (74.17) | 70.92 (70.48) | 19.38 (20.70) | 0 (0) |
| | 72.12 | 76.84 | 23.50 | 50.95 | 72.89 | 69.59 | 21.03 | 0 |
| 7 | 93.64 | 79.59 | 8.27 | 18.68 | 105.20 | 84.66 | 16.72 | 0 |
| | 97.04 (95.65) | 79.19 (79.85) | 5.75 (7.15) | 9.00 (14.72) | 102.48 (106.67) | 85.98 (84.95) | 18.09 (18.12) | 0 (0.31) |
| | 96.28 | 80.76 | 7.43 | 16.47 | 112.34 | 84.21 | 19.56 | 0.93 |
| 8 | 75.89 | 78.80 | 13.91 | 30.91 | 78.37 | 82.88 | 16.53 | 3.69 |
| | 78.53 (80.42) | 78.41 (80.86) | 13.91 (13.75) | 39.23 (34.36) | 89.33 (85.13) | 82.88 (82.59) | 15.61 (16.62) | 5.88 (4.45) |
| | 86.84 | 85.37 | 13.43 | 32.95 | 87.68 | 82.00 | 17.73 | 3.79 |
| M ± SD | 78.55 ± 9.16 | 78.41 ± 2.58 | 20.17 ± 9.49 | 40.03 ± 16.16 | 86.66* ± 10.94 | 80.62 ± 4.99 | 17.19** ± 2.77 | 1.86** ± 1.70 |

*Significant at .05 level.
**Significant at .001 level.

# Results

### Peak Forces

The results of the analysis of variance showed, first of all, that the new start increased horizontal peak force in the front leg significantly. The horizontal force at start was $78.55 \pm 9.16$kg for the conventional one, and $86.66 \pm 10.94$kg for the new start (Table 2). Pressure on the hands during the "set" position was reduced greatly. For the conventional start, pressure on the hands was $27.05 \pm 2.87$kg, while it was $21.79 \pm 2.78$kg for the new start (Table 3).

The two starts differed in direction and magnitude of the horizontal forces exerted by the rear leg. The conventional start had a backward direction with a peak force of $20.17 \pm 9.49$kg, and Chen's start had a forward direction with a peak force of $17.19 \pm 2.77$kg. A small upward directional force from the rear leg existed in Chen's start, and this force turned downward as the runner began to pull after the sound of the gun (Figure 3).

The total peak force in the conventional start at the time of the start from both legs was 118.44kg in a vertical direction, whereas force from the rear leg was 40.03kg (33.80%). In the horizontal direction, the total peak force was 98.72kg and the force from the rear leg amounted to 20.17kg (20.43%). In the new start the total peak vertical force was 82.48kg, of which the force from the rear leg comprised 1.86kg (2.26%). The total peak horizontal force in the new start was 103.85kg, with a rear leg force of 17.19 kg (16.55%) in a forward direction during "set" position. The significant increase in the front leg's horizontal force at the start is one of the most important factors enhancing mechanical efficiency for a good start.

### Form

Analysis of film taken with a high speed cinecamera showed that the two starts manifested different starting profiles during the "set" position and when beginning to take the first step after the gun was fired. In Chen's start the runner raised his hip higher and placed his front leg closer to the starting line than

**Table 3.** Comparison of pressure on hands (kg) at start between two starts

| Subject | Conventional start | Chen's start |
|---|---|---|
| 1 | 25.39 | 22.73 |
| 2 | 30.19 | 20.72 |
| 3 | 22.40 | 18.84 |
| 4 | 25.62 | 26.94 |
| 5 | 27.81 | 22.49 |
| 6 | 24.38 | 18.62 |
| 7 | 30.18 | 25.20 |
| 8 | 30.50 | 19.17 |
| M | 27.05 | 21.79* |
| SD | 2.87 | 2.87 |

*Significant at .01 level.

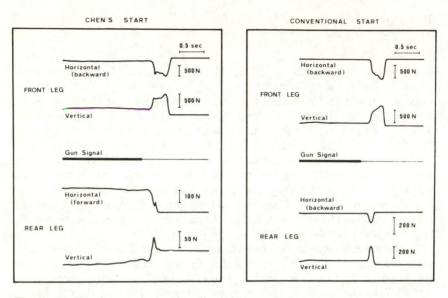

**Figure 3.** The forces during "set" position and at start.

in the conventional start. At the same time, while in the "set" position, the runner moved his shoulder farther away from the starting line in Chen's start than he did for the conventional start. The angle between the line from the hands and the vertical line down from the acromion to the ground was greater in Chen's start, which meant the upper portion of the body could move for-

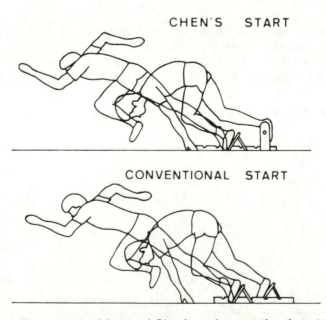

**Figure 4.** Comparison of forms of Chen's and conventional starts.

ward farther. The angles between the trunk and the horizontal at the time just before the leg broke contact with the front block were smaller in Chen's start (Figure 4).

### Performance

The time for the 30 m dash was shortened when using Chen's start. Time for the conventional start was $4.475 \pm 0.127$ s, and for the new start it was $4.446 \pm 0.150$ s. Average running time was reduced by 0.029 s, even though the runner did not have much time to practice Chen's start (Table 4).

### Length of the First Step

Parameters for a reasonably good sprint start should be that, while moving fast, the runner can take a long first step while keeping a low body profile. In Chen's start the first step was lengthened by 5.24 cm over the conventional start. This lengthening was due to an increase in the horizontal thrust forces from the front leg at the start (Table 5).

**Table 4.** Comparison of 30 m dash times (s) between two different starts

| Subject | Conventional start | | | | Chen's start | | | |
|---|---|---|---|---|---|---|---|---|
| | 1 | 2 | 3 | M | 1 | 2 | 3 | M |
| 1 | 4.38 | 4.33 | 4.33 | 4.35 | 4.27 | 4.29 | 4.27 | 4.28 |
| 2 | 4.44 | 4.43 | 4.45 | 4.44 | 4.45 | 4.32 | 4.41 | 4.39 |
| 3 | 4.49 | 4.52 | 4.57 | 4.53 | 4.54 | — | — | 4.54 |
| 4 | 4.34 | 4.46 | 4.46 | 4.42 | 4.45 | 4.41 | 4.47 | 4.44 |
| 5 | 4.47 | 4.40 | 4.37 | 4.41 | 4.27 | 4.35 | 4.42 | 4.35 |
| 6 | 4.54 | 4.50 | 4.52 | 4.52 | 4.52 | 4.51 | 4.58 | 4.53 |
| 7 | 4.41 | 4.33 | 4.33 | 4.36 | 4.25 | 4.33 | 4.27 | 4.28 |
| 8 | — | 4.77 | — | 4.77 | 4.71 | 4.79 | 4.78 | 4.76 |
| M | | | | 4.475 | | | | 4.446 |
| SD | | | | 0.127 | | | | 0.150 |

**Table 5.** Length (cm) of the first step of the two different starts

| Subject | Conventional start | | | | Chen's start | | | |
|---|---|---|---|---|---|---|---|---|
| | 1 | 2 | 3 | M | 1 | 2 | 3 | M |
| 1 | 44.5 | 40.5 | 34.4 | 39.8 | 57.4 | 54.4 | 55.0 | 55.6 |
| 2 | 54.0 | 59.1 | 44.5 | 52.5 | 32.0 | 47.3 | 49.0 | 42.8 |
| 3 | 41.5 | 53.0 | 44.0 | 46.2 | 56.0 | — | — | 56.0 |
| 4 | 43.5 | 34.5 | 37.0 | 38.3 | 46.0 | 45.0 | 49.5 | 46.8 |
| 5 | 47.5 | 48.3 | 50.8 | 48.9 | 47.5 | 41.1 | 50.3 | 46.3 |
| 6 | 56.5 | 51.0 | 59.0 | 55.0 | 55.0 | 61.2 | 40.5 | 52.2 |
| 7 | 49.0 | 43.0 | 42.0 | 44.7 | 60.1 | 47.3 | 50.5 | 52.6 |
| 8 | 29.5 | 29.0 | — | 29.3 | 46.5 | 52.4 | 35.6 | 44.8 |
| M | | | | 44.39 | | | | 49.63 |
| SD | | | | 7.91 | | | | 4.75 |

## EMGs

Electromyographic study indicated that while the runner was in the "on your mark" position, muscles of rectus femoris and tibialis anterior in the front leg worked intensively during the conventional start (Figure 5), while in Chen's start the tibialis anterior in the rear leg showed a moderately low continuous

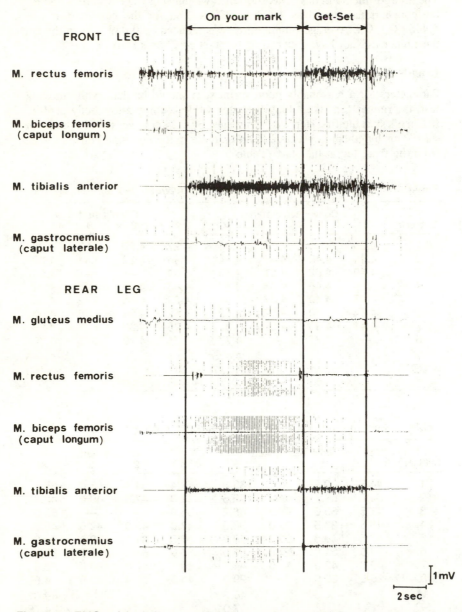

**Figure 5.** EMGs of the lower extremities' muscles during "on your mark" and "set" positions in conventional start.

electrical activity (Figure 6). EMGs showed an increased voltage in all muscles for the ''set'' position in the two starts. The pretensed pulling leg in Chen's start increased amplitude from the rectus femoris and tibialis anterior muscles in the rear leg, and the pulling action of the rear leg in Chen's start strengthened the thrusting action of the front leg (see Figures 5 and 6).

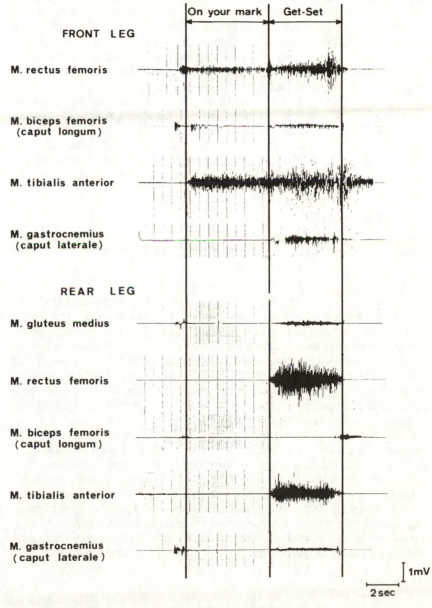

**Figure 6.** EMGs of the lower extremities' muscles during ''on your mark'' and ''set'' positions in Chen's start.

# Discussion

The isometrical contraction of the rectus femoris and tibialis anterior muscles shifted part of the weight of the upper trunk back, resulting in reduced pressure on the hands. This allowed the runner to move his hands freely at the start. A strong and effective hand movement gave the thrusting leg a great deal of help in pushing the body away from the block when the gun was heard (Chaffin, Lee, & Freivalds, 1980; Moore & Hutton, 1980). The pulling leg retained some tension during the "set" position, which accelerated the vigorous forward drive of the rear leg, and a strongly driving rear leg strengthened the thrusting force of the front leg (Cavagna, 1975; Cavagna, Komapek, & Mazzolen, 1971; Cavagna & Saibene, 1964).

These EMG findings provided evidence that Chen's start had two main advantages. Firstly, isometric pulling of the rear leg during the "set" position stored energy for the following driving action once the gun was heard and reduced the weight of the upper trunk on the runner's hands. Secondly, the horizontal force of the front leg was increased by the counter action of the pulling leg, which also lengthened the first step of the sprint start (Frishburg, 1984; Luhtanen & Komi, 1979).

## Performance Time

Time in the 30 m dash was improved by use of the new start. This result confirmed our hypothesis that a good start is vital in sprint events.

## Forces

Chen's start increased the forces while the runner was on the starting block. The dorsa of the rear foot was used to pull the body from the rear block isometrically, and this counter action against the push of the front leg significantly strengthened the horizontal thrust force from the "set" position until the time when the runner started to drive forward. This force increase in the front leg greatly contributed to lengthening the first step, as well as lowering the angle of decline of the starting position. These conditions are vital for a good sprint. The pulling rear leg in the "set" position provided the means of satisfying these requirements.

From the viewpoint of strength exercise, the pulling rear leg is effectively conditioned by a kind of isometric weight training. This increases thrusting force and trains the neuromotor pattern appropriate for the sprint start.

In summary, the results of this study support our hypothesis that a pretensed pulling rear leg during the "set" position strenghthens the thrust, particularly the peak horizontal force, in the front leg. It also reduces the amount of pressure on the hands and prevents the runner from unintentionally breaking away too soon. The new start also has the advantage of being easy to learn and of providing a kind of isometric exercise to improve muscle strength for sprinters.

# References

Cavagna, G.A. (1975). Force platform as ergometer. *Journal of Applied Physiology*, **39**(1), 174-179.

Cavagna, G.A., Komapek, L., & Mazzolen, S. (1971). The mechanism of sprint running. *Journal of Applied Physiology*, **217**, 709-721.

Cavagna, G.A., & Saibene, P.P. (1964). Mechanical work in running. *Journal of Applied Physiology*, **19**, 249-256.

Chaffin, D.B., Lee, M., & Freivalds, A. (1980). Muscle strength assessment from EMG analysis. *Medicine and Science in Sports*, **12**(3), 205-211.

Fenn, W.O. (1930). Work against gravity and work due to velocity change in running. *American Journal of Physiology*, **93**, 433-462.

Frishburg, B.A. (1984). An analysis of overground and treadmill sprinting. *Medicine and Science in Sport*, **15**(6), 478-485.

Kinbara, I. (1964). *Track & field*. Tokyo, Japan: T. Suzuki.

Luhtanen, P., Komi, P.V. (1979). Mechanical power and segmental contribution to force impulse in long jump take-off. *European Journal of Applied Physiology*, **41**, 267-274.

Mascurier, J.L. (1974). *Hurdling*. London: British Amateur Athletic Board.

Moore, M.A., & Hutton, R.S. (1980). Electromyographic investigation of muscle stretching techniques. *Medicine and Science in Sports*, **12**(3), 205-211.

Wilt, F., & Ecker, T. (1971). *International track & field coaching encyclopedia*. New York: Parker.

# 6

# *Elite and Subelite Female Middle- and Long-distance Runners*

*Jack Daniels and Nancy Scardina*
EUGENE, OREGON, USA

*John Hayes*
TEMPE, ARIZONA, USA

*Peter Foley*
WEST LAFAYETTE, INDIANA, USA

Research involving female runners has been sparse compared with the amount of information that has been accumulated relative to male runners. Undoubtedly, this is largely a function of the lack of opportunities for women in athletics in general, and until recently, a particular lack of competitive opportunities in long-distance running events. The marathon has finally been accepted as an Olympic event for women and 5 km and 10 km races are becoming very popular and established at nearly every level of competition. With the recent improvement in their world-best marathon time to 2 h 21 min 6 s, women now race the marathon comparatively as well as they do the 1500 m and 3000 m (see Table 1 for comparison of male and female middle- and long-distance world bests), and with more emphasis on 5 km and 10 km track races, women's performances in these races will undoubtedly show considerable improvement also. Because competitive long-distance running for women has achieved worldwide acceptance, it seemed appropriate to describe a sample of proven female runners. Therefore the purpose of this study was to attempt to identify some characteristics that might discriminate between elite and subelite ath-

Our sincere appreciation is extended to Dr. Sam Smith, Department of Animal Sciences, University of New Hampshire, Durham, NH, for his technical and laboratory assistance in the determination and evaluation of serum-ferritin data.

**Table 1.** Comparisons of world-best times for various running distances for males and females

| Event | Male times | Female times | Difference % | Female time at + 11.0%[a] | Female time Re: 1500[b] |
|---|---|---|---|---|---|
| 800 | 1:41.7 | 1:53.3 | + 11.35 | 1:52.9 | 1:53.4 |
| 1500 m | 3:29.5 | 3:52.5 | + 11.00 | 3:52.5 | 1:52.5 |
| 3000 m | 7:32.1 | 8:22.7 | + 11.17 | 8:21.8 | 8:17.5 |
| 5000 m | 13:00.4 | 14:48.1 | + 13.80 | 14:26.2 | 14:26.3 |
| 10 km | 27:13.8 | 30:59.9 | + 13.84 | 30:13.5 | 30:01.2 |
| 42 km | 2:07:11 | 2:21:06 | + 10.94 | 2:20:10 | 2:20:40[c] |

[a]Least difference between male and female times.
[b]See Daniels et al. (1977).
[c]Track equivalent converted to road terrain.

letes, and to describe some of the common physical, hematological, and physiological characteristics that successful female middle- and long-distance runners exhibit.

# Procedures

## Subjects

Well-trained female runners ($N=30$) served as subjects. Twenty-eight of the subjects were American and two were foreigners currently living and competing in the United States. The subjects were divided into categories of proficiency and specialty. Those runners who had won a national championship, represented their countries in international competition, or who held a national or world record in their specialties were considered elite (E). Subelite runners (S) made up the remainder of the subjects, all of whom were successful at the collegiate level as demonstrated by having won major competitions and having participated in at least one national championship event in their specialties. In addition to the E and S proficiency categories, the total subject pool was also divided into middle-distance (M) and long-distance (L) event categories. M runners included subjects who primarily competed in races up to 5000 m in distance; L runners specialized in races of 10 km to the marathon (42 km). Of the 30 subjects 17 were considered E, 13 were S, 16 were M, and 14 were L. More detailed identification of the subjects showed 8 to be EM, 9 EL, 8 SM, and 5 SL. Also included among the 20 subjects were four sets of identical twins.

## Preexercise tests

Following an explanation of all tests and the signing of an informed consent, and before a series of submax and max runs on a treadmill, each subject had two blood samples drawn. One was analyzed for red cells (RBC), white blood cells (WBC), hematocrit (HCT), and hemoglobin (Hb). The serum was separated from the other sample, frozen, and stored for subsequent analysis of serum ferritin using a two-site immune-radiometric assay procedure (Ramco fer-iron kit). After having her blood drawn, each subject was measured for height and weight and had skinfold measurements recorded for six sites—tricep, subscapular, suprailiac, umbilical, posterior thigh, and anterior thigh.

## Exercise tests

Following the blood tests and body measurements each subject performed a series of runs on a treadmill. The first of four 6-min, submax runs was at a velocity of 230 m•min$^{-1}$ (7:00 per mile pace). Subsequent runs were at 248 m•min$^{-1}$ (6:30 pace), 268 m•min$^{-1}$ with a 4- to 7-minute recovery given between submax runs. A 2-minute expired-gas sample was collected during the fifth and sixth minute of each submax run, using the equipment and procedure described by Daniels (1971). A 10-s heart rate, taken by palpation immediately upon completion of each run, was used to calculate exercise heart rate for the intensity of running just completed. Applied Electrochemistry S3-A oxygen and Beckman LB2 carbondioxide gas analyzers were used to determine expired fractions of $O_2$ and $CO_2$. Reference gases and approximately one third of the expired gas samples were also analyzed by a Gallenkamp-Lloyd volumetric gas analyzer. Expired-gas volumes were determined by emptying the collection balloons into a Collins 350-liter gasometer.

Following the final submax run, each subject was given a 15- to 20-minute recovery and then asked to perform a $\dot{V}O_2$ max test. The first minute of the $\dot{V}O_2$ max test was run on a 0% grade at a pace that was approximately 30 m•min$^{-1}$ slower than 5000 m race pace. The second minute of the continuous max test was on 0% grade, at a velocity approximating current 5000 m race pace; the remainder of the test was at this pace. Starting at the beginning of the third minute a 1% grade was added to the treadmill each minute until the test was ended by the subject's indication that she could not run 30 s longer. Continuous balloons of expired gas were collected from 3:30 to 4:15, 4:15 to 5:00, and every 30 s thereafter until test termination. Following analysis of all gas samples the results of the 2-minute collections were accepted as representative of the demands of each submax run and the highest $\dot{V}O_2$ max reached during the max test was considered $\dot{V}O_2$ max.

# Results

## Physical and Hematological Characteristics

Age, height, weight, skinfolds (6-site sum), and blood-test data are presented in Table 2. Table 2 also indicates the number of subjects in each proficiency and performance category. No significant differences ($p>.05$) existed among categories of runners for any of the characteristics shown in Table 2. The elite runners appear to have a tendency toward higher iron stores as reflected by serum ferritin (S Fe) data, but the rather large variations in values prevented any differences from being statistically significant. From Table 2 it can be seen that event specialty and degree of success do not appear to be related to any of the standard physical or hematological variables considered in this study.

**Table 2.** Mean physical and hematological characteristics of female runners of different performance and event categories

| Category[b] | N | Age yr | Ht cm | Wt kg | SF[a] mm | RBC $10^6(mm^3)^{-1}$ | HCT % | Hb $g \cdot dl^{-1}$ | WBC $10^3(mm^3)^{-1}$ | SFe $ng \cdot ml^{-1}$ |
|---|---|---|---|---|---|---|---|---|---|---|
| EM | 8 | 23.0 | 165 | 50.3 | 52.8 | 4.45 | 39.9 | 13.6 | 5.7 | 28.6 |
| EL | 9 | 22.8 | 167 | 53.2 | 54.0 | 4.45 | 40.6 | 13.6 | 4.6 | 35.5 |
| SM | 8 | 21.0 | 166 | 52.5 | 62.6 | 4.48 | 41.6 | 14.0 | 5.4 | 21.1 |
| SL | 5 | 23.4 | 168 | 54.7 | 49.2 | 4.46 | 39.6 | 13.2 | 5.2 | 16.0 |
| E | 17 | 22.9 | 166 | 51.9 | 53.4 | 4.45 | 40.3 | 13.6 | 5.1 | 32.4 |
| S | 13 | 21.9 | 167 | 53.4 | 57.5 | 4.48 | 40.8 | 13.8 | 5.4 | 18.5 |
| M | 16 | 22.0 | 165 | 51.4 | 57.7 | 4.47 | 40.7 | 13.9 | 5.6 | 24.2 |
| L | 14 | 23.0 | 167 | 53.8 | 52.3 | 4.45 | 40.3 | 13.5 | 4.8 | 30.1 |
| ALL | 30 | 22.5 | 166 | 52.5 | 54.9 | 4.46 | 40.5 | 13.6 | 5.2 | 26.8 |
| Minimum | | 19 | 159 | 44.4 | 33.9 | 4.04 | 37.6 | 12.4 | 3.4 | 7.4 |
| Maximum | | 28 | 177 | 63.1 | 76.8 | 4.72 | 44.9 | 15.3 | 7.4 | 70.0 |

[a]SF = skinfold sum of 6 sites: tricep, subscapular, suprailiac, umbilical, posterior thigh, anterior thigh.
[b]E = elite S = subelite M = middle distance L = long distance.

## Submax Running

Mean $\dot{V}O_2$ max and heart rate (HR) data for the four submax running velocities are shown in Table 3. The elite long-distance (EL) runners performed with significantly lower $\dot{V}O_2$ max and HR at all running intensities than did the subelite middle-distance (SM) runners ($p<.05$). Also, as a group, the elite (E) runners had lower $\dot{V}O_2$ max and HR values at all speeds than did the subelite (S) runners, and the long-distance (L) runners had lower $\dot{V}O_2$ max and HR values at all speeds than did the middle-distance (M) runners ($p<.05$). Among the total 30 subjects, large differences exist among even well-trained runners

**Table 3.** Mean $\dot{V}O_2$ and HR data during submax running for female runners of different performance and event categories

| Category | N | $\dot{V}O_2$ (ml·min$^{-1}$·kg$^{-1}$) 230[a] | 248 | 268 | 293 | HR (B·min$^{-1}$) 230 | 248 | 268 | 293 |
|---|---|---|---|---|---|---|---|---|---|
| EM | 8 | 42.3 | 46.7 | 51.5 | 57.7 | 144 | 152 | 161 | 174 |
| EL* | 9 | 41.5 | 45.5 | 50.3 | 56.5 | 126 | 142 | 155 | 168 |
| SM* | 8 | 45.6 | 50.0 | 54.6 | 60.9 | 151 | 162 | 173 | 182 |
| SL | 5 | 44.1 | 48.4 | 53.4 | 58.8 | 141 | 154 | 166 | 180 |
| E* | 17 | 41.9 | 46.1 | 50.9 | 57.0 | 134 | 147 | 158 | 171 |
| S* | 13 | 45.0 | 49.4 | 54.1 | 60.0 | 148 | 158 | 170 | 181 |
| M* | 16 | 44.0 | 48.4 | 53.0 | 59.3 | 148 | 157 | 167 | 178 |
| L* | 14 | 42.4 | 46.5 | 51.4 | 57.3 | 131 | 146 | 159 | 172 |
| All | 30 | 43.2 | 47.5 | 52.3 | 58.4 | 140 | 153 | 163 | 175 |
| Minimum | | 36.3 | 39.5 | 44.7 | 49.8 | 96 | 132 | 140 | 148 |
| Maximum | | 48.9 | 53.6 | 57.3 | 64.0 | 168 | 180 | 192 | 204 |

[a]Velocity (m·min$^{-1}$).
*All $\dot{V}O_2$ and HR data significantly different ($p<.05$).

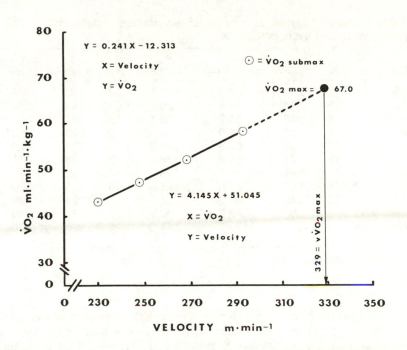

**Figure 1.** Mean $\dot{V}O_2$ max and relationship between $VO_2$ and treadmill-running velocity for 30 female runners. Also shown is the velocity which mathematically corresponds to $VO_2$ max ($vVO_2$ max).

in $\dot{V}O_2$ max and HR reactions to steady-state running (greater than a 24% range in $\dot{V}O_2$ and over 31% in HR, as calculated from the minimum and maximum values given at the bottom of Table 3).

Figure 1 shows the mean relationship between running velocity and $\dot{V}O_2$ (ml•min$^{-1}$•kg$^{-1}$) for the 30 subjects. The average $\dot{V}O_2$ max is also presented along with the running velocity related to $\dot{V}O_2$ max ($vVO_2$ max—329 m•min$^{-1}$) as calculated from the regression equation(s) presented in Figure 1.

### $\dot{V}O_2$ Max Test Data

All subjects endured at least 5 min in the max test; none continued for longer than 8 min. Mean max-test data for $\dot{V}O_2$, VE, R, and HR are presented for the various categories of subjects in Table 4. In addition, the velocity related to $VO_2$ max (a variable which seems appropriately termed velocity at $VO_2$max, or $vVO_2$ max for each of the categories is also presented in Table 4. The only differences between any of the categories which were significant were in $vVO_2$ max ($p<.05$). In this variable, EM runners were higher than SM runners, EL higher than SM, and EL were also higher than SL. Further, E and S runners differed as did M and L runners, in $vVO_2$ max ($p<.05$). Only 1 of the 30 subjects had a $\dot{V}O_2$ max below 60 ml•min$^{-1}$•kg$^{-1}$ (an SM subject) and one EL runner had a $\dot{V}O_2$ max of 78.6 ml•min$^{-1}$•kg$^{-1}$.

**Table 4.** Mean $\dot{V}O_2$ max data for 30 female runners of different performance and event categories

| Category | N | $\dot{V}O_2$ max 1·min⁻¹ | $\dot{V}O_2$ max ml·min⁻¹·kg⁻¹ | $\dot{V}_E$ 1·min⁻¹ | R | HR B·min⁻¹ | $v\dot{V}O_2$ max m·min⁻¹ |
|---|---|---|---|---|---|---|---|
| EM | 8 | 3.37 | 67.0 | 111.5 | 1.12 | 195 | 332* |
| EL | 9 | 3.71 | 68.8 | 126.2 | 1.09 | 188 | 344* |
| SM | 8 | 3.45 | 65.7 | 126.1 | 1.13 | 196 | 313* |
| SL | 5 | 3.61 | 66.0 | 124.3 | 1.12 | 202 | 322* |
| E | 17 | 3.55 | 67.9 | 119.3 | 1.10 | 191 | 338* |
| S | 13 | 3.51 | 65.8 | 125.4 | 1.13 | 198 | 317* |
| M | 16 | 3.41 | 66.4 | 118.8 | 1.13 | 195 | 322* |
| L | 14 | 3.67 | 67.8 | 125.5 | 1.10 | 193 | 336* |
| All | 30 | 3.48 | 67.0 | 121.9 | 1.11 | 194 | 329 |
| Minimum | | 2.92 | 59.8 | 90.9 | .97 | 180 | 298 |
| Maximum | | 4.18 | 78.6 | 147.2 | 1.22 | 228 | 370 |

*Differences significant ($p<.05$).

## Twin Subjects

Table 5 shows skinfold sums, blood test data, $\dot{V}O_2$ submax at 268 m·min⁻¹ (6:00·mile⁻¹ pace), max-test data and calculated $v\dot{V}O_2$ max for the four sets of twins. With the exception of Subjects 7 and 8, results of the blood tests were very similar within each set of twins. Running economy, as measured by $\dot{V}O_2$ max at 268 m·min⁻¹ varied very little within sets. This relative demand of steady-state submax running was also reflected by similar heart rates in three of the four sets of twins. As was true with the resting and submax data, the results of the max tests also show the twins to be very similar within sets. Subjects 3 and 4 demonstrated nearly identical $v\dot{V}O_2$ max values as a result of one twin being more economical with a lower $\dot{V}O_2$ max and the other less economical with a higher $\dot{V}O_2$ max. Subject 3 had been involved more in running than had her sister and had achieved greater success, but was recovering from injury at the time of testing, a factor which may have led to a somewhat lower $\dot{V}O_2$ max.

## Discussion

### Physical Characteristics

The relative homogeneity in age among the categories of subjects is not surprising since the majority were still college students. However, the similarities that existed in height, weight, and 6-site-skinfold sums were somewhat surprising. There certainly does not appear to be any tendency for elite female runners to be different in these physical characteristics from other serious female runners who have not reached quite as high a level of success. Nor do there appear to be any differences in these physical characteristics between middle- and long-distance female runners. Compared to some other well-trained female runners of similar age (Daniels, Krahenbuhl, Foster, Gil

Table 5. Selected resting, submax and max data for four sets of identical twin female runners

| Set | ID | SF[a] mm | RBC $10^6$ $(mm^3)^{-1}$ | HCT % | Hb g·$dl^{-1}$ | WBC $10^3$ $(mm^3)^{-1}$ | SFe ng·$ml^{-1}$ | $\dot{V}O_2$-268 ml·$min^{-1}$·$kg^{-1}$ | HR-268 B·$min^{-1}$ | $\dot{V}O_2$ max ml·$min^{-1}$·$kg^{-1}$ | HRmax B·$min^{-1}$ | $\dot{V}_E$max l·$min^{-1}$ | R | v$\dot{V}O_2$ max m·$min^{-1}$ |
|---|---|---|---|---|---|---|---|---|---|---|---|---|---|---|
| A | 1 | 68.7 | 4.41 | 41.0 | 13.8 | 6.5 | 34.0 | 55.0 | 180 | 62.2 | 194 | 137 | 1.19 | 300 |
|   | 2 | 70.9 | 4.25 | 39.5 | 13.8 | 6.2 | 16.0 | 55.0 | 184 | 64.2 | 192 | 142 | 1.13 | 307 |
| B | 3 | 65.7 | 4.52 | 41.0 | 13.9 | 5.3 | 32.0 | 54.8 | 176 | 63.7 | 208 | 98 | 1.08 | 303 |
|   | 4 | 62.9 | 4.40 | 40.0 | 13.3 | 5.1 | 21.5 | 57.4 | 176 | 67.5 | 216 | 100 | 1.06 | 306 |
| C | 5 | 59.7 | 4.31 | 39.2 | 13.1 | 4.3 | 11.0 | 53.5 | 160 | 67.0 | 210 | 134 | 1.13 | 324 |
|   | 6 | 66.3 | 4.28 | 38.7 | 13.1 | 4.3 | 11.0 | 52.4 | 160 | 67.1 | 204 | 147 | 1.13 | 330 |
| D | 7 | 74.8 | 4.43 | 41.5 | 13.7 | 6.9 | 22.5 | 54.4 | 156 | 66.7 | 180 | 136 | 1.10 | 317 |
|   | 8 | 76.5 | 4.69 | 44.2 | 14.7 | 5.1 | 35.0 | 54.4 | 174 | 66.6 | 186 | 132 | 1.03 | 317 |

[a]Skinfold sum of six sites—tricep, subscapular, suprailiac, umbilical, posterior thigh, anterior thigh.

bert, & Daniels, 1977; Saltin & Åstrand, 1967; Upton et al., 1984; Wells, Hecht, & Krahenbuhl, 1981), the current subjects were nearly identical in height; however, the current runners were somewhat lighter than were the Swedish athletes studied by Saltin and Åstrand (1967). The women runners studied by Wilmore and Brown (1974) were also heavier, considerably older, and a little taller, and the data reported by Conley, Krahenbuhl, Burkett, and Millar (1981) showed their runners to be shorter and lighter than were the present subjects. The 6-site-skinfold data, shown in Table 2, are very similar to those reported by others (Bransford & Howley, 1977; Conley, Krahenbuhl, Burkett, & Millar, 1981; Daniels et al., 1977) who have also studied well-trained female runners. Even though the mean physical appearance of various groups of trained female runners are similar, the variations in height and weight are considerable; elite subjects in this study were among the tallest, shortest, heaviest, and lightest of the total sample. It is also interesting to note that the three most successful long-distance runners among our subjects were all equal to or greater than the mean in skinfold sums.

## Hematological Characteristics

As was the case with common physical characteristics, differences between the various categories of runners in the several hematological variables were virtually nonexistent. Only a few individuals fell outside the normal range of values expected of females of this age group. The mean HCT and Hb values for the current subjects were similar to findings of other recent investigators (Parr, Bachman, & Moss, 1984; Upton et al., 1984), but higher than reported by Nickerson and Tripp (1983) before their runners were treated for low iron stores, as indicated by low serum ferritins. The importance of measuring serum ferritins for identification of iron deficiency (Nickerson & Tripp, 1983; Parr et al., 1984) is supported by our findings. We had satisfactory (although not particularly high) serum ferritin values among our subjects, but of the eight subjects below 20 ng•ml$^{-1}$ (four were 11.0 or less), the lowest hemoglobin recorded was 13.1 g•dl$^{-1}$ and the mean for the group was 13.5 g•dl$^{-1}$, not different from the overall mean for the 30 subjects (Table 2). The mean 39.3% HCT for these lowest eight serum-ferritin (SFe) subjects, however, was lower than the overall mean of our subjects and lower than reported by Parr et al. (1984), but identical to the young marathoners studied by Upton et al. (1984). Although not significantly different from other categories of runners (Table 2), it is possible that only the rather large variations found in the SFe values prevented the mean reading of 16.0 ng•ml$^{-1}$ for the SL athletes from being significantly lower than for some of the other categories. Whether low SFe values would themselves contribute to the prevention of any SL athletes from being more successful is not particularly evident from the information available, but there does seem to be cause for concern regarding these female runners as a group, and their low iron stores. No attempt was made to evaluate diet, either from a qualitative or a quantitative perspective.

## Heart Rate During Submax and Max Running

The variations in heart rate response to the various intensities of exercise were large, but significant differences during submax running did exist (Table 3).

It might be expected that elite runners had lower heart rates at all submax runs than did subelite runners; it is not unlikely that the elite runners had trained harder and longer than their subelite counterparts, although no effort was made in this study to document years of training or typical training regimens for any of the subjects. Although not significant, a somewhat lower max heart rate was reached by the E athletes, compared with S runners. The L runners also exhibited a lower submax HR than M runners, although max HR was not different (Table 4). Interestingly, as the intensity of the submax run increased, the difference in HR submax decreased between the M and L runners. That this might be the result of a better adaptation to different training intensities of the two groups is not reflected in a similar pattern in $\dot{V}O_2$ submax, where equal differences existed at all submax speeds.

Even though rather large mean differences existed among some of the smaller subcategories of runners (EM, EL, SM, SL) during the submax runs, only the EL and SM runners differed significantly ($p<.05$). Undoubtedly the small sample sizes and great variations prevented other differences from reaching significance at the .05 level. The HR max data for our subjects are very similar to those reported by other investigators (Brown & Wilmore, 1971; Daniels et al., 1977; Drinkwater & Horvath, 1971; Wilmore and Brown, 1974) even for female runners who were only 12-13 years old (Brown, Harrower, & Deeter, 1972) or between 14 and 18 (Drinkwater & Horvarth, 1971). Even though the mean HR max for EL and SL runners were 188 and 202, respectively, the variations in HR data were likely responsible for nonsignificant differences ($p>.05$). The highest HR reached by any of the 30 subjects was 228 (an SM runner); 180 was the lowest HR max, a value that was attained by six different runners who represented both elite and subelite categories. A final note about heart rates—one of our subjects had a heart rate of 96 $B \cdot min^{-1}$ while running at 230 $m \cdot min^{-1}$ (7:00 $mile^{-1}$ pace), a characteristic one might expect to see from an Olympic marathon champion.

## $\dot{V}O_2$ Submax and $\dot{V}O_2$ max

The $\dot{V}O_2$ submax data in Table 3 appear to almost directly reflect the HR data from the same table—differences between E and S, M and L, and EL and SM were significant at all running velocities ($p<.05$).

From the data of Falls and Humphrey (1976) and Bransford and Howley (1977), the $\dot{V}O_2$ max at 268 $m \cdot min^{-1}$ for their trained females was 52.9 and 52.3 $ml \cdot min^{-1} \cdot kg^{-1}$, respectively; our women averaged 52.3 $ml \cdot min^{-1} \cdot kg^{-1}$. However, the slopes of the regression curves in the above studies were somewhat flatter and at 322 $m \cdot min^{-1}$ the respective $\dot{V}O_2$ max $ml \cdot min^{-1} \cdot kg^{-1}$ calculate to be 60.9 and 62.1, compared with our 65.3 $ml \cdot min^{-1} \cdot kg^{-1}$ (Figure 1). That our current regression equation generates a steeper slope is most likely a function of our data being collected over higher running velocities, a phenomenon that has been reported earlier (Daniels et al., 1977).

In comparing our submax $\dot{V}O_2$ max data with that from elite male runners (Pollock, 1977) we find that our female subjects are of equal running economy to the men ($ml \cdot min^{-1} \cdot kg^{-1} \dot{V}O_2$)—53.0 men versus 52.3 our women at 268 $m \cdot min^{-1}$ and 65.0 men versus 65.3 our women at 322 $m \cdot min^{-1}$. In fact the most economical male runner in the study reported by Pollock (1977) used

57.0 ml•min⁻¹•kg⁻¹ at 322 m•min⁻¹, and our most economical female runner would use 58.7 ml•min⁻¹•kg⁻¹ by extrapolation of her $\dot{V}O_2$ velocity regression curve beyond the 293 m•min⁻¹ fastest test-speed. This same female runner had only a 44.7 ml•min⁻¹•kg⁻¹ $\dot{V}O_2$ at 268 m•min⁻¹, well below the meansof both our current study and that reported by Pollock (1977). Still, current findings in our lab suggest that elite male runners may be capable of even greater economy than we have yet seen among women, even though an earlier direct comparison of economy between male and female runners did not produce a significant difference (Daniels et al., 1977).

That long-distance male runners are more economical (consume significantly less oxygen per kilogram per minute at the same submax speed) than are middle-distance runners, has been reported earlier (Costill, Thomason, & Roberts, 1973; Dill, 1965; Pollock, 1977) and is supported by our findings with female runners (Table 3). However, it is still not clear whether the better economy displayed by runners who primarily race longer distances has come about as a function of training and/or competing at longer distances or if more economical runners have just found more success over longer races. In view of the high mileage run by even middle-distance runners, it would appear that the latter explanation is the more feasible. Further, running economy has been shown to vary considerably (Farrell, Wilmore, Coyle, Billings, & Costill, 1979), even among runners who specialize in the same events (Daniels, 1974; Daniels et al., 1977), and to correlate significantly with performance among runners of near equal performance (Conley & Krahenbuhl, 1980), and, even though improvements in economy have been associated with training (Conley, Krahenbuhl & Burkett, 1981; Conley, Krahenbuhl, Burkett, & Millar, 1984), Daniels, Scardina, and Foley (1984) have suggested that the differences that exist among individuals are to a great extent a function of inherent anatomical and/or physiological design; training seems to play a minimal, if any, role in narrowing the between-individual variations that exist. If, in fact, good running economy is more advantageous for longer than for shorter distance races, testing economy may be helpful in determining the direction of some running careers. Certainly among the 30 subjects in this study, running economy did differ among various categories of runners (Table 3), and $\dot{V}O_2$ max did not (Table 4), even though E runners did show a tendency to have a somewhat higher $\dot{V}O_2$ max when expressed in ml•min⁻¹•kg⁻¹. This lack of significant difference in $\dot{V}O_2$ max and presence of difference in economy between categories of runners supports the earlier findings of Conley and Krahenbuhl (1980) that economy becomes more important when runners are of near equal performance.

The overall mean $\dot{V}O_2$ max of 67.0 ml•min⁻¹•kg⁻¹, the lowest mean sub category $\dot{V}O_2$ max of 65.7 (SM runners), and the 78.6 ml•min⁻¹•kg⁻¹ value for one of the EL runners (Table 4) speaks well for the caliber of the subjects who participated in this study. When comparing these max data with results of earlier work involving elite female distance runners (Brown et al., 1972; Brown & Wilmore, 1971; Daniels et al., 1977; Saltin & Åstrand, 1967; Wilmore & Brown, 1974), it is clear that the current subjects are of a high quality that is not at all surprising given the advancements in interest and participation by female athletes during the past decade. In general, when looking at the aerobic factors that differ most between male and female runners it certainly appears that $\dot{V}O_2$ max is more discriminating than is $\dot{V}O_2$ submax (running economy).

### Velocity at $\dot{V}O_2$ max (v$\dot{V}O_2$ max)

By extrapolation of the regression curve relating running velocity and $\dot{V}O_2$ max, to $\dot{V}O_2$ max, the velocity of running that corresponds to $\dot{V}O_2$ max can be identified (see Figure 1). We refer to this velocity as v$\dot{V}O_2$ max, a variable that combines economy and $\dot{V}O_2$ max into a single value which more completely describes aerobic fitness of a runner. $\dot{V}O_2$ max has received the bulk of attention as the most important single variable related to success in endurance running. However, more recently $\dot{V}O_2$ submax, (Conley & Krahenbuhl, 1980; Conley, Krahenbul, & Burkett, 1981; Conley et al., 1984; Daniels, 1974; Daniels et al., 1977; Daniels et al., 1984), fractional utilization (Costill, Branam, Eddy, & Sparks, 1971; Costill & Fox, 1969; Costill et al., 1973), and anaerobic threshold (Farrell et al., 1979; Komi, Ito, Sjödin, Wallenstein, & Karlsson, 1981; Kumagai, et al., 1982) have all received considerable attention and have been shown to correlate highly with distance-running success.

Figures 2 and 3 illustrate the usefulness of plotting $\dot{V}O_2$ submax and $\dot{V}O_2$ max data when attempting to identify possible differences in the aerobic charac-

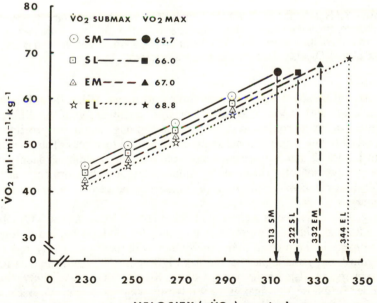

**Figure 2.** Relationships of $\dot{V}O_2$ and treadmill-running velocity for four subcategories of female runners: subelite middle distance (SM) subelite long distance (SL), elite middle distance (EM), and elite long distance (EL). Also shown are the mean $\dot{V}O_2$ max and v$\dot{V}O_2$ max values for the four subcategories.

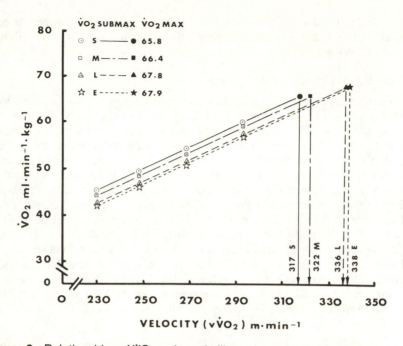

**Figure 3.** Relationships of $\dot{V}O_2$ and treadmill-running velocity for different performance and event categories of female distance runners: subelite (S), elite (E), middle distance (M), and long distance (L). Also shown are the mean $\dot{V}O_2$ max and $v\dot{V}O_2$ max data for the four categories.

teristics of two or more runners or groups of runners. The slight differences (nonsignificant) in $\dot{V}O_2$ max among groups, combined with the differences (some significant, some not) in $\dot{V}O_2$ submax among categories, project $v\dot{V}O_2$ max data points which become significant in more instances (Table 4). From both Figures 2 and 3 it becomes more obvious that running economy plays a very important role in determining endurance-running performance, and that $v\dot{V}O_2$ max can be a useful means of comparing the aerobic characteristics of runners.

Figure 4 carries the usefulness of identifying both $\dot{V}O_2$ max and $\dot{V}O_2$ submax even further. This figure plots the data points for the least and most economical runners in the present study, the runner with the highest $\dot{V}O_2$ max (78.6 ml•min$^{-1}$•kg$^{-1}$) and highest $v\dot{V}O_2$ max (370 m•min$^{-1}$), the mean data for all 30 runners, and data for the runner with the lowest $v\dot{V}O_2$ max − 298 m•min$^{-1}$. Runner B (whose $\dot{V}O_2$ max is 12.9 ml•min$^{-1}$•kg$^{-1}$ less than A), because of her superior economy, projects a $v\dot{V}O_2$ max nearly equal to A and within 1 m•min$^{-1}$ of the mean $v\dot{V}O_2$ max of the total group, which has a $\dot{V}O_2$ max over 10% greater than is B's. Runner D, although equal in economy to runner C, is at a great disadvantage to C because of a much lower $\dot{V}O_2$ max, and, as shown in Figure 4 a $v\dot{V}O_2$ max some 72 m•min$^{-1}$ less. Figure 4 also indicates the $\dot{V}O_2$ max that would project a $v\dot{V}O_2$ max equal to the 370 m•min$^{-1}$ of runner C, for A, B, and the average subject. Also, the average subject would project

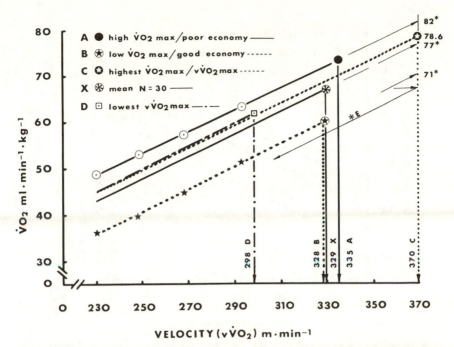

**Figure 4.** Relationships of $\dot{V}O_2$ and treadmill-running velocity for selected individuals, from among 30 female runners, showing various combinations of $\dot{V}O_2$ max and running economy ($\dot{V}O_2$ submax) and resulting $v\dot{V}O_2$ max values.

a $v\dot{V}O_2$ max of 370 m·min$^{-1}$ without a change in $\dot{V}O_2$ max if economy could be improved to a level somewhat better than demonstrated by runner B (indicated by *E).

Finally, Figure 5 compares three of the subjects in the current study who have performed nearly identical times for 3000 m. Two of the subjects (A and B) were presented in Figure 4 also. Subject F falls between A and B, both in $\dot{V}O_2$ max and $\dot{V}O_2$ submax. It is interesting to compare the best 3000 m times of the three runners (two are EL, one is SM)—9:07, 9:06, and 9:06, with the 3,000 m = times that their $v\dot{V}O_2$ max would produce—9:09, 8:57, and 8:56, respectively. The $v\dot{V}O_2$ max values certainly suggest that these three runners are nearly equal, whereas the differences in $\dot{V}O_2$ max and running economy, singly, would not. Knowing which characteristics of a runner's physiological makeup are strengths and which are weaknesses may provide considerable insight into not only the event(s) of greatest potential, but also the types of training that are best suited for the individual.

## Conclusion

Within the limits of this study the following conclusions have been reached regarding well-trained female middle- and long-distance runners.

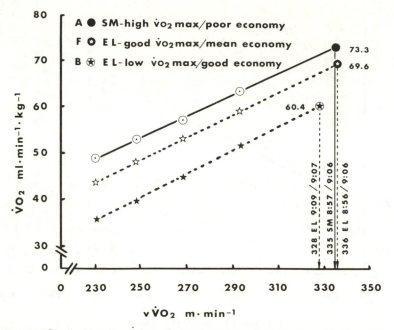

**Figure 5.** Similarities in vVO₂ max among three female runners of equal 3000m performance who vary considerably in VO₂ max and running economy (VO₂ submax).

1. Long-distance (L) runners are more economical than are middle-distance (M) runners.
2. Elite runners (E) are more economical than are subelite (S) runners.
3. No differences exist between L and M or between E and S runners in common physical or hematological characteristics.
4. No differences exist in VO₂ max nor HR max between L and M runners or between E and S runners.
5. Velocity at max (vVO₂ max) is a useful variable that combines VO₂ max and economy into a single factor which shows good potential for identifying aerobic differences between various runners or categories of runners.

# References

Bransford, D.R., & Howley, E.T. (1977). Oxygen cost of running in trained and untrained men and women. *Medicine and Sciences in Sports*, **9**, 41-44.

Brown, C.H., Harrower, J.R., Deeter, M.F. (1972). The effects of cross-country running on pre-adolescent girls. *Medicine and Science in Sports*, **4**, 1-5.

Brown, C.H., & Wilmore, J.H. (1971). Physical and physiological profiles of champion women long-distance runners (abstract). *Medicine and Science in Sports*, **3**(1).

Conley, D.L., & Krahenbuhl, G. (1980). Running economy and distance running performance of highly trained athletes. *Medicine and Science in Sports*, **12**, 357-360.

Conley, D.L., Krahenbuhl, G.S. & Burkett, L.N. (1981). Training for aerobic capacity and running economy. *Physician and Sportsmedicine*, **9**(4), 107-115.

Conley, D.L., Krahenbuhl, G.S., Burkett, L.N., & Millar, A.L. (1981). Physiological correlates of female road racing performance. *Research Quarterly for Exercise and Sport*, **52**, 441-448.

Conley, D.L., Krahenbuhl, G.S., Burkett, L.N., & Millar, A.L. (1984). Following Steve Scott: Physiological changes accompanying training. *Physician and Sportsmedicine*, **12**(1), 103-106.

Costill, D.L., Branam, G., Eddy, D., & Sparks, K. (1971). Determinants of marathon running success. *International Zeitschrift Agnew. Physiology*, **29**, 249-254.

Costill, D.L., & Fox, E.L. (1969). Energetics of marathon running. *Medicine and Science in Sports*, **1**, 81-86.

Costill, D.L., Thomason, H. & Roberts, E. (1973). Fractional utilization of the aerobic capacity during distance running. *Medicine and Science in Sports*, **5**, 248-252.

Daniels, J. (1971). Portable respiratory gas collection equipment. *Journal of Applied Physiology*, **31**, 164-167.

Daniels, J. (1974). Physiological characteristics of champion male athletes. *Research Quarterly*, **45**, 342-348.

Daniels, J., Krahenbuhl, G. Foster, C. Gilbert, J., & Daniels, S. (1977). Aerobic responses of female distance runners to submaximal and maximal exercise. In P. Milvy (Ed.), *The marathon: Physiological, medical, epidemiological and psychological studies* pp. 726-733). New York: Annals NY Academy Sciences.

Daniels, J.T., Scardina, N.J. & Foley, P. (1984). VO₂ submax during five modes of exercise. In N. Bachl, L. Prokop, & R. Suckert (Eds.), *Current topics in sports medicine: Proceedings of the World Congress of Sports Medicine*, Vienna: Urban and Schwarzenberg.

Dill, D.B. (1965). Oxygen used in horizontal and grade walking and running on a treadmill. *Journal of Applied Physiology*, **20**, 19-22.

Drinkwater, B.L., & Horvath, S.M. (1971). Responses of young female track athletes to exercise. *Medicine and science in Sports*, **3**, 56-62.

Falls, H.B., & Humphrey, L.D. (1976). Energy cost of running and walking in young women. *Medicine and Science in Sports*, **8**, 9-13.

Farrell, P.A., Wilmore, J.H., Coyle, E.F., Billings, J.C., & Costill, D.L. (1979). Plasma lactate accumulation and distance running performance. *Medicine and Science in Sports*, **11**, 338-344.

Komi, P.V., Ito, A. Sjödin, B., Wallenstein, R., & Karlsson, J. (1981). Muscle metabolism, lactate breaking point, and biomechanical features of endurance running. *International Journal of Sports Medicine*, **2**, 148-153.

Kumagai, S., Tanaka, K. Matsuura, Y., Matsusaka, A., Hirakoba, K., & Asano, K. (1982). Relationships of the anaerobic threshold with the 5 km, 10km, and 10 mile races. *European Journal on Applied Physiology*, **49**, 13-23.

Nickerson, H.J., & Tripp, A.D. (1983). Iron deficiency in adolescent cross country runners. *Physicians and Sportsmedicine*, **11**(6), 60-66.

Parr, R.B., Bachman, L.A., & Moss, R.A. (1984). Iron deficiency in female athletes. *Physician and Sportsmedicine*, **12**(4), 81-86.

Pollock, M.L. (1977). Submaximal and maximal working capacity of elite distance runners. Part 1: Cardiorespiratory aspects. In P. Milvy (Ed.), *The marathon, Physiological, medical, epidemiological and psychological studies* (pp. 310-322). New York: Annals N.Y. Academy Sciences.

Saltin, B., & Åstrand, P.O. (1967). Maximal oxygen uptake in athletes. *Journal of Applied Physiology*, **23**, 353-358.

Sjödin, B., & Jacobs, I. (1981). Onset of blood lactate accumulation and marathon running performance. *International Journal of Sports Medicine*, **2**, 23-36.

Upton, S.J., Hagan, R.D., Lease, B., Rosentswieg, J., Gettman, L.R., Duncan, J.J. (1984). Comparative physiological profiles among young and middle-aged female distance runners. *Medicine and Science in Sports and Exercise*, **16**, 67-71.

Wells, C.L., Hecht, L.H., & Krahenbuhl, G.S. (1981). Physical characteristics and oxygen utilization of male and female marathon runners. *Research Quarterly for Exercises and Sport*, **52**, 281-285.

Wilmore, J.H., & Brown, C.H. (1974). Physiological profiles of women distance runners. *Medicine and Science in Sports*, **6**, 178-181.

# 7

# *Psychological Characteristics of Elite and Nonelite Marathon Runners*

*Shirley K. Durtschi and Maureen R. Weiss*
UNIVERSITY OF OREGON
EUGENE, OREGON, USA

Sport psychologists are interested in understanding what motivates elite athletes to excel and to discern what preparational techniques and psychological skills need to be implemented to achieve exceptional performance. Recent investigations have recognized the complex nature of various sport personalities and have utilized multivariate techniques to provide a more comprehensive assessment of individual athletes (Gould, Weiss, & Weinberg, 1981; Highlen & Bennett, 1979; Silva, Schultz, Haslam, & Murray, 1981). These studies assessed cognitive strategies, mental practice, anxiety, self-confidence levels and other personality characteristics of elite and nonelite athletes. In general, they found that varying patterns of cognitions and mental preparation techniques were strongly correlated with elite performance. The elite athletes differed significantly from the nonelite athletes on variables of self-confidence, attentional focus, and maximum potential.

Morgan and his colleagues (Morgan & Costill, 1972; Morgan & Johnson, 1978; Morgan & Pollock, 1977) studied the psychophysiological distinctions between elite and nonelite athletes. As a result of their comprehensive research, the mental health model was developed (Morgan, 1978a). The model predicts that an athlete who is anxious, depressed, introverted, confused, fatigued, and low on psychic vigor will tend to be less successful than an athlete who is characterized by the absence of such traits. The mental health model has been accurate in predicting success and failure and has been replicated in several research studies on various elite athletes who competed in wrestling, rowing, and distance running (Morgan & Johnson, 1978; Morgan & Pollock, 1977).

Based on previous personality research on elite versus nonelite athletes (Morgan, 1980a; Morgan & Costill, 1972; Morgan & Johnson, 1978; Morgan & Pollock, 1977) and on mental preparation techniques differentiating athletes of varying ability levels (Gould et al., 1981; Highlen & Bennett, 1979; Silva et al., 1981), the present study investigated the psychological characteristics, cognitive strategies, and training methods of elite and nonelite marathoners.

## Method

### Subjects

Elite (11 male, 7 female) and nonelite (27 males, 21 females) runners who competed in the 1982 Nike OTC Marathon in Eugene, Oregon, participated in the study. A male elite runner was defined as one who had run a marathon under 2 hr, 20 min, while an elite female runner was one who had run under a 2 hr, 50 min marathon. These times were based on the average U.S. Olympic Trial qualifying standards. All elite runners in this study were invited to compete in the 1982 Nike OTC Marathon. The nonelite runners were randomly selected from the entries of individuals not meeting the specifications of an elite distance runner.

A total of 132 consent forms were sent out to elite and nonelite distance runners participating in the marathon. Ninety letters (68%) were returned. Psychological assessment packets were mailed to these 90 participants. A total of 66 completed packets were received in the weeks following the marathon, for a 73% response rate.

### Measures

The psychological assessment packet sent to each participant in this study contained five questionnaires. These questionnaires were designed to measure various personality characteristics, training methods, running involvement patterns, competitive goals and expectations, cognitive strategies, anxiety levels, and mood profiles of the athletes in preparation for competition. A short description of the questionniare completed by each participant is outlined below.

The Running History Questionnaire consisted of background questions concerning the runner's current training program, motives for starting to run, motives for continuing to run competitively, and thought processes experienced during race competition.

The Distance Runner Questionnaire was adapted from Mahoney and Avener (1977), who developed a comprehensive assessment tool to evaluate the cognitive, emotional, and behavioral aspects of an athlete's response to competition. This questionnaire identified situations in which cognitive strategies were used in preparation for coping with the stress of marathon racing. Specific categories focused on attentional style, arousal levels at various intervals leading up to the marathon, self-confidence, and mental imagery.

The Sport Competition Anxiety Test (SCAT) was designed by Martens (1977) as a reliable and valid instrument for measuring competitive trait anxiety (A-Trait). The Competitive State Anxiety Inventory (SCAI-1), also developed by

Martens (1977), measures situational anxiety or the anxiety that an athlete feels at the time he or she completes the inventory.

The Profile On Mood States (POMS) inventory using the "right now" response set, was to be completed by elite and nonelite runners at the end of each day of training during the 10-day period prior to the race. The POMS is a psychological profile that measures tension, depression, anger, fatigue, confusion, and vigor (Morgan & Johnson, 1978). A POMS profile that registers low scores in all attributes except vigor has been called the *iceberg profile* because the negative variables fall below the 50th percentile, and the one positive variable, vigor, is well above the 50th percentile.

Performance was assessed according to each distance runner's official time and finish place obtained from the final results of the 1982 Nike OTC Marathon.

## Procedures

The elite males and elite females invited to race in the 1982 Nike OTC Marathon were sent a cover letter explaining the purpose of the study and an informed consent form that was to be signed and returned if the runners were willing to participate. At the same time, an informed consent and a cover letter were sent to a random selection of 30 male and 30 female nonelite distance runners who registered to run the marathon. The psychological assessment packets were mailed to those who agreed to participate. Explicit instructions were provided for completing each of the items in the packet.

Participants were instructed to compile all of the questionnaires, put them in the special envelope within 10 days after the completion of the marathon, and send them to the investigator.

# Results

The psychological assessment packet generated a vast amount of information about elite and nonelite male and female distance runners preparing to participate in the Nike OTC Marathon. Responses to the five questionnaires were analyzed using descriptive statistics and two-way (sex by ability) analyses of variance to compare elite and nonelite male and female marathoners.

## Running History Questionnaire

Runners responded to the questions regarding their motives for involvement in competitive running and their thought patterns during the marathon. Answers to the questions Why run? and Why continue to run? demonstrated diverse motives for the runner groups. The elites were motivated to excel in their sport and to capitalize on their natural talent, physical attributes, and psychological strength to endure. They were also motivated by the rewards successful racing brings (e.g., travel, gifts, monetary incentive, new experiences, and new acquaintances). The nonelites found satisfaction in attaining personal goals, developing positive self-images, and mentally and physically feeling better about themselves. For the nonelites, racing was exciting as an enjoyable social interaction with other runners.

A major theme reflected in the responses of all four groups was that running offered the individual a means of self-fulfillment by providing challenges in training and goals to attain through racing. Distance running demanded self-control and discipline that was rewarded by a feeling of satisfaction and accomplishment.

Responses to the use of cognitive strategies showed that all four groups used some form of association: attending to bodily input; constantly monitoring respiration, temperature, heaviness in calves and thighs, neck and shoulder tightness; and making a conscious effort to stay loose. However, nonelites were more likely to report using dissociative strategies. Morgan (Morgan, 1978a; Morgan & Pollock, 1977) found that the use of an associative cognitive strategy differentiates the elite from the nonelite runner of lesser ability. The elite runner "reads his or her body" and can adjust the pace, while the nonelite uses the dissociative process (fantasies and creative thoughts) to alleviate the pain (Morgan & Pollock, 1977).

A profile of male and female marathoners in this study with regard to motives for running, thoughts during running, training mileage, and performance, is summarized in Table 1.

## Distance Runner Questionnaire

The Distance Runner Questionnaire provides information on how individual athletes employed cognitive strategies (attentional style, arousal levels, self-confidence, and mental imagery) in training and performance situations and distinguishes these behaviors in elite and nonelite distance runners. Patterns of anxiety levels for elite and nonelite runners are shown in Figure 1. Significant differences between elite and nonelite runners were found on four of the seven anxiety ratings.

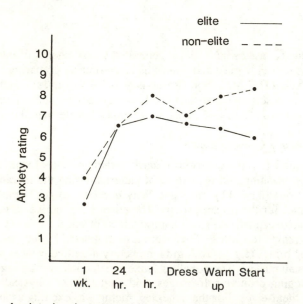

**Figure 1.** Anxiety levels reported in preparation for the marathon.

**Table 1.** Profile of male and female elite and nonelite marathoners: Motives for running, thoughts during running, training mileage, and performance predictions and results

| Item | Elite | | Nonelite | |
| --- | --- | --- | --- | --- |
| | Male | Female | Male | Female |
| Motive for running | Natural talent, body type; desire to excel in running | Challenge, discipline, self-improvement, goal = success | Get in shape, healthy recreation, reduce stress | Physical and social benefits, feel good about oneself |
| Thoughts during running | Concentrate on race competition, monitor body signals, relax and stay loose | Positive energetic thoughts, visualize efficiency, focus on breathing and pace | Push through feelings of pain and work hard to maintain pace | Creative thoughts; enjoy scenery, look for friends in the crowd, figure split times, seek aid stations |
| Training mileage (miles per week) | 111.4 | 87.4 | 64.9 | 57.1 |
| Performance predictions and actual results: | | | | |
|   Predicted pace | 5:03 | 6:10 | 6:38 | 7:03 |
|   Predicted goal (finish time) | 2:12:32 | 2:41:41 | 2:54:57 | 3:16:15 |
|   Actual pace | 5:10 | 6:21 | 6:57 | 7:29 |
|   Actual finish time | 2:15:30 | 2:46:34 | 3:01:52 | 3:19:28 |

Anxiety levels were relatively low the week prior to competition for both ability groups. As the race approached, anxiety levels increased and peaked about 1 hour before the race began. The anxiety rating graph (see Figure 1) shows that the nonelite competitors were one to two points higher on the scale than the elites. One hour before competition, anxiety in nonelite runners peaked and then dropped during the dressing phase. They returned to a crest even higher the hour before competition and again immediately before the start of the race. Elite runners showed a steady drop in anxiety from 1 hour before the race to the start of the race. Once the race started, both groups experienced lowered anxiety levels. These findings support previous research on anxiety levels of elite and nonelite performers (Epstein & Fenz, 1962; Fenz, 1975; Mahoney & Avener, 1977).

## The Sport Competition Anxiety Test (SCAT)

The runners responded to items on the SCAT, revealing their general feelings about competitive sport situations. Elite females ($M=17.2$) were significantly lower on trait anxiety than male elites ($M=24.5$).

## The Competitive State Anxiety Inventory (CSAI-1)

The CSAI-1 was completed on days 10, 7, 4, and the day of the race so that an analysis of the factors sensitive to changes in A-state during that precompetition period could be made. A two-way analysis of variance for the state anxiety inventory revealed no significant main effects or interactions for any of the four administrations of the test. No consistent patterns of state anxiety were found in any of the four groups.

## The Profile On Mood States (POMS)

The POMS was given to all of the marathon runners to complete on each of the 10 days prior to competition. The total of the scores in the six general categories on each of the 10 POMS formed the individual mood profiles. The successful psychological profiles for athletes, defined as the iceberg profile by Morgan (1978b), is characterized by scores that show vigor well above average and anger, tension, depression, confusion, and fatigue all below the mean.

The POMS revealed that only 9% of the elite males had an iceberg profile on each of the 10 days, 18% had an iceberg profile on the day prior to competition, and the average number of iceberg profiles during the 10-day period was 2.73. For nonelite males, 7% had iceberg profiles on each of the 10 days, 19% had icebergs on the 10th day, and an average number of 2.82 iceberg profiles per nonelite male were recorded during the 10-day period. None of the elite or nonelite females had an iceberg profile on each of the 10 days. Twenty-nine percent of the elite females had an iceberg on the day before competition, and the average number of iceberg profiles per elite female during the 10-day period was 3.57. Fourteen percent of the nonelite females had an iceberg on the 10th day, and the average number of iceberg profiles during the 10-day period was 3.09. Even though none of the elite or nonelite females had an iceberg profile on each day leading up to the race, their average of iceberg profiles over the 10-day period was greater than both elite and nonelite males.

No major variations existed between elite and nonelite mood profiles. Thus the predicted iceberg findings were not evident. Overall, the elite and nonelite profiles were more similar than different on this particular measure.

## Discussion

The results of this study suggest that differences exist between elite and nonelite distance runners on a number of psychological variables in preparation for a marathon. Elites and nonelites differ in their levels of commitment to running, as well as their motives for running. Elites also ran more miles and trained more intensely than the nonelites.

The anxiety ratings at various intervals revealed that elite athletes experienced heightened levels of anxiety 1 hour before the race, but gradually reduced their anxiety as the starting time drew near. Nonelite runners, in contrast, showed a continuous increase in anxiety all the way to the start of the race. Significant differences were found on four of the seven anxiety ratings. The elites were significantly less anxious than the nonelites 1 week before competition, 1 hour before competition, while warming up at the race, and at the starting line. Once the race started, both groups experienced lowered anxiety levels. These findings support previous research on anxiety levels of elite and nonelite performers (Epstein & Fenz, 1962; Fenz, 1975; Mahoney & Avener, 1977).

The POMS profiles of the four runner groups were more similar than different. This finding is consistent with Morgan and Pollock's (1977) study which compared POMS results of world class distance and middle distance runners to those of competitive college runners. Instead of finding the iceberg profile only in the world-class runners, they found that the runners did not differ significantly on any of the mood variables. They concluded that running long distances either produces or requires positive mental health and that distance runners of differing abilities do not differ in this respect.

This study was an initial attempt to gather data regarding pyschological characteristics and cognitive strategies of marathoners using a number of comprehensive psychological measures. Morgan found that regular testing of elite athletes with the POMS can give early warnings of psychological problems, but accurate prediction of behavior cannot rely on one single measurement. Testing elite athletes with POMS, MMPI, and state and trait anxiety measures (Morgan, 1979; Morgan & Johnson, 1978) showed that no single measure of psychological characteristics was sufficient for predicting the performance of athletes. Rather, a truly effective selection model would have to be based on a combination of physiological, psychological, and past performance measures (Morgan, 1980b).

Further research is needed in the areas of sport personality and prediction of athletic performance. A psychophysiological model may be the most comprehensive way to assess athletes. Specifically, psychological measures should be used with other measures, such as field observations, self-reports, physiological characteristics, and social and environmental variables.

# References

Epstein, S., & Fenz, W.D. (1962). Theory and experiment on the measurement of approach-avoidance conflict. *Journal of Abnormal and Social Psychology*, **64**, 97-112.

Fenz, W. (1975). Strategies for coping with stress. In I.G. Sarason & C.D. Spielberger (Eds.), *Stress and anxiety* (Vol. 2). New York: Wiley.

Gould, D., Weiss, M., & Weinberg, R. (1981). Psychological characteristics of successful and nonsuccessful Big 10 wrestlers. *Journal of Sport Psychology*, **3**, 69-81.

Highlen, P., & Bennett, B. (1979). Psychological characteristics of successful and nonsuccessful elite wrestlers: An exploratory study. *Journal of Sport Psychology*, **1**, 123-137.

Mahoney, M.J., & Avener, M. (1977). Psychology of the elite athlete: An exploratory study. *Cognitive Therapy and Research*, **1**, 135-141.

Martens, R. (1977). *Sport Competition Anxiety Test*. Champaign, IL: Human Kinetics.

Morgan, W.P. (1978a). The mind of the marathoner. *Psychology Today*, **11**, 38-39.

Morgan, W.P. (1978b). Sport personality: The credulous-skeptical argument in perspective. In W. Straub (Ed.), *Sport Psychology: An analysis of athlete behavior*. Ithaca, New York: Mouvement Press.

Morgan, W.P. (1979). Anxiety reduction following acute physical activity. *Psychiatric Annals*, **9**, 141-147.

Morgan, W.P. (1980a). Prediction of performance in athletes. In P. Klavora & J.V. Daniel (Eds.), *Coach, athlete and the sport psychologist*. Champaign, IL: Human Kinetics.

Morgan, W.P. (1980b). The trait psychology controversy. *Research Quarterly for Exercise and Sport*, **51**, 50-76.

Morgan, W.P., & Costill, D.L. (1972). Psychological characteristics of the elite distance runner. *Journal of Sports Medicine and Physical Fitness*, **12**(1), 42-46.

Morgan, W.P., & Johnson, R.W. (1978). *Psychological characterization of the elite wrestler: A mental health model*. Paper presented at the Annual Meeting of the American College of Sports Medicine, Chicago.

Morgan, W.P., & Pollock, M.L. (1977). Psychological characterization of the elite distance runner. *Annals of the New York Academy of Science*, 301.

Silva, J.M., Schultz, B.B., Haslam, R.W., & Murray, D.A. (1981). Psychophysiological assessment of elite wrestlers. *Research Quarterly for Exercise and Sport*, **52**(3), 348-358.

# 8

# Mechanical Efficiency in Rowing

*Tetsuo Fukunaga, Akifumi Matsuo, Keizo Yamamoto, and Toshio Asami*
UNIVERSITY OF TOKYO
MEGURO-KU TOKYO, JAPAN

Mechanical efficiency is defined as the ratio of the energy expended to do a given amount of work. Many different values for mechanical efficiency in rowing exercises were observed in previous studies (Asami, Adachi, & Yamamoto, 1981; Cunningham, Goode, & Critz, 1975; Hagerman, Connors, Gault, Hagerman, & Polinski, 1978; Henderson & Haggard, 1925; di Prampero, Cortili, Celentano, & Cerretelli, 1971). Gaesser and Brooks (1975) attempted to compare different methods of calculating the mechanical efficiency of gross, net, work, and delta efficiencies and reported that the highest value was delta efficiency.

The purpose of the present study was to estimate the gross, net, work, and delta efficiencies during a rowing exercise and to investigate similarities and differences of the rowing efficiency reported previously.

## Method

The subjects of the present study were five varsity oarsmen. The mean and standard deviation for age, height, and weight of the subjects were 20.8 ± 1.5 yrs, 67.1 ± 4.0 kg, and 173.6 ± 4.0 cm, respectively. Maximal oxygen uptake was 3.92 ± 0.47 l/min (58.3 ± 4.9 ml/kg min).

The measurement was carried out by using a rowing tank in which water was circulated by a motor-driven pump. The flow rate of the tank water was set at 3 m/s. The oarsman sat in the normal rowing position with the seat/slide assembly and foot braces adjusted to conform to his wishes.

After 10 min of resting on the seat, the subject was requested to row with the stepwise incremental loading method in which rowing intensity was increased subjectively from zero to maximum effort. This was done under the instruction of a coxswain who used an oscillograph to monitor the force exerted on an oarlock pin. Each oarsman performed a 13-min rowing exercise.

Heart rate was recorded by telemetry (SAN-EI 2E3IA). Oxygen consumption was measured during resting and exercise conditions every 30 s by an automatic oxygen analyzer (ERGO OXYSCREEN, Jeager, West Germany).

Anaerobic threshold (AT) during tank rowing was determined from plots of $\dot{V}E$ and gas exchange variables of $\dot{V}CO_2$, $\dot{V}E/\dot{V}O_2$, and $FECO_2$ against the exercise time. According to Wasserman, Whipp, Koyal, and Beaver (1973), $\dot{V}O_2$ measured just below the nonlinear increment of $\dot{V}O_2$ was designated as the AT.

A strain gauge transducer (SHINKOH LC-200KE58) measured the force applied to the oarlock pin ($\bar{F}_c$). The transducer was mounted on a modified pin which was rigidly connected to the floor with the longer side of the basis parallel to the water flow. The angular displacement of the oar in a horizontal direction (OH) was measured with an electropotentiometer mounted on the pin. An electrical switch was attached to the edge of the oar blade to indicate whether the blade was in or out of the water.

The outputs of all transducers were directly connected to an oscillograph, and data was recorded on magnetic tape. The stored data were analyzed by using a microprocessor (SAN-EI 7T07).

The mechanical work calculated from the force and displacement of the oar was obtained for every stroke during the whole rowing exercise. Mechanical work in rowing ($\dot{W}_o$) was calculated from the following equation:

$$\dot{W}_o = \bar{F}_c \times \frac{a \cdot b}{a + b} \times \sin \Theta$$

$F_c$ was the mean force applied to the pin, $a$ was the lever arm of the force exerted by the hand grip on the oar, and $b$ was the lever arm of applied force on the blade, and $\Theta$ was the angle between the oar and the line perpendicular to the water flow. The mechanical work in a minute ($\dot{W}_o$) was calculated from

$$\dot{W}_o = \dot{W}_o \times f$$

where f was stroke frequency per minute.

The mechanical efficiency was determined by the following equations defined by Gaesser and Brooks (1975).

$$\text{gross efficiency} = \frac{W}{E} \times 100$$

$$\text{net efficiency} = \frac{W}{E} \times 100$$

$$\text{work efficiency} = \frac{W}{E_1 - E_u} \times 100$$

$$\text{delta efficiency} = \frac{dW}{dE} \times 100$$

W represented caloric equivalent of external work performance, E was the gross caloric output including resting metabolism, $e$ was the resting caloric output, $E_1$ was the caloric output from loaded rowing, $E_u$ was the caloric output from unloaded rowing, $dW$ was the caloric equivalent of an increment in work performed above the previous work rate, and $dE$ was the increment in caloric output above the previous work rate performance.

## Results

Figure 1 shows the typical recordings of the angular displacement of the oar on a horizontal plane ($\Theta H$), the force applied to the pin ($F_c$), and the signal showing the time when the oar blade was in or out of the water (SW) when rowing maximally. $\Theta H$ indicated about $45°$ at the moment the blade entered the water and about $30°$ when it exited the water. The peak value of $F_c$ in a stroke was about 1500 N.

In the present study the rowing intensity was increased continuously as determined by the judgment of the oarsman. $\Theta H$ and $\bar{F}_c$ during 13 min of rowing are shown in Figure 2. $\bar{F}_c$ increased gradually to a maximum of 1500 N, while $\Theta H$ indicated almost constant values.

The relationship between oxygen uptake ($\dot{V}O_2$) and mechanical work ($\dot{W}_o$) in various rowing intensities under the condition of anaerobic threshold is shown in Figure 3. At the unloaded rowing ($\dot{W}_o = 0$) $\dot{V}O_2$ was $1.12 \pm 0.11$ l/min (mean $\pm$ SD). It was observed that $\dot{W}_o$ increased linearly with the increase of $\dot{V}o_2$ above about 2 l/min of $\dot{V}o_2$, and the gross efficiency was 15-20%.

The stroke frequency per minute increased from $16.2 \pm 3.7$ f/min at unloaded rowing to about 23 f/min at the rowing intensity of anaerobic threshold.

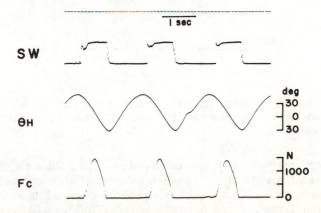

**Figure 1.** Typical recordings of the angular displacement of the oar in the horizontal plane ($\Theta H$), the force applied to the pin ($\bar{F}_c$), and the signal showing the time in which the oar blade was in or out of the water (SW) during maximum rowing.

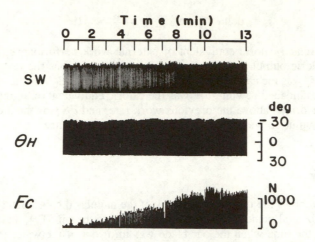

**Figure 2.** Continuous recordings of SW, ΘH, and $\bar{F}_c$ during 13 min of rowing when the intensity was increased from zero to maximum.

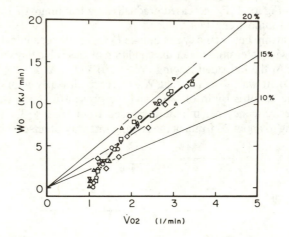

**Figure 3.** Relation between $\dot{W}_o$ and $\dot{V}O_2$ during stepwise incremental loading under anaerobic threshold. Numbers expressed as % represent the gross efficiency.

When rowing maximally a stroke frequency of $33.7 \pm 1.5$ f/min was observed.

Because the range of ΘH in a stroke was independent of the intensity (Figure 2), the increment of $\dot{W}O_2$ was caused by the increase of $F_c$ and stroke frequency

The relation between $\bar{F}_c$ and the gross efficiency ($\dot{W}o/\dot{V}o_2$) is shown in Figure 4. The efficiency increased linearly with increasing $\bar{F}_c$ under the low rowing intensities, while at the moderate intensities above 500 N of $F_c$ the efficiency indicated nearly constant values.

Gross efficiency: $17.5 \pm 1.3\%$
Net efficiency: $19.8 \pm 1.4\%$
Work efficiency: $27.5 \pm 2.9\%$
Delta efficiency: $22.8 \pm 2.2\%$

## Discussion

Different values of the mechanical efficiency during rowing were reported as follows: 20-26% (Henderson & Haggard, 1925), 18-23 (di Prampero et al., 1971), $18.1 \pm 1.9\%$ (Cunningham et al., 1975), 14% (Hagerman et al., 1978), and $16.2 \pm 1.6\%$ (Asami et al., 1981). Differences of these reported values could be explained in terms of the measurement of work done and the calculation of efficiency. Reports of di Prampero et al. (1971) and Asami et al. (1981), in which the force applied to the oar was measured by using a strain gauge while rowing in the water, used the same experimental method as the present study. The gross efficiency of di Prampero et al. (1971) and the net efficiency of Asami et al. (1981) agreed with the present data. Hagerman et al. (1978) and Cunningham et al. (1975) used a rowing ergometer and calculated a gross efficiency of 14% and 18.1%, respectively. The present gross efficiency agreed with that reported by Cunningham et al. (1975) and was a little higher than that reported by Hagerman et al. (1978). The higher gross efficiency separated by Henderson and Haggard (1925), compared to other results, may be due to methodological problems in measuring mechanical work that was calculated from the force of pumping water against the rowing machine resistance.

The increment of efficiency with increasing $F_c$ or work in the present study agreed with previous studies of bicycle pedaling exercises in which the gross, net, and work efficiency increased with an increase in work rate (Åstrand 1960; Gaesser & Brooks, 1975).

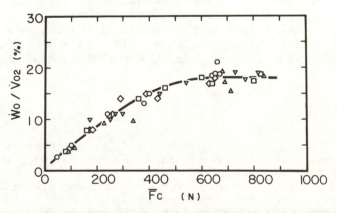

**Figure 4.** Changes in the gross efficiency ($\dot{W}_o/\dot{V}O_2$) with the force applied to the pin ($\bar{F}_c$).

To obtain an accurate measurement of efficiency it is necessary to measure the mechanical work exerted by the muscle and the energy consumed for that work only. In a rowing exercise not only leg muscles, but arm and trunk muscles are activated, resulting in a more recruited muscle mass than other types of exercise such as bicycling and running. Net efficiency has been a frequently used method in calculating what has also been termed *mechanical efficiency*. In this calculation the energy cost of moving the leg, arm, and trunk was not considered in the estimation of work done by the exercising subject. In the rowing exercise this energy cost could not be ignored, because approximately 1 l/min of $Vo_2$ was used in unloaded rowing. In consideration of this unloaded energy cost, the work or delta efficiency is good in theory. Whipp and Wasserman (1969) reported 10% higher values for the work (30%) compared to the net (20%) for the bicycle exercise. Gaesser and Brooks (1975) also indicated that the delta efficiency (24.4-34%) was considerably higher than gross efficiency (7.5-20.4%) and net efficiency (9.8-24.1%) and slightly higher than work efficiency (24.8-30.3%) for the bicycle exercise. The present study in which the highest value was observed in work efficiency (27.5%) compared to the gross (17.5%), net (19.8%), and delta (22.8%) efficiencies agreed with the results of Gaesser and Brooks (1975) and Whipp and Wasserman (1969).

## Conclusion

The mechanical efficiency of the oarsmen was estimated by using a rowing tank in which water flow was set at 3 m/s. The mechanical work was calculated from the force applied to the oarlock pin using a strain gauge transducer and the angular displacement of the oar. Work intensity was increased with a stepwise incremental loading method from unloaded rowing to maximum effort. $Vo_2$ was measured every 30 s by an automatic oxygen analyzer.

The gross efficiency increased linearly with increasing $F_C$ under the low rowing intensities, while, at the moderate intensities of above approximately 500 N of $F_C$, the efficiency indicated nearly constant values.

The mechanical efficiency, which remained nearly constant, was indicated as follows: $17.5 \pm 1.3\%$ of gross efficiency, $19.8 \pm 1.47\%$ of net efficiency, $27.5 \pm 2.9\%$ of work efficiency, and $22.8 \pm 2.2\%$ of delta efficiency.

## References

Asami, T., Adachi, N., & Yamamoto, K. (1981). Biomechanical analysis of rowing performances. In A. Morecki et al. (Eds.), *Biomechanics VII-B* (pp. 442-446). Baltimore: University Park Press.

Åstrand, I. (1960). Aerobic work capacity in men and women with special reference to age. *Acta Physiologica Scandinavia*, **169**, 7-92.

Cunningham, D.A., Goode, P.B., & Critz, J.B. (1975). Cardiorespiratory response of exercise on a rowing and bicycle ergometer. *Medicine and Science in Sports*, **7**(1), 37-43.

di Prampero, P.D. di, Cortili, G., Celentano, F., & Cerretelli, P. (1971). Physiological aspects of rowing. *Journal of Applied Physiology*, **31**(6), 853-857.

Gaesser, G.A., & Brooks, G.A. (1975). Muscular efficiency during steady rate exercise: Effects of speed and work rate. *Journal of Applied Physiology*, **36**(6), 1132-1139.

Hagerman, F.C., Connors, M.C., Gault, J.A., Hagerman, G.R., & Polinski, W.J. (1978). Energy expenditure during simulated rowing. *Journal of Applied Physiology*, **45**(1), 87-93.

Henderson, Y., & Haggard, H.W. (1925). The maximum of human power and its fuel. *American Journal of Physiology*, **72**, 264-282.

Wasserman, K., Whipp, B.J., Koyal, S.N., & Beaver, W.L. (1973). Anaerobic threshold and respiratory gas exchange during exercise. *Journal of Applied Physiology*, **35**, 236-243.

Whipp, B.J., & Wasserman, K. (1969). Efficiency of muscular work. *Journal of Applied Physiology*, **26**(5), 644-648.

# 9

# *The Relationship Between Worry, Emotionality, and Sport Performance*

David M. Furst and Gershon Tenenbaum
WINGATE INSTITUTE FOR PHYSICAL EDUCATION
WINGATE POST, ISRAEL

The purpose of this study was to investigate the relationships between sport performance and state anxiety, specifically the anxiety components of cognitive worry and emotionality (awareness of somatic arousal). High levels of anxiety contribute to people's failure to maximize physical as well as mental potential. Anxiety and performance have therefore been studied by numerous researchers in a laboratory setting; however, a call was recently made for more field research (Martens, 1979). Field studies using a variety of global anxiety measures have now been conducted, but the results are mixed. Relationships between precompetitive anxiety and sport performance have been found, for example, in basketball (Klavora, 1978; Sonstroem & Bernardo, 1982), golf (Weinberg & Genuchi, 1980), parachuting (Powell & Verner, 1982), riflery (Burton, 1971), and softball (Gershon & Deshaies, 1978). However, other researchers have failed to find relationships between the two factors when studying male distance runners (Sanderson & Reilly, 1983), bowling (Burton, 1971), or when controlling for ability in golf (Cook et al., 1983).

Not only can anxiety be divided into an immediate state and a more stable trait (Spielberger, Gorsuch, & Lushene, 1970), but it is now generally accepted that both state and trait are multidimensional phenomena (Endler & Okada, 1975; Liebert & Morris, 1967; Schwartz, Davidson, & Goleman, 1978). What has not been established is which component or components of anxiety are related to sport performance. This delineation is needed in order to construct specific anxiety-reduction programs.

Recently a pencil and paper test, published by Morris, Davis, and Hutchings (1981), was designed to measure specific components of state anxiety.

Their 10-item questionnaire has two scales—one measures worry (negative expectations and cognitive concerns), and the other measures emotionality (awareness of physiological arousal). For research studies in academic test anxiety, the worry component has been associated with poor expected or actual performance (Doctor & Altman, 1969; Liebert & Morris, 1967; Morris & Liebert, 1970). In a test of physical performance (typing), worry was again negatively related to performance (Morris, Smith, Andrews, & Morris, 1975). One explanation for this association has been based on Easterbrook's (1959) cue-utilization theory: as arousal increases, the range of utilized cues decreases. At first this results in enhanced performance as irrelevant cues are ignored, but under higher arousal the relevant cues also are not utilized, and performance deteriorates. Wine (1971, 1982) suggests that this difference between high- and low-anxiety individuals in the utilization of task cues is in line with her division of attention hypothesis. She postulates that when people worry they redirect the focus of attention toward negative thoughts and away from task-relevant aspects of performance. The resulting anxiety/performance relationship is thought to resemble an inverted-U (Yerkes & Dodson, 1908), and this curvilinear relationship has been found in sport (Klavora, 1978; Sonstroem & Bernardo, 1982).

Based on this inverted-U relationship, Oxendine (1970) postulated that different levels of optimal arousal (of which anxiety is one type) would be associated with different sports. According to Oxendine, sports requiring fine motor control (golf, table tennis) would be affected by high levels of arousal more than sports requiring a larger strength or speed component (swimming, weight lifting). Various sports placed along this continuum were therefore examined using two subcomponents of anxiety and a more global anxiety measure to examine the anxiety/sport performance relationship.

## Method

### Subjects

Subjects were team ($n = 199$) and individual sport ($n = 61$) athletes from six different sports. Basketball players ($n = 67$) were tested either during regular league games or during an international tournament. All other athletes were tested during their national championships. This included swimmers ($n = 37$), virtually all national-level boxers ($n = 9$), the majority of the top table tennis players ($n = 15$), and nationally rated team handball squads ($n = 29$).

### Questionnaires

Four anxiety questionnaires were used in this study. To establish basal trait anxiety, Spielberger's 20-item, 4-point scale (TAI, 1970) and Martens's (1977) 15-item, 3-point scale (SCAT) were used. State anxiety measures were Spielberger's 20-item, 4-point scale (SAI) and Morris's (Morris et al., 1981) 10-item, 5-point Worry-Emotionality Scale (W-E Scale). All questionnaires were translated into Hebrew (during which time the word "test" was changed to "competition" in the W-E Scale). Two additional questions were included as part of the study. Athletes were asked to rate their perceived levels of ability on a Likert type scale from 1 to 10, and to rate their expected level of success in the upcoming competition on a scale from 1 to 9.

Performance was the difference (delta) between the coach's expectation of the individual athlete's readiness to compete (skill level, conditioning, health) and the athlete's actual performance as rated by the coach. This method, while more "subjective," avoids the problems of recording output of seemingly more objective measures and, thus, was adopted for its ecological validity. For example, a basketball player who is put into the game for defense and who does not score would get a low performance rating if total points were used as the measure of performance. Similarly, without knowing the athlete's ability, conditioning, and health, finishing position (Sanderson & Reilly, 1983) or score (Burton, 1971) may not be an adequate measure of what the athlete is capable of doing on that specific day. Coaches' ratings, used successfully by previous researchers (Apitzsch, 1973; Klavora, 1978; Passer & Gallo, 1981; Powell & Verner, 1982), are also the only way to measure performance in team sports where scoring may be low (soccer) or where a player is not directly part of the scoring (soccer, team handball, or American football).

## Procedure

Athletes were given the TAI and the SCAT trait anxiety measures during a time not connected with an upcoming competition. The athletes completed the SAI, the W-E Scale, the success, and the ability questions within 30 min prior to competition. The coach rated each athlete's readiness to compete the morning before the game and then rated the performance within 24 hr after the competition on percent scales.

## Results and Discussion

The data were analyzed using the six sports separately, when divided into team and individual sports, and into those who won or lost. Pearson product-moment correlations, ANOVAs, and a procedure developed by Klavora (1978) were used in the analysis.

In order to investigate the possibility of an inverted-U relationship between anxiety levels (SAI, W, E) and performance, the procedure used by Klavora was adopted (see Klavora, 1978 for details). Basically this method involves first calculating the mean state anxiety associated with all performances above expectations (AEP; delta greater than five). Next, two means are calculated for expected performance (EP; delta between five and minus five). All EPs with anxiety scores above the AEP mean are averaged to yield a high-anxiety group that performed as expected (EP2), and all EPs with anxiety scores below the AEP mean were averaged to yield a low-anxiety group that performed as expected (EP1). The same procedure was then used to establish the two anxiety groups (high/low) that performed below expectations (BEP; delta below minus five). The means at these five points were calculated on a cross-sectional rather than a repeated measures sample; however, in support of

Klavora's results with basketball players, the mean SAI scores of BEP1 = 24.4, EP1 = 26.9, AEP = 33.3, EP2 = 39.2, and BEP2 = 42.2 for Israeli basketball players formed an inverted-U (see Figure 1). In addition, the soccer scores for SAI of 31.6, 32.6, 38.5, 42.1, and 44.9 also formed an inverted-U. That is, low- as well as high-anxiety levels were associated with poor performance. However, for swimming and handball the inverted-U relationship was not obtained. Using swimming as an example, the means of 39.5, 33.5, 40.8, 50.7, and 54.7 show that while expected performance was associated with moderate anxiety (33.5), both below- and above-expected performances were associated with nearly the same anxiety levels (39.5 and 40.8, respectively) (see Figure 2). This same V shape connecting BEP1, EP1, and AEP instead of an ascending or descending line was also found for handball and for all four sports when using W or E as the anxiety measures. Possibly not enough data was available to provide a stable sample for use with this procedure.

The six sports were examined in a test of Oxendine's (1970) hypothesis that sports lying on a continuum of fine to gross motor skills require differing levels of arousal for optimum performance. Table tennis was hypothesized to require a high level of fine motor coordination, then boxing and team sports, with swimming demanding the least fine motor coordination and the most speed/strength. A calculation of the mean anxiety levels for optimum performance failed to support Oxendine's hypothesis. Optimum performance for boxing, team handball, and basketball was found to be associated with the lowest SAI 28.3, 32.3, and 33.3, respectively. Table tennis was next with 38.3, along with soccer (38.5), and then swimming (40.8). The worry and emotionality scores were virtually all clustered along the lower end of the scale (low W and E), and it is possible that this concentration led to the failure to show any differentiation between sports. Several explanations exist: the W-E Scale itself may not be able to distinguish the existing levels of worry and somatic

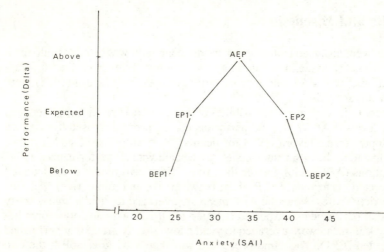

**Figure 1.** Precompetitive anxiety (SAI) and performance for basketball players showing the inverted-U relationship.

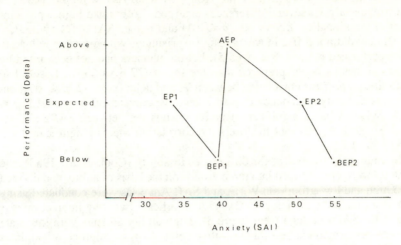

**Figure 2.** Precompetitive anxiety (SAI) and performance for swimmers.

arousal in athletes, Israeli athletes may not be willing to report their anxiety, or worry and emotionality may not play a major role in sport. The low means for both W and E for each sport suggest that Israelis either are not worried/emotional, or that they are unwilling to record their anxiety. This conclusion is supported by the results of an Israeli study of academic test anxiety using the W-E Scale (Furst, Tenenbaum, & Weingarten, 1984) in which students also recorded low W and E scores compared with their American counterparts.

In order to examine any relationships between performance (as measured by delta) and the three state anxiety measures for each sport, one-way ANOVAs were performed. For athletes who performed better than expected (delta above five), the good swimmers as a group had higher state anxiety (45.3) than the boxers (30.3) or basketball players (33.3). Therefore, for a sport needing high strength/endurance, higher SAI was associated with good performance. When comparing athletes who performed more poorly than expected, basketball players had lower state anxiety (29.2) than poor soccer players (43.5) or swimmers (51.3), and these basketball players also had lower emotionality scores (6.5) than swimmers who did poorly (12.3). When comparing athletes who had played below or at (and above) expectations, the only difference found was that soccer players who played better had lower state anxiety (38.2) than those who played poorly (43.5).

The sample was then divided into individual and team sport athletes. One-way ANOVAs, with each factor analyzed separately, showed that the individual sport athletes were more worried (10.7 vs 8.0), more aware of physiological arousal (10.4 vs 8.0), and higher on SAI (43.1 vs 37.0), $p \leqslant .01$. For individual but not team sport athletes, worry was inversely related to expected success ($r = .47$ vs 0.0). Individual sport athletes have greater direct observable responsibility for their performances, and this may be connected to their higher levels of precompetitive anxiety.

When the teams were divided into groups by win/loss (swimmers were left out of the analysis) several differences emerged. Losers had higher precompetitive emotionality (8.9 vs 7.8, $p \leqslant .01$) and higher SAI (41.4 vs 35.7, $p \leqslant .01$) but did not differ in worry. Not surprisingly, winners were judged to have performed better (78.2 vs 65.5), but the winners had not been rated by their coaches as better prepared than the losers (77.6 vs 75.6). Losers had a significant *positive* correlation between W and delta ($r = .32, p \leqslant .01$), but winners had only a tendency toward a negative correlation ($r = -.12, p \leqslant .08$). Winners had a significant negative correlation between SAI and delta ($r = -.19, p \leqslant .02$), but for losers the correlation was not significant ($r = .15, p \leqslant .16$).

In an attempt to control for differences in ability (Cook et al., 1983), the athletes were both divided into three groups on the basis of ability and divided into high and low groups on W, E, and SAI. Analyses were conducted using a $3 \times 2$ (ability $\times$ anxiety) ANOVA. A significant two-way interaction was found for SAI and delta (see Figure 3). High-ability athletes with low state anxiety performed the best (high positive delta, 4.0), but high-ability athletes with high state anxiety were judged to have performed the worst (large negative delta, $-10$). Athletes who rated themselves low in ability performed slightly worse than their coaches expected, regardless of high or low state anxiety ($-1.5, -2.2$). Athletes with a medium level of ability and low state anxiety performed as their coaches expected (.65), but when highly state anxious they performed very poorly (large negative delta, $-8.8$). Low state anxiety was therefore associated with better performance, but low ability athletes performed poorly regardless of anxiety. High and medium ability athletes (with higher expectations), who also had high anxiety, performed worse than high and medium ability athletes who had low anxiety.

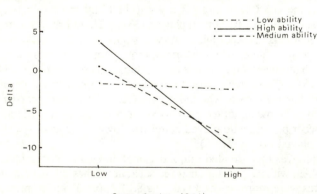

**Figure 3.** Interaction of ability, precompetitive anxiety (SAI), and performance (delta).

## Summary and Conclusions

An attempt was made to relate the subcomponents of worry and emotionality and a more global measure of state anxiety to sport performance (as evaluated by the coach). Worry and emotionality, as measured by the W-E Scale, while having associations with other state and trait anxiety factors, failed to show any meaningful relationships with performance. However, the more global measure of state anxiety was found to be related to performance such that an inverted-U was formed for basketball and soccer but not for team handball and swimming (possibly due to an inadequate subsample size). Israeli athletes scored very low in the W-E Scale, showing that either they are not worried/ emotional, or that they are unwilling to report that they are worried/emotional.

## References

Apitzsch, E. (1973). Pre-start anxiety in competitive swimmers. *Proceedings of the 3rd International Congress of Sport Psychology* (pp. 50-57). Madrid, Spain: National Institute of Education.

Burton, E. (1971). State and trait anxiety, achievement motivation and skill attainment in college women. *Research Quarterly, 42*, 139-144.

Cook, D., Gansneder, B., Rotella, R., Malone, C., Bunker, L., & Owens, D. (1983). Relationship among competitive state anxiety, ability, and golf performance. *Journal of Sport Psychology, 5*, 460-465.

Doctor, R., & Altman, F. (1969). Worry and emotionality as components of test anxiety: Replication and further data. *Psychological Reports, 24*, 563-568.

Easterbrook, J. (1959). The effect of emotion on cue utilization and the organization of behavior. *Psychological Review, 66*, 183-201.

Endler, N., & Okada, M. (1975). A multidimensional measure of trait anxiety: The S-R Inventory of General Trait Anxiousness. *Journal of Consulting and Clinical Psychology, 43*, 319-329.

Furst, D., Tenenbaum, G., & Weingarten, G. (1984). *Test anxiety, gender, and exam type*. Manuscript submitted for publication.

Gershon, R., & Deshaies, P. (1978). Competitive trait anxiety and performance as predictors of precompetitive state anxiety. *International Journal of Sport Psychology, 9*, 16-26.

Klavora, P. (1978). An attempt to derive inverted-U curves based on the relationship between anxiety and athletic performance. In D. Landers & R. Christina (Eds.), *Psychology of motor behavior and sport—1977* (pp. 369-377). Champaign, IL: Human Kinetics.

Liebert, R., & Morris, L. (1967). Cognitive and emotional components of test anxiety: A distinction and some initial data. *Psychological Reports, 20*, 975-978.

Martens, R. (1977). *Sport competition anxiety test*. Champaign, IL: Human Kinetics.

Martens, R. (1979). About smocks and jocks. *Journal of Sport Psychology, 1*, 94-99.

Morris, L., Davis, M., & Hutchings, L. (1981). Cognitive and emotional components of anxiety: Literature review and a revised Worry-Emotionality Scale. *Journal of Educational Psychology, 73*, 541-555.

Morris, L., & Liebert, R. (1970). Relationship of cognitive and emotional components of test anxiety to physiological arousal and academic performance. *Journal of Consulting and Clinical Psychology, 35*, 332-337.

Morris, L., Smith, L., Andrews, E., & Morris, N. (1975). The relationship of emotionality and worry components of anxiety to motor skills performance. *Journal of Motor Behavior, 7*, 121-130.

Oxendine, J. (1970). Emotional arousal and motor performance. *Quest, 13*, 23-32.

Passer, M., & Gallo, F. (1981). Arousal and performance among intercollegiate soccer players [Abstract]. *Proceedings of the North American Society for the Psychology of Sport and Physical Activity*, p. 75.

Powell, F., & Verner, J. (1982). Anxiety and performance relationships in first time parachutists. *Journal of Sport Psychology, 4*, 184-188.

Sanderson, F., & Reilly, T. (1983). Trait and state anxiety in male and female cross-country runners. *British Journal of Sports Medicine, 17*, 24-26.

Schwartz, G., Davidson, R., & Goleman, D. (1978). Patterning of cognitive and somatic processes in the self-regulation of anxiety: Effects of meditation versus exercise. *Psychosomatic Medicine, 40*, 321-328.

Sonstroem, R., & Bernardo, P. (1982). Intraindividual pregame state anxiety and basketball performance: A re-examination of the inverted-U curve. *Journal of Sport Psychology, 4*, 235-245.

Spielberger, C.D., Gorsuch, R.L., & Lushene, R.E. (1970). *Manual for the state-trait anxiety inventory*. Palo Alto, CA: Consulting Psychologists Press.

Weinberg, R., & Genuchi, M. (1980). Relationship between competitive trait anxiety, state anxiety, and golf performance: A field study. *Journal of Sport Psychology, 2*, 148-154.

Wine, J. (1971). Test anxiety and direction of attention. *Psychological Bulletin, 76*, 92-104.

Wine, J. (1982). A cognitive-attentional construct. In H. Krohne & L. Laux (Eds.), *Achievement, stress, and anxiety* (pp. 207-219). Washington, DC: Hemisphere.

Yerkes, R., & Dodson, J. (1908). The relation of strength of stimulus to rapidity of habit formation. *Journal of Comparative and Neurological Psychology, 18*, 459-482.

# 10

# *Age, Experience, and Gender as Predictors of Psychological Response to Training in Olympic Speedskaters*

*Mary C. Gutmann, Dorothy N. Knapp, Carl Foster,*
*Michael L. Pollock, and Barbara L. Rogowski*
MOUNT SINAI MEDICAL CENTER
MILWAUKEE, WISCONSIN, USA

Although psychological factors and personality characteristics have been found to differentiate between a successful and an unsuccessful athlete (Johnson & Morgan, 1981; Mahoney & Avener, 1977; Morgan & Johnson, 1978; Nagle, Morgan, Hellickson, Serfass, & Alexander, 1975), relatively little is known about the athlete's psychological response to training and its effects on outcome.

A longitudinal, prospective study of 11 male speedskaters suggested two distinct patterns of mood changes over the 6 months of training prior to the 1980 Winter Olympic Trials (Gutmann, Pollock, Foster, & Schmidt, 1984). Older, more experienced skaters showed a decrease in depression and an increase in vigor from June to December, reaching a "psychological peak" just before the trials. Younger skaters who were less successful showed greater mood fluctuations and higher levels of fatigue, which may reflect "overtraining." Since the 1980 study involved only male skaters, it was not possible to evaluate the effects of gender on psychological response to training. The purpose of the present study is to replicate the previous design with both male and female skaters competing in the 1983 Winter Olympic Trials.

# Methods

## Subjects and Design

Candidates for the 1984 U.S. Olympic Speedskating Team ($N = 48$) were followed during the summer (June to September) preceding the 1983 Winter Olympic Trials to assess psychological response to high-intensity training. Out of this group, 32 subjects were evaluated at least 3 of the 4 months. The results reported are from the subsample of 32 subjects, with 17 male and 15 female skaters. Ages ranged from 14-27 years, with a mean of 19.9 years. Average length of experience in metric skating was 5.8 years, with 5.3 years at national level competition. Males and females did not differ significantly in age or number of years of experience.

The June and July evaluations were conducted at the Parkside Sport and Fitness Center near Chicago; the August evaluation was done at the end of the 2-week training phase at the U.S. Olympic Training Center in Colorado. All subjects were evaluated again in September at the Human Performance Laboratory at Mount Sinai Medical Center in Milwaukee.

## Procedures

Psychological evaluations were done concurrently with physiological studies, which will be reported elsewhere. The psychological evaluation consisted of a battery of paper and pencil tests including the Profile of Mood States (POMS) (McNair, Lorr, & Droppleman, 1971), Ratings of Perceived Exertion (RPE) (Borg & Noble, 1974) on training, and an adherence questionnaire. Other instruments were also administered in June and September to assess self-motivation, health perception, and attitude toward health care utilization.

Analysis of variance (ANOVA) with repeated measures was used to evaluate within- and between-group differences. For comparison purposes, the skaters were divided into two age groups, giving us 18 subjects (8 males and 10 females) at or below 20 years of age and 14 subjects (9 males and 5 females) 21 years or older.

# Results

## Training Intensity

Most skaters trained an average of 4 hr a day, 6 to 7 days a week. Training concentrated on both physical conditioning and development of specific skills. Activities included uphill running, cycling (continuous and tempo), slide board, low walks, and weight work. Skaters did not begin ice training until mid-October in Norway.

Significantly higher RPEs were obtained toward the end of summer, indicating a progressive increase in perceived training intensity, $F(2, 60) = 6.84$, $p = .003$. Mean RPEs were 15.9 in July, 16.8 in August, and 16.5 in September. Younger skaters ($\leqslant 20$ years old) reported their highest RPEs in August at the Colorado training camp, while older skaters ($> 20$ years old) showed a linear increase in their highest RPEs in September. No significant RPE differences were rated between the male and female skaters.

## Mood Changes

The POMS results show moderate levels of tension, depression, anger, confusion, and total mood disturbance (TMD) at the beginning of summer, although the group profile was similar to that of other college populations. A progressive decrease occurred in these negative moods from June to August, then a slight rise occurred in September.

Changes in mood states were unrelated to gender, but age was a significant factor. Skaters over 20 years of age had significantly lower mean scores on anger, fatigue, confusion, and TMD, and a higher mean score on vigor. Younger skaters showed some improvement in negative moods from June to August, then increased again in September. Older skaters showed a consistent drop in negative moods throughout the entire summer. A significant interaction was also found on vigor, in which older skaters showed a general increase in vigor over time, while the younger skaters remained the same or decreased slightly from June to September. The results of the POMS are summarized in Table 1.

## Illness and Injury

Overall, 66% of the subjects experienced some illness, and 69% reported some injury during the 4 summer months. Within each month, 15-38% of the subjects reported illnesses, and 19-34% reported injuries. The reported incidence of illness and injury was lowest in August, but increased again in September.

Age and gender did not affect the reported incidence of illness. However, significant age differences existed in reported injuries, $F(1, 30) = 6.48$, $p = .016$. An average of 44% of the older subjects reported injuries over the 3 months, compared to 18% of the younger skaters. Males and females did

**Table 1.** Mean *t* scores on the profile of mood states by age group

| Time | TEN | DEP | ANG | Factor VIG* | FAT | CON* | TMD* |
|------|-----|-----|-----|------|-----|------|------|
| Subjects ≤ 20 years old (*n* = 18) | | | | | | | |
| June, 1984 | 51.5 | 46.7 | 54.0 | 52.1 | 50.2 | 46.9 | 197.3 |
| July, 1984 | 47.1 | 45.7 | 51.1 | 49.4 | 48.4 | 46.3 | 189.2 |
| Aug., 1984 | 41.0 | 43.0 | 43.7 | 50.9 | 48.5 | 38.5 | 163.8 |
| Sept., 1984 | 46.6 | 45.3 | 48.7 | 49.8 | 47.3 | 41.3 | 179.3 |
| Subjects > 20 years old (*n* = 14) | | | | | | | |
| June, 1984 | 46.7 | 46.3 | 48.6 | 53.0 | 45.8 | 43.5 | 178.1 |
| July, 1984 | 43.6 | 41.5 | 47.0 | 60.0 | 43.7 | 40.1 | 155.9 |
| Aug., 1984 | 41.5 | 41.0 | 43.7 | 56.8 | 46.8 | 35.9 | 152.1 |
| Sept., 1984 | 41.0 | 41.9 | 43.3 | 57.9 | 43.5 | 38.3 | 150.1 |

*Note.* TEN = tension, DEP = depression, ANG = anger, VIG = vigor, FAT = fatigue, CON = confusion, TMD = total mood disturbance.
*$p < .05$ for between group comparisons.

not differ on frequency of injuries, but a significant interaction did occur over time, $F(2, 60) = 4.22, p = .019$. In September 53% of the males reported injuries, which represents a sharp increase from August. Only 13% of the females reported injuries in September.

### Adherence to Training

Eighty-one percent of the subjects reported missing training in July, 46% in August, and 66% in September. As a group, the skaters missed an average of 2.5 days in July, 0.9 days in August, and 2.9 days in September, giving an overall average of 2.1 days per month, $F(2.60) = 3.40, p = .039$. Younger skaters missed significantly more days of training (2.8 days per month) than the older skaters (1.2 days per month), $F(1, 30) = 5.07, p = .030$. Males also tended to miss more training than females (2.7 vs 1.5 days, respectively), $F(1, 30) = 2.82, p = .100$. All subjects showed better adherence to training in August, regardless of age or gender.

Most of the days missed were because of tiredness and fatigue. Injuries accounted for 32% of the days missed, and minor illnesses accounted for 16%. As noted above, older skaters had more injuries ($p = .016$), but missed fewer days of training ($p = .030$) than the younger skaters. Males also reported an increase in injuries and missed more days of training in September because of fatigue.

# Discussion

The results of the present study are consistent with those obtained from the 1980 Olympic candidates. In the earlier study, skaters selected for the 1980 U.S. Olympic team responded to training with decreased depression and increased vigor, while those who were not selected fluctuated in mood and showed increasing fatigue (Gutmann et al., 1984). Age and experience contributed to a positive response to training and success at the Trials.

Skaters in this subsample generally showed an improvement in mood over the 4 months of summer training, while scores on vigor and fatigue remained fairly constant. As in the previous study, significant differences were found between age groups. Skaters 21 years of age or older had overall lower scores on the negative mood dimensions at each time point. In addition, older skaters increased in vigor from June to September, while the younger skaters remained the same or decreased slightly. Thus younger skaters were only able to maintain their energy levels during training, while older, more experienced skaters were able to develop mentally as well as physically. It remains to be seen if these differences continue during ice training, and if they affected outcome at the Winter Trials.

Increased tension and fatigue found in the younger skaters may reflect stress associated with high-intensity training. The skaters were training consistently at near maximum levels of intensity, 4 hours a day, 6-7 days a week. Their average rating of 16.4 on the Borg scale may be an underestimate of their actual training intensity because it was obtained retrospectively. ''Overtraining'' is a risk at such high intensities, especially with well-motivated, adherent athletes.

Experienced athletes might have learned to regulate their training to avoid ''overtraining'' and excessive anxiety. Evidence suggests that scheduled practice sessions elicit the same levels of arousal and state anxiety as actual competition (Huddleston & Gill, 1981). However, more successful athletes are able to ''use'' their anxiety as a stimulant to perform better (Mahoney & Avener, 1977).

Overtraining may also result in illness, injury, and nonadherence to training. Injuries were prevalent, especially among older male skaters, while younger skaters were more likely to report minor illnesses. However, illness accounted for only 16% of the days of training missed, and 32% were attributed to injuries. The remainder of training days missed were due mostly to tiredness and fatigue. Thus time off of training may well have been one way skaters coped with the stress of their summer schedules. Here again, age differences were apparent. Older skaters missed significantly fewer days despite a higher incidence of injuries.

Although age and experience influenced psychological response to training, few significant differences were found between males and females. Both groups had similar results on the POMS and showed parallel changes over time. Males did report more injuries and tended to miss more days of training, but the two groups were remarkably similar in all other aspects of their psychological responses to training.

One notable finding was the consistently positive response of skaters to the Colorado training camp. Scores on the negative mood scales were lowest in August, although vigor and fatigue remained the same. This pattern was most evident with younger skaters, but they showed a relapse in September with an increase in negative moods and nonadherence to training. In contrast, older skaters maintained the positive changes throughout. It appears that the structured setting and group training in Colorado benefited the younger, less experienced skaters the most. However, some intervention is needed to help skaters maintain the benefits and prevent relapses.

## Summary and Conclusions

1. The group as a whole had moderate levels of tension, depression, anger, confusion, and TMD at the beginning of the summer, but showed a significant decrease in these negative moods over the 4 months of training.
2. Males and females did not differ in their emotional responses to training, but age and experience had a major effect on moods and training behavior (adherence).
3. Skaters over 20 years of age ($n = 14$) were significantly less distressed, had higher vigor, and responded positively to training with an accentuation of the POMS ''iceberg'' profile from June to September. In contrast, younger skaters ($n = 18$) fluctuated in negative moods and never achieved a peak in vigor.

4. Older skaters also missed fewer days of training despite more injuries. The group as a whole missed an average of 2.1 days of training per month. Over half of the days missed were because of tiredness or fatigue. Age and gender were unrelated to illness patterns, but males tended to report more injuries and miss more training days.
5. Younger skaters benefited the most from the structured, group training camp in Colorado. They trained harder, missed fewer days, had less illnesses and injuries, and improved significantly in mood. However, relapse prevention is needed to maintain optimal psychological and physical conditioning.

# References

Borg, G., & Noble, B.J. (1974). Perceived exertion. In J. Wilmore (Ed.), *Exercise and sport sciences reviews* (pp. 131-153). New York: Academic Press.

Gutmann, M.C., Pollock, M.L., Foster, C., & Schmidt, D. (1984, December). Training stress in Olympic speed skaters: A psychological perspective. *The Physician and Sportsmedicine, 12*(12), 45-57.

Huddleston, S., & Gill, D.L. (1981). State anxiety as a function of skill level and proximity to competition. *Research Quarterly for Exercise and Sport, 52*, 31-34.

Johnson, R.W., & Morgan, W.P. (1981). Personality characteristics of college athletes in different sports. *Scandinavian Journal of Sports Sciences, 3*, 41-49.

Mahoney, M.J., & Avener, M. (1977). Psychology of the elite athlete: An exploratory study. *Cognitive Therapy & Research, 1*, 135-141.

McNair, D.M., Lorr, M., & Droppleman, L.F. (1971). *Profile of Mood States manual*. San Diego: Educational and Industrial Testing Service.

Morgan, W.P., & Johnson, R.W. (1978). Personality characteristics of successful and unsuccessful oarsmen. *International Journal of Sport Psychology, 9*, 119-133.

Nagle, F.J., Morgan, W.P., Hellickson, R.O., Serfass, R.C., & Alexander, J.F. (1975). Spotting success traits in Olympic contenders. *The Physician and Sportsmedicine, 3*, 31-34.

# 11

# Perceived Vulnerability to Illness and Injury Among Olympic Speedskating Candidates: Effects on Emotional Response to Training

*Dorothy N. Knapp, Mary C. Gutmann,*
*Barbara L. Rogowski, Carl Foster, and Michael L. Pollock*
MOUNT SINAI MEDICAL CENTER
MILWAUKEE, WISCONSIN, USA

Illness, injury, adherence, and emotional response to training may all affect athletic performance. Although increasing interest exists within sport psychology in athletes' emotional responses to training and competition (Huddleston & Gill, 1981; Morgan & Pollock, 1977; Silva, Schultz, Haslam, & Murray, 1981), little attention has been paid to psychological (as opposed to situational) factors which may affect or predict emotional response.

One factor that may influence emotional response to training is the athlete's perception of his or her own vulnerability to illness and injury. A review of the literature revealed no systematic study of perceived vulnerability to illness and injury in athletes. Literature on the illness behavior of medical patients

This study was supported in part by a grant from the United States Olympic Committee, Sports Medicine Division, Elite Athlete Project. The USOC is not responsible for the authors' findings or the authors' interpretations of these findings.

We gratefully acknowledge the assistance of Dianne Holum, coach of the United States' National Speedskating Team, and the skaters themselves whose cooperation and support made this project possible, and Drs. Barry Blackwell and Len Sperry for their review of a draft of this article.

Requests for reprints should be sent to Dorothy Knapp, PhD, Human Performance Laboratory, University of Wisconsin Medical School, Milwaukee Clinical Campus, Mount Sinai Medical Center, P.O. Box 342, Milwaukee, WI 53201.

suggests that somatic concern may exert a considerable influence on behavior and emotions, including illness reporting, expressions of emotional distress, and limitations of "healthy" activities (Blackwell, 1981; Wooley, Blackwell, & Winget, 1978).

The purpose of this study is to assess perceived vulnerability to illness and injury and recent history of illness in elite athletes and to determine whether these factors predicted self-reported illness and injury, adherence to training, or emotional status during training.

## Method

Members of the U.S. National Speedskating Team, training for the 1984 Olympic Trials, were followed for four consecutive months of summer training. A total of 48 speedskaters (26 male, 22 female; mean age = 19.4) were seen at least once, with 32 skaters (17 male, 15 female; mean age = 19.9) being assessed at least three of the four time periods. Skaters were assessed in June (T1) and in July (T2) at 2-day training camps in Chicago, at the end of a 2-week August (T3) training camp in Colorado, and finally in September (T4) at Mount Sinai Medical Center's Human Performance Laboratory in Milwaukee. Summer training included high-intensity, varied work containing little actual ice-skating, as summarized in Table 1. Training intensity increased from T1 to T4, reaching a peak at T3.

Skaters' perceptions of their health, vulnerability to illness and injury, and past incidence of illness were obtained at T1 using the questionnaire items shown in Table 2. Skaters' responses to the questions regarding worry about getting sick, worry about getting hurt, and how often they got sick compared to others their own age (items 1, 2, and 3) were significantly interrelated ($p < .01$), using Fisher's exact probability test: skaters who worried more about getting sick also believed they got sick more often than others their own age, and were more inclined to worry about getting injured.

Skaters were grouped into four different sets of high- and low-perceived illness/injury vulnerability groups based on their responses to items 1, 2, 3,

**Table 1.** Descriptive summary of speedskaters' summer training

| Description | Frequency |
| --- | --- |
| 90 min workout | 2 times daily |
| (1 rest day every 10 days) | |
| 3 hard weeks, 1 easier week | |
| Varied high-intensity workouts including: | |
|   Bicycling (continuous and tempo) | 3 times weekly |
|   Running (uphill tempos) | 1-2 times weekly |
|   Weights (strength and endurance) | 2-3 times weekly |
|   Slideboard/rollerskates | 2-3 times weekly |
|   "Downtimes"—dry skate | 3-4 times weekly |
|    (Specific skating exercises) | |

or 4, and repeated measures ANOVA were used to assess differences in illness, injury, emotional response, and adherence to training. Similar results were obtained in the analyses using items 1, 2, or 3. This pattern of positive correlation and very similar effects on the dependent variables suggested that items 1, 2, and 3 were all measuring essentially the same thing, which will be called perceived vulnerability to illness and injury (PIV). Answers to Item 4 did not predict illness, injury, emotional response, or adherence to summer training.

Specific results reported will be those for PIV groups based on Item 1 (worry about becoming ill). These results are representative of the effects of differences in Item 2 (worry about injury) and Item 3 (estimation of frequency of personal illness compared to others). Skaters responding that they "almost never" worry about getting sick formed the Low PIV group ($n = 23$), whereas those who worried "sometimes" or "a lot" formed the High PIV group ($n = 9$) in these analyses.

Skaters were also grouped according to their reports of the number of times they had to stay home during the previous year because of sickness (Item 6, Table 2). Ten skaters reported that they had had zero to one such sicktimes (Few ST); 14 reported two to four sicktimes (Moderate ST); and 8 reported five or more sicktimes in the past year (Many ST). As with the PIV groups, analyses of variance with repeated measures were performed to determine whether significant differences existed between ST groups on illness, injury, training adherence, or emotional response using the subsample of 32 skaters who were seen at least three out of four assessment times. Means for the subsample were inserted where there was missing data.

Skaters' emotional states were assessed at the beginning of training and each month thereafter using the Profile of Moods States (POMS) form which asks subjects to rate how they have been feeling for the past week. The POMS gives measures of tension, depression, anger, vigor, fatigue, and confusion. A total mood disturbance score (TMD) was calculated by summing the T-scores of these subscales, with vigor weighted negatively (McNair, Lorr, & Droppleman, 1971, p. 9). In addition, at T2, T3, and T4, skaters responded to a questionnaire that asked if they had been sick or injured since the last assessment or had missed training days for other reasons, noting the number of training days missed.

## Results

### Illness, Injury, and Adherence

Most skaters reported that they almost never worried about becoming ill or injured, and that they were sick or injured less often than others their own age (Table 2). None rated their overall health as less than "average," with the majority giving a rating of "very good." Responses to these items were not significantly related to age, self-motivation scores, or gender, with the exception of a trend for female skaters to be somewhat more worried about getting hurt than male skaters (chi-square = 3.01, $df = 1$, $p < .10$). As a

**Table 2.** Skaters' rating of health and vulnerability to illness and injury

| Question | Rating | | |
| --- | --- | --- | --- |
| | A lot | Sometimes | Almost never |
| 1. How often do you worry about getting sick? | 6 | 3 | 23 |
| 2. How often do you worry about getting hurt? | 3 | 10 | 19 |

| | More often | About the same | Less often |
| --- | --- | --- | --- |
| 3. Do you think you get sick more often, about the same, or less often than others your age? | 4 | 9 | 19 |
| 4. Do you think you get hurt more often, about the same, or less often than others your age? | 4 | 9 | 19 |

| | Very good | Good | Average | Poor | Very poor |
| --- | --- | --- | --- | --- | --- |
| 5. How would you rate your overall health? | 22 | 8 | 2 | 0 | 0 |

| | | M | SD |
| --- | --- | --- | --- |
| 6. In the past year, how many times did you have to stay home because you were sick? | | 6.06 | 10.48 |

group, skaters reported a mean of six times when they had to stay home because of illness in the previous year.

No significant overall differences in self-reported illness or injury during summer training were found between High and Low PIV skaters, with one exception: there was a trend, $F(2, 60) = 2.78$, $p = .0687$, for more Low than High PIV skaters to report illness in September (48% vs 11%). However, no difference was found in the number of training days missed due to illness. Between 15% and 38% of all skaters reported illness each month, with a trend for illness reporting increasing at T4. Most illnesses were relatively minor problems such as colds, flu, etc. Ill skaters missed a mean of 0.87-1.9 days of training due to illness each month. Between 19% and 34% of skaters reported injury each month, with injured skaters missing a mean of 0.15-3.09 days of training per month because of injury.

Low and High PIV skaters did not differ in reported adherence to training. Although between 46% and 81% of the skaters reported missing training each month (38 to 62% for nonhealth reasons), the average number of training days missed was low (0.9 to 2.9 per month). Prominent among the reasons given for missing training were fatigue and being "mentally not into it," particularly at T3 and T4. Training adherence was greater at T3, both in a lower percent of skaters reporting missed training, $F(2, 60) = 8.86, p = .0007$, and a lower average number of days missed, $F(2, 60) = 3.41, p = .0383$. T3 included the Colorado 2-week training camp.

Thus, perceived vulnerability to illness did not predict adherence or injury during summer training in the group of 32 speedskaters. Furthermore, it bore only a weak and somewhat paradoxical relationship to illness-reporting at T4 when more *Low* PIV skaters reported illness. This is in contrast to the finding that High PIV skaters reported having been home sick more often in the past year than Low PIV skaters, $Ms = 13.6$ vs $3.1$ times, $t(30) = 10.48, p < .001$.

Similarly, no significant difference was found between Few, Moderate, and Skaters in the Many ST group injury or training adherence. However, the groups differed significantly in self-reported illness during training: Moderate ST skaters had the highest incidence of illness, $F(2, 29) = 7.67, p = .0024$ (Figure 1). On the average, 44% of the Moderate ST skaters reported having been ill at each time point, compared to 12% and 13% of Few and Many ST skaters, respectively.

To summarize, neither PIV nor ST influenced training adherence or injury reporting; they affected only illness reporting. PIV showed only a weak interaction effect on illness reporting whereas Moderate ST skaters reported significantly more illness throughout the summer.

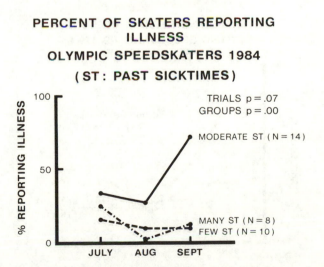

**Figure 1.** Percent of skaters reporting illness each month as a function of number of sicktimes in the year preceding summer training. (Few St = 0-1 sicktimes, Moderate ST = 2-4 sicktimes, Many ST = 5 or more sicktimes.)

## Emotional Status

Despite high and increasing intensity of training, relatively frequent report of injuries, and increased illness reporting toward the end of summer, the skaters as a group showed decreasing emotional distress as the summer progressed, with the lowest distress in August. Decreasing TMD scores were due to similarly decreasing tension, depression, anger, and confusion ratings. No significant change in vigor or fatigue was observed in the skaters as a group.

No significant overall difference in emotional response was found between ST groups; however, a significant group-by-trials interaction was observed, $F(6, 87) = 2.34$, $p = .0376$ (Figure 2). Skaters in the Many ST group were considerably more emotionally distressed (particularly more depressed, angry, and fatigued) early in summer training (T1 and T2) than Few and Moderate ST skaters, but no difference was found at T3 and T4. Thus, skaters who had had many sicktimes in the year preceding training were more emotionally distressed, but only early in summer training.

Low PIV skaters reported less emotional distress throughout summer training than High PIV skaters ($M$ TMD 163.2 vs 195.2), $F(1, 30) = 9.41$, $p = .0047$: Low PIV skaters were significantly less tense, depressed, angry, fatigued, and confused, and felt more vigor than the High PIV skaters. A significant interaction between groups over time was also observed $F(3, 90) = 3.70$, $p = .0144$ (Figure 3). High PIV skaters showed much higher emotional distress at T1 and T2. This approached the level of Low PIV skaters at T3 and rose somewhat again at T4. The POMS scales that contributed most to this interaction effect were tension, depression, and anger, which all showed similar interaction effects.

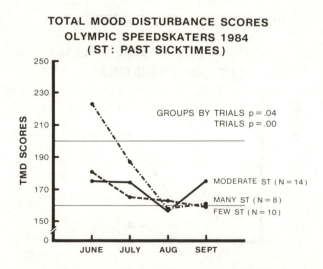

**Figure 2.** Mean Total Mood Disturbance (TMD) scores for each month, as a function of number of sicktimes in the year preceding summer training. (Few ST = 0-1 sicktimes, Moderate ST = 2-4 sicktimes, Many ST = 5 or more sicktimes.)

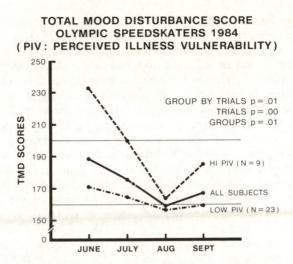

**Figure 3** Mean Total Mood Disturbance (TMD) scores for each month, among all skaters, and as a function of percieved vulnerability to illness (PIV). (High PIV = Worry about getting sick "sometimes" or "a lot"; Low PIV = Worry about getting sick "almost never".)

In summary, both ST and PIV were significantly related to emotional status during training. Skaters in the Many ST group showed greater emotional distress, but only early in training. In contrast, High PIV skaters experienced more emotional distress throughout summer training, but also appeared to emotionally benefit the most during the Colorado training camp experience.

## Discussion

Neither recent past history of sickness nor perceived vulnerability to illness and injury affected injury reporting or adherence to training, but their sphere of influence was upon illness reporting and, especially, emotional response to training.

Effects upon illness reporting were somewhat paradoxical. Skaters who reported an *intermediate* number of sicktimes in the preceding year reported significantly more illness during summer training than those skaters who reported many past illnesses. No information regarding the nature or season of the sicktimes experienced in the preceding year was obtained. It may be that winter colds and flu were overrepresented among skaters with many past sicktimes. If this were true, they would not necessarily be expected to replicate their past reported frequency of illness until the next winter season.

However, the strongest effect of perceived vulnerability to illness and injury, and past sicktimes was on emotional status during training. Skaters with a high frequency of confining sicktimes in the previous year showed much higher emotional distress at the beginning of summer training. Conversation with some skaters suggested that the distress was attributable to an awareness of loss of conditioning due to illness, and concern that frequent illness might continue and therefore disrupt training. But as the Many ST skaters experienced little illness through the summer, their emotional distress also lessened until at midsummer it was no different from that of the other skaters. One may hypothesize that the effects of frequent confining illness in the recent past on emotional status during training will be transitory as long as the bouts of illness do not continue. An alternate hypothesis is that the Many ST skaters had more confining sicktimes in the previous year as a consequence of being more emotionally distressed, and that as their moods improved during the summer training, their illness reporting also decreased.

In contrast, perceived vulnerability to illness and injury had a sustained strong effect on emotional distress during summer training. High PIV skaters (comprising about one third of the sample) experienced substantially more emotional distress than those who perceived themselves to be relatively invulnerable (Figure 3). This effect was observed in all POMS subscales including vigor and fatigue. Previous studies suggest POMS scores may be related to performance (Gutmann, Pollock, Foster, & Schmidt, 1984; Morgan & Johnson, 1978; Nagle, Morgan, Hellickson, Serfass, & Alexander, 1975; Silva et al., 1981). Whether perceived vulnerability to illness and injury and/or emotional status during training were significantly related to performance in the present study remains to be determined. Assessment of skaters' perceived vulnerability to illness and injury may be useful in identifying skaters who are more vulnerable to emotional distress during training and who may benefit from intervention to reduce their distress.

Worry about getting sick, worry about getting hurt, and estimations of how frequently one gets sick compared to others one's age were positively correlated in this sample of skaters and produced similar effects on the dependent variables studied. In contrast, estimations of how frequently one gets hurt compared to others one's age were unrelated to the above items and did not significantly influence any of the dependent variables studied. Perhaps one reason for this difference is that injuries produce more discreet, less ambiguous symptoms than sickness. This item may have reflected the individual skater's past history of actual injuries, but such data was not collected. This item was not significantly related to injury reporting during the time of the study.

Perceived vulnerability to illness and injury, as defined in this study, contains a cognitive component which may reflect the skater's estimate of probability of becoming ill during training, as well as the emotional component of worry. Worry about illness/injury may be influenced by cognitive estimates of likelihood of becoming injured or ill, perceived consequences of such events, and perhaps overall emotional status. Further work will be needed to refine the measurement of these concepts and to determine their relative influence on athletes in training. Results of the present study suggest that this may be an important area of study.

Note that High PIV skaters experienced their lowest levels of emotional distress at T3, the time of the 2-week summer training camp. At this time the skaters, many of whom usually trained in relative isolation without benefit of a coach's supervision, gathered to train as a group. The presence of a supportive coach and teammates, and a training schedule which made clear what was expected of them, seemed to be particularly important. All skaters were most adherent and least distressed at this time, despite the fact that they also worked hardest, but High PIV skaters apparently found this training camp to be especially beneficial. Interestingly, their emotional distress increased again in September although it remained lower than at the beginning of the summer. These findings suggest that group training with clear expectations and under the close and supportive supervision of one's coach may be especially helpful in reducing emotional distress in skaters who perceive themselves to be more vulnerable to injury and illness.

# References

Blackwell, B. (1981). Illness behaviour labelling and compliance. *Clinical and Investigative Medicine, 4*, 209-214.

Gutmann, M.C., Pollock, M.L., Foster, C., & Schmidt, D. (1984, December). Training stress in Olympic speed skaters: A psychological perspective. *The Physician and Sportsmedicine, 12*(12), 45-57.

Huddleston, S., & Gill, D.L. (1981). State anxiety as a function of skill level and proximity to competition. *Research Quarterly for Exercise and Sport, 52*, 31-34.

McNair, D.M., Lorr, M., & Droppleman, L.F. (1971). *EdITS manual for the Profile of Mood States* (1st ed.). San Diego: Educational and Industrial Testing Service.

Morgan, W.P., & Johnson, R.W. (1978). Personality characteristics of successful and unsuccessful oarsmen. *International Journal of Sport Psychology, 9*(2), 119-133.

Morgan, W.P., & Pollock, M.L. (1977). Psychologic characterization of the elite distance runner. *Annals of the New York Academy of Sciences, 301*, 382-403.

Nagle, F.J., Morgan, W.P., Hellickson, R.O., Serfass, R.C., & Alexander, J.F. (1975). Spotting success traits in Olympic contenders. *The Physician and Sportsmedicine, 3*, 31-34.

Silva III, J.M., Schultz, B.B., Haslam, R.W., & Murray, D. (1981). A psychophysiological assessment of elite wrestlers. *Research Quarterly for Exercise and Sport, 52*, 348-358.

Wooley, S., Blackwell, B., & Winget, C. (1978). A learning theory model of chronic illness behavior: Theory, treatment, and research. *Psychosomatic Medicine, 40*, 379-401.

# 12

# The Relationship Between %$\dot{V}O_2$ max and Running Performance Time

*Luc Léger, Daniel Mercier, and Lise Gauvin*
UNIVERSITY OF MONTREAL
MONTREAL, QUEBEC, CANADA

In an attempt to pinpoint factors affecting running performance, researchers have devoted some attention to examining the relationship between %$\dot{V}O_2$ max and running performance time. Such an endeavor is relevant since resultant regression equations are useful in establishing specific and accurate training loads as well as in predicting $\dot{V}O_2$ max from running performance when running's $O_2$ expenditure is known (that is, %$\dot{V}O_2$ and $\dot{V}O_2$ are computed from performance times and then $\dot{V}O_2$ max or 100% is extrapolated from %$\dot{V}O_2$ and $\dot{V}O_2$). However, preliminary efforts designed to describe %$\dot{V}O_2$ max by time curves (Åstrand & Rodahl, 1970; Costill & Fox, 1969) were based on limited data, and no regression equations were developed. In addition, running distance rather than running time was used as a prediction variable in at least one of these studies (Costill & Fox, 1969). This seems inappropriate since metabolic events are a function of running time rather than running distance in heterogeneous populations. Although more recent investigations (Davies & Thompson, 1979) properly reported %$\dot{V}O_2$ max according to running time, they comprised lengthy performance time ranges (0.5-24 hr) and only high-caliber athletes. Other researchers (Purdy, 1974) focused mainly on world records and thus employed running speed and running distance as their dependent and independent variables, respectively.

Therefore in order to overcome these difficulties, a reexamination of the %$\dot{V}O_2$ max-performance time link was conducted. The purpose of the study was to analyze regression equations predicting %$\dot{V}O_2$ max from running performance time. A subsidiary purpose was to compare the accuracy of various mathematical models pertaining to the analysis.

This study was supported by FCAC EQ-2335.

## Method

### Subjects

Data were collected from 311 runners who performed 521 running distances ranging from 0.2-42.2 km within 3 weeks of a $\dot{V}O_2$ max test. The sample was comprised of 251 males and 60 females with a $\dot{V}O_2$ max of 61.3 $\pm$ 6.1 ml kg$^{-1}$min$^{-1}$ ($M \pm SD$).

### Computation of $\dot{V}O_2$ max and %$\dot{V}O_2$ max

$\dot{V}O_2$ max was determined by a maximal multistage running track test in which $\dot{V}O_2$ max was predicted from maximal running speed ($r = 0.96$, $SEE = 5\%$, Léger & Boucher, 1980). Starting speed was set at 8 km h$^{-1}$ and increased 1 km h$^{-1}$ (or 1 met) every 2 min; subjects adjusted their running speeds by passing 50 m post marks placed around the track as they heard an auditory signal emitted by a prerecorded tape. The test score corresponds to the last stage called on the tape prior to exhaustion (i.e., when the runner can no longer keep up with the pace). In addition, since gross $\dot{V}O_2$ estimates of horizontal track running in calm air can be graded according to running speed when variables are converted into proper units (Léger & Mercier, 1984), it follows that

$$\dot{V}O_2, \text{met} = \text{SPEED}, \text{km}^{-1} \tag{1}$$

Thus the test score may be expressed as maximal aerobic speed in km h$^{-1}$ or as maximal aerobic power in mets (1 met = 3.5 ml kg$^{-1}$min$^{-1}$). Percent $\dot{V}O_2$ max was subsequently obtained by computing average performance $\dot{V}O_2$/$\dot{V}O_2$ max ratio. The average performance $\dot{V}O_2$ was determined from average running speed by using Equation 1.

### Regression Analyses

In an attempt to accurately describe the relationship between %$\dot{V}O_2$ max (Y) and performance time (X), various regression models were fitted to the data points. Linear, logarithmic, exponential, and polynomial regression equations were derived through the least squares method. Other models were developed through trial-and-error hand fitting and were later verified with the least squares method by comparing predicted %$\dot{V}O_2$ max with observed %$\dot{V}O_2$ max. Accuracy of the resulting regression equations was assessed according to the size of correlation coefficients ($r$), the standard errors of the estimate ($SEE$), and the comparison of regression curves with the eye-fitting curve.

## Results and Discussion

Although $\dot{V}O_2$ max was not directly assessed, its prediction from running maximal aerobic speed obtained via the multistage track test appears to constitute an accurate and unbiased estimate ($r = 0.96$, $SEE = 5\%$, Léger & Boucher, 1980). For this study it was assumed that each individual had the same mechanical efficiency in running the track test and various road races. Such an assumption allowed for compensation of interindividual variations. In addition, as indicated in Equation 1, %V̇O₂ max and % maximal aerobic running speed were equivalent. Thus, using indirectly rather than directly measured VO₂ max in regression analyses seems justified.

Fitting traditional mathematical models to the data yielded unsatisfactory results. Among the linear, polynomial, semi-logarithmic, and double logarithmic regression models, only the double logarithmic regression (Equation 5, Table 1) explained significant portions of the variance for performance times longer than 2 min (Table 1 and Figure 1). However, better regression fits were obtained with more complex models (Equations 6, 7, and 8 in Table 1, and Figure 2). Specifically, as indicated in Table 1, Equations 7 and 8 explained the most variance (r and SEE) and very closely hugged the eye-fitting curve over the entire range of performance times. In fact, Equation 7 is composed of four separate equations and is preferred over Equation 8 since predictor and criterion variables can be used interchangeably with greater ease.

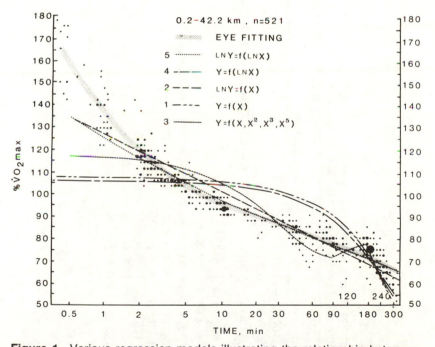

**Figure 1.** Various regression models illustrating the relationship between % V̇O₂ max (Y) and performance time (X). Regression coefficient are listed in Table 1. Abcissa is expressed on a logarithmic scale. Thus linear regression 5., Y = f(X), appears curvilinear whereas semilogarithmic regression, 3., Y = f(ln X), appears linear. Only log-log regression 2., ln Y = f(ln X), compared favorably with eye fitting for performance longer than 2 min. Equation numbers are the same as in Table 1. Size of dots increases with the number of observations having the same coordinates (n = 1-9).

**Table 1.** Accuracy ($r$ and $SEE$) of various regressions describing %$\dot{V}O_2$ max (Y) as function of the running performance time (X, min) for times ranging between 0.33-300 min (521 observations)

| Equation | Regression Equation | $r$ | $SEE$ %$\dot{V}O_2$ max (%$\bar{Y}$) |
|---|---|---|---|
| 1 | $Y = 107.92 - 0.191X$ | -0.749 | 15.0 (15.8) |
| 2 | $\ln Y = 4.67 - 0.00214X$ | -0.817 | 13.0 (13.7) |
| 3 | $Y = 118.42 - 1.375X + 0.01372X^2 - 0.00004489X^3 + 0.1352 \times 10^{-9}X^5$ | -0.869 | 11.2 (11.8) |
| 4 | $Y = 126.69 - 11.056 \ln X$ | -0.936 | 7.9 (8.3) |
| 5 | $\ln Y = 4.86 - 0.115 \ln X$ | -0.952 | 7.1 (7.5) |
| 6 | $Y = 70 + 20.2973e^{-0.006478X} + 41.5589e^{-0.16926X} + 75.79954e^{-1.35955X}$ | -0.967 | 5.8 (6.1) |
| 7 | < 4.6 min: $\ln Y = 4.93 - 0.186 \ln X$<br>4.6-70.4 min: $\ln Y = 4.79 - 0.096 \ln X$<br>70.4-173.7 min: $\ln Y = 4.90 - 0.121 \ln X$<br>> 173.7 min: $\ln Y = 5.08 - 0.156 \ln X$ | -0.970 | 5.5 (5.8) |
| 8 | $Y = 85.22 - 0.0667X + 26.1178e^{-0.0863X} + 66.694e^{-0.7988X}$ | -0.971 | 5.2 (5.5) |

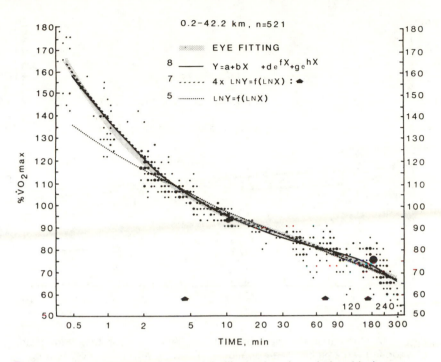

**Figure 2.** Various regression models illustrating the relationship between % VO₂ max (Y) and performance time (X). Regression coefficients are listed in Table 1. Abcissa is expressed on a logarithmic scale. Only logarithmic regression (no. 8) and the set of 4 log-log regressions (no. 7) are very close to the eye-fitting curve for the entire range of performance times (0.5 to 300 min). Equation numbers are the same as in Table 1. Size of dots increases with the number of observations having the same coordinates (*n* = 1-9).

dot v

The fact that both Equations 7 and 8 are comprised of multiple components may reflect the involvement of various metabolic sources in energy production as performance duration increases. Short performances (< 4.6 min) seem to be regulated by neuromuscular functions (speed and power) and anaerobic metabolism (ATP and PC reserves as well as the anaerobic glycolysis); medium length performances (4.6-70.4 min) appear to be governed by V̇O₂ max and glycogen reserves; lengthy performance (70.4-173.7 min) are seemingly linked to V̇O₂ max, endurance, and fat oxidation; and extra-long events (< 173.7 min) appear to be determined by endurance, fat oxidation, ionic balance, and thermoregulation (Costill, 1979; Keul, Doll, & Keppler, 1972; Péronnet, Thibault, Ledoux, & Brisson, 1983). In accordance with this principle, point dispersion in the %V̇O₂ max-performance time scattergram (Figure 2) was smaller for middle range performances and became gradually larger as performance times increased or decreased. Despite this variation in spread, average values should remain unbiased.

Nevertheless, data in this study were collected from average-caliber athletes. For example, male subjects averaged 530 ± 160 points, which is roughly

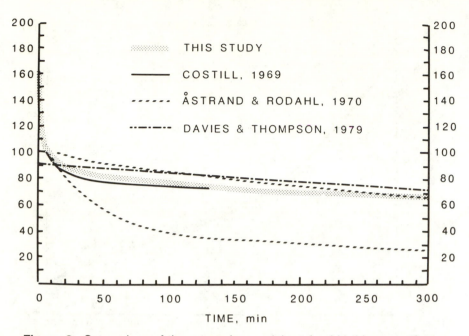

**Figure 3.** Comparison of the regression model retained in this study (Set of 4 log-log regressions, see equation 7, Table 1) with other curves published in the literature. % $\dot{V}O_2$ max (Y) as a function of performance time (X) is plotted on linear scales.

equivalent to running 800 m in 2:19, 3 km in 10:39, or 10 km in 39:04. The marathoners had lower performance scores, with 355 ± 190 points and a time of 3:57:22. Superior class runners may have greater endurance and consequently may be able to maintain higher % $\dot{V}O_2$ max especially in longer events. This information may explain why other curves reported in the literature are slightly more elevated (Figure 3). As a corollary, a runner who specializes in endurance training for a particular distance may be able to maintain a higher % $\dot{V}O_2$ max for this particular distance than the % $\dot{V}O_2$ max predicted by the average curve. The average curve could thus be used to determine a runner's relative endurance and to properly guide the athlete in developing his or her endurance at appropriate intensities.

As a final observation, the running performance time and average speed permit the calculation of % $\dot{V}O_2$ max (Equation 7) and $\dot{V}O_2$ requirement (Equation 1), and then $\dot{V}O_2$ max with good accuracy ($r > 0.85$ and $SEE < 6\%$ for races ranging from 0.6-42.2 km, Léger & Mercier, 1983.)

# References

Åstrand, P.-O., & Rodahl, K. (1970). *Textbook of work physiology*. New York: McGraw Hill.

Costill, D.L. (1979). *A scientific approach to distance running*. Los Altos, CA: Tafnews.

Costill, D.L., & Fox, E.L. (1969). Energetics of marathon running. *Medicine and Sciences in Sports, 1*, 81-86.

Davies, C.T.M., & Thompson, M.W. (1979). Aerobic performance of female marathon and male ultramarathon athletes. *European Journal of Applied Physiology, 41*, 233-245.

Keul, J., Doll, E., & Keppler, D. (1972). *Energy metabolism of human muscle*. Baltimore: University Park Press.

Léger, L., & Boucher, R. (1980). An indirect continuous running multistage field test: The Université de Montréal Track Test. *Canadian Journal of Applied Sports Sciences, 5*, 77-84.

Léger, L., & Mercier, D. (1983). Regressions between V̇O₂max and running performances on distance from 0.2 to 42.2 km. Unpublished manuscript.

Léger, L., & Mercier, D. (1984). Gross energy cost of horizontal treadmill and track running. *Sports Medicine, 1*, 270-277.

Péronnet, F., Thibault, G., Ledoux, M., & Brisson, G. (1983). *Le marathon: Équilibre énergétique, endurance et alimentation du coureur sur route*. Montréal: Décarie.

Purdy, J.G. (1974). Least squares model for the running curve. *Research Quarterly, 450*, 224-238.

# 13

# Ventilation Limitations to Performance Among Elite Male Distance Runners

*David E. Martin, Donald F. May, and Susan P. Pilbeam*
GEORGIA STATE UNIVERSITY
ATLANTA, GEORGIA, USA

Olympic-caliber endurance runners are characterized by maximum oxygen up-take ($\dot{V}O_2$max) values far in excess of those reported commonly for age- and sex-matched untrained controls (Pollock, 1977). The explanation for this relates to genetic endowment and successful long-term training. Two organ systems well-known for sizable adaptive changes to endurance exercise are the skeletal muscles (Holloszy, 1976) and the cardiovascular system (Clausen, 1977). The respiratory system interfaces with the environment and these organ systems to provide adequate gas exchange for the primarily aerobic metabolism that permits the extraordinary endurance performance potential demonstrated by elite runners.

The question of whether ventilation may be a limiting factor either for optimal performance during race-pace aerobic running or during maximum-intensity performance is of interest. The operating capabilities of the cardiovascular, pulmonary, and skeletal muscle systems are all developed with endurance training, and the system most limited in its abilities should first begin to limit performance. The training stress imposed by endurance runners, and the extent of adaptation will determine the limitation. If a measurable ventilatory limitation to such work exists, then specific training of the ventilatory system to enhance its performance capabilities could be beneficial.

Support for this work was provided by funds from the Urban Life Foundation of Georgia State University and by the United States Olympic Committee Council of Sports Medicine. Appreciation also goes from the authors to the athletes studied, whose great desire to learn more about themselves inspired a close-working interaction of mutual benefit.

121

We were interested in studying the ventilatory capabilities of endurance runners from three points of view. First, we wanted to characterize the various lung function parameters among elite runners in peak physical condition and thereby validate the work of Raven (1977) on a similarly elite group of runners.

Second, we wanted to compare the expired ventilation for elite runners during treadmill running at their anaerobic thresholds ($\dot{V}_E$-AT) and at their maximum performance ($\dot{V}O_2$max). This was not done in the study by Raven (1977). It would provide an approximation of maximum sustainable ventilation during competitive racing, since the work intensity at AT corresponds to the athletes' race paces in endurance events.

Third, we wanted to ascertain whether the ($\dot{V}_E$) of endurance runners could be a factor limiting their ability to deliver a maximum performance during treadmill running. Determination of the maximum voluntary ventilation (MVV) over a brief (12 s) period provides a clinical indication of short-term maximum ventilatory capacity of the breathing system. If breathing itself was an important limiting factor during the final moments of a treadmill run to $\dot{V}O_2$max, it was hypothesized that $\dot{V}_E$ at $\dot{V}O_2$max might approach MVV. This report describes the results of our examination of these problems.

## Methods

Ten elite male distance runners came to our laboratory periodically for comprehensive longitudinal physiological profiling to evaluate whether various regimes of training produced measurable changes in preselected laboratory indices of performance. Prior to participation in the evaluative procedures, all athletes read and signed a consent form based upon guidelines developed by the American College of Sports Medicine. The procedures relevant to this report included basic anthropometry (height, weight, percent body fat), pulmonary function assessment (spirometry, plethysmography, lung diffusing capacity), and determination of $\dot{V}O_2$max and AT using an incremental workload treadmill run.

Height and weight were determined with the athletes wearing running shorts and a T-shirt. Skinfold measurements were made from seven sites (triceps, thigh, pectoralis, midaxillary, suprailiac, abdominal, subscapular) as described by Behnke and Wilmore (1974). A Harpenden skinfold caliper was utilized for these determinations. The mean of three separate measurements at each skinfold site was recorded. The quadratic equation of Jackson and Pollock (1978) allowed prediction of body density (BD), since it has been validated for people of similar structure. From this density value, percent body fat was estimated from the relationship of Siri (1961), which assumes a fat-free body density of 1.10 gm/cc.

Spirometric measurements—forced vital capacity (FVC), forced expiratory volume after 1 s (FEV$_1$), expiratory reserve volume (ERV), inspiratory capacity (IC), maximum voluntary ventilation (MVV), forced midexpiratory flow (FEF$_{25-75}$), and peak expiratory flow rate (PEFR)—were obtained using a Collins Survey Computer (Model 06031). Plethysmographic measurements—residual volume (RV) and total lung capacity (TLC)—were obtained using a Collins Body Plethysmograph. Pulmonary diffusing capacity (D$_L$CO) was measured using a Collins Modular Lung Analyzer System (Model P-1280). For all of these measurements, the subjects were seated with good posture. All subjects were taught how to perform these various diagnostic tests prior to actual data collection to reduce error from unfamiliarity with equipment and protocol.

Treadmill tests were conducted in a ventilated room under relatively uniform conditions (temperature = 18-20° C, $P_B$ = 98-99 kPa; relative humidity 30-35%). All tests were done between 1045 and 1145 hr biological clock time for the athletes which sometimes varied with local time since some crossed time zones to get to Atlanta. All subjects developed experience in our laboratory concerning treadmill running at the work intensities used during the diagnostic test. This included running with our expired gas collection equipment in place and on-line. We (as well as the athletes) considered this prior learning essential to ensure a maximum effort treadmill run would occur in familiar circumstances.

Subjects were prepped for electrocardiographic monitoring using leads II and V5. Headgear for obtaining expired gases was affixed, and 5 min of resting metabolic and cardiac performance data were collected. Subjects were seated for these determinations, and were at least 4 hr postprandial and 18 hr post-previous-training.

Following this, the athletes warmed up prior to the actual test, which prepared them both physiologically and mentally for their competitive efforts. This consisted of general flexibility exercise and then a few kilometers of running outdoors or on the treadmill. This activity required approximately 25 min. Athletes then rested for approximately 5 min while the headgear was affixed; finally, the actual test was begun.

The test protocol consisted of 2-min incremental workload increases, beginning with 215 m/min and proceeding through 242 m/min to 268 m/min, all at 0% grade. The grade was then increased, with running velocity constant, to 2%, 6%, 8%, 10%, 11%, and 12%. McMiken and Daniels (1976) showed that, at treadmill velocities up to 260 m/min, $O_2$ consumption between over-ground and treadmill running is similar. Thus, we chose to increase grade rather than velocity beyond 268 m/min. Subjects were verbally encouraged during the run, and ran to voluntary exhaustion. Recovery was active, consisting first of walking and then running easily (215 m/min, 0% grade) for 5-7 min until their heart rates returned to 100-110 beats per minute (b/m) and respiratory exchange ratios (RER) fell below 0.90.

Cardiac activity was monitored continuously during the test using a multiple-lead cable system connected to a single-channel Hewlett-Packard electrocardiograph (1500A)-oscilloscope (7803B). Heart rate (HR) was recorded every 30 s, and 6-s EKG strips were obtained.

The athletes breathed freely through a low-resistance valve (Otis-McKerrow). Expired gases passed into a 10-l mixing chamber according to the method of Wilmore and Costill (1974). Accumulated $\dot{V}_E$ was obtained by an infrared rotating vane pneumotachygraph (Pneumoscan #S-301). Expired $CO_2$ ($F_ECO_2$) and $O_2$ ($F_EO_2$) were measured continuously by infrared (Beckman LB-2) and polarographic (Beckman OM-11) analyzers, respectively. These analyzers were calibrated against standardized gases prior to testing. Measurements were obtained every 30 s.

Calculations from these raw data allowed a determination of $\dot{V}_E$, $CO_2$ output ($\dot{V}CO_2$), $O_2$ uptake ($\dot{V}O_2$), and the ventilatory equivalents for each gas ($\dot{V}_E$ BTPS/$\dot{V}CO_2$ STPD and $\dot{V}_E$ BTPS/$\dot{V}O_2$ STPD). Ventilatory and gas exchange measurements alone were used to estimate AT and $\dot{V}O_2$max, without simultaneous monitoring of blood lactic acid. Numerous studies (Caiozzo et al., 1982; Ivy, Withers, Van Handel, Elger, & Costill, 1980; Reinhard, Muller, & Schmulling, 1979; Wasserman, Whipp, Koyal, & Beaver, 1973; Yoshida, Nagata, Maro, Takeuchi, & Sada, 1981) have shown that the AT occurs at essentially the same $O_2$ uptake whether measured via ventilatory gas exchange variables or blood lactic acid. The rising blood lactic acid levels bring about the ventilatory changes.

This procedure reduced the need for on-line sampling for lactic acid analysis and permitted noninvasive determination of the AT, using the definition of Wasserman and McIlroy (1964), as the increasing work intensity point at which the calculated ratio of $\dot{V}_E$/$\dot{V}O_2$ started increasing systematically at a faster rate than the ratio of $\dot{V}_E$/$\dot{V}CO_2$. This criterion was found by Caiozzo et al. (1982) as the most sensitive indicator of the gas exchange AT. It was also observed by graphing $\dot{V}_E$ versus $\dot{V}O_2$ and observing the breakpoint marking a departure from previous linear rise. At this point $CO_2$ elimination and $\dot{V}_E$ begin to rise out of proportion to the increasing $O_2$ consumption, such that the $\dot{V}_E$/$\dot{V}CO_2$ ratio is maintained while the $\dot{V}_E$/$\dot{V}O_2$ ratio increases. This excessive yield of $CO_2$ occurs through buffering of lactic acid by bicarbonates during muscular work. Lactic acid produced by working tissues accumulates in the blood faster than it can be metabolized. (Naimark, Wasserman, & McIlroy, 1964; Volkov, Shirkavets, & Boulkevich, 1975).

Criteria for achievement of $\dot{V}O_2$max were an RER $\geqslant 1.0$ and either a plateau in $\dot{V}O_2$ or a decrease despite a constant or increased workload. These plateau values were averaged to give the $\dot{V}O_2$max value. For some tests this plateau lasted as long as 2.5 min. $\dot{V}_E$ at $\dot{V}O_2$max was reported as the highest value observed during the plateau period. The extent to which $\dot{V}_E$-AT and $\dot{V}_E$ max approached MVV were expressed as percentages.

# Results

Table 1 summarizes the physical characteristics of the 10 elite athletes studied. Spirometric, plethysmographic, and diffusion capacity data are summarized in Table 2. Lung volumes, flow rates, and diffusing capacity ($D_L CO$) were recorded as the mean of three separate determinations done 5 min apart to minimize the effects of fatigue. FVC and TLC were also reported as a ratio to height, since lung volumes develop in proportion to the cube of body height (Bjure, 1971).

To compare this group of subjects with a height/age/sex-matched sedentary population, Table 3 summarizes the percentage that each pulmonary function variable the athletes approached a normative predicted value. The prediction equations of Morris, Koski, and Johnson (1971) were used for FVC, $FEV_1$, and $FEF_{25-75}$. Those of Cherniack and Raber (1972) were utilized for MMV and PEFR. For $D_L CO$, TLC, IC, ERV, and RV, the equations of Bates, Mack-

**Table 1.** Physical and athletic performance characteristics of 10 elite distance runners

| Subject | Age (yr) | Height (cm) | Sum of skinfolds* (mm) | Body fat (%) | Lean body mass (kg) | Fat mass (kg) | Event specialty | Best performance closest to testing |
|---|---|---|---|---|---|---|---|---|
| 1 | 26 | 178 | 38.9 | 5.68 | 57.9 | 3.49 | Steeplechase | 8:25.36 |
| 2 | 27 | 173 | 36.3 | 5.70 | 53.2 | 3.21 | Marathon | 2:10:19 |
| 3 | 22 | 185 | 45.9 | 6.69 | 70.8 | 5.07 | Steeplechase | 8:23.62 |
| 4 | 22 | 185 | 30.8 | 2.68 | 62.8 | 1.73 | Marathon | 2:12:01 |
| 5 | 23 | 170 | 32.8 | 4.42 | 54.5 | 2.52 | Marathon | 2:13:25 |
| 6 | 26 | 178 | 33.5 | 4.23 | 62.0 | 2.53 | Marathon | 2:14:09 |
| 7 | 27 | 185 | 43.8 | 7.08 | 68.3 | 5.21 | Mile | 3:50.84 |
| 8 | 26 | 178 | 39.0 | 5.83 | 62.3 | 3.85 | 10,000 meters | 27:29.16 |
| 9 | 26 | 180 | 32.2 | 4.75 | 58.9 | 2.94 | Marathon | 2:09:53 |
| 10 | 23 | 182 | 33.8 | 4.68 | 58.1 | 2.85 | 10,000 meters | 28:04.31 |
| M | 25 | 179 | 36.7 | 5.17 | 60.9 | 2.24 | | |
| ± SD | 1.94 | 4.86 | 4.84 | 5.30 | 1.05 | | | |

*Triceps, Thigh, Pectoralis, Midaxillary, Suprailiac, Abdominal, Subscapular.

**Table 2.** Selected pulmonary function parameters of 10 elite distance runners

| Subject | Spirometry | | | | | | | | Plethysmography | | | | |
|---|---|---|---|---|---|---|---|---|---|---|---|---|---|
| | IC (l) | ERV (l) | FVC (l) | $FEV_1$/FVC (%) | FVC/Ht (ml/cm) | MVV (l/s) | $FEF_{25-75}$ (l/s) | PEFR (l/s) | RV (l) | TLC (l) | TLC/Ht (ml/cm) | RV/TLC (%) | $D_LCO$ (ml/min/kPa) |
| 1 | 3.46 | 2.66 | 6.08 | 87 | 34.2 | 3.67 | 6.36 | 12.4 | 1.03 | 7.15 | 40.2 | 14 | 5.44 |
| 2 | 2.79 | 1.82 | 4.89 | 79 | 28.3 | 3.08 | 3.40 | 10.2 | 1.87 | 6.48 | 37.5 | 29 | 5.92 |
| 3 | 4.27 | 2.10 | 6.88 | 91 | 37.2 | 4.23 | 8.93 | 15.1 | 1.33 | 7.70 | 41.6 | 17 | 6.48 |
| 4 | 4.15 | 1.68 | 6.06 | 78 | 33.7 | 1.97 | 4.20 | 8.2 | 2.36 | 8.19 | 45.5 | 29 | 5.13 |
| 5 | 3.33 | 1.78 | 5.35 | 87 | 31.5 | 3.05 | 5.40 | 11.5 | 1.49 | 6.60 | 39.8 | 23 | 5.61 |
| 6 | 3.46 | 1.68 | 5.20 | 80 | 29.2 | 3.15 | 3.82 | 10.6 | 1.73 | 6.87 | 38.6 | 25 | 5.05 |
| 7 | 3.45 | 2.49 | 5.90 | 78 | 31.9 | 3.40 | 4.22 | 12.2 | 1.43 | 6.37 | 34.4 | 22 | 4.91 |
| 8 | 4.40 | 1.61 | 6.16 | 90 | 34.6 | 3.80 | 8.10 | 15.5 | 1.41 | 7.42 | 41.7 | 19 | 4.72 |
| 9 | 3.78 | 1.82 | 5.92 | 76 | 32.9 | 2.47 | 3.68 | 11.1 | 1.47 | 7.39 | 41.1 | 20 | 5.03 |
| 10 | 4.04 | 2.19 | 6.35 | 69 | 34.8 | 2.92 | 3.69 | 9.4 | 2.28 | 8.51 | 46.8 | 27 | 6.47 |
| M | 3.71 | 1.98 | 5.88 | 82 | 32.8 | 3.17 | 5.18 | 11.62 | 1.64 | 7.27 | 40.7 | 23 | 5.48 |
| ± SD | 0.48 | 0.34 | 0.56 | 6.7 | 2.55 | 0.62 | 1.88 | 2.19 | 0.40 | 0.68 | 3.43 | 4.8 | 0.60 |

*Note.* IC = inspiratory capacity, ERV = expiratory reserve volume, FVC = forced vital capacity, $FEV_1$ = one-second forced expiratory volume, MVV = maximum voluntary ventilation, $FEF_{25-75}$ = forced midexpiratory flow, PEFR = peak expiratory flow rate, RV = residual volume, TLC = total lung capacity, $D_LCO$ = diffusing capacity.

**Table 3.** Percentage deviation of elite distance runners from predicted normal age/size-matched values for selected pulmonary function parameters

| Subject | Spirometry | | | | | | Plethysmography | | |
|---|---|---|---|---|---|---|---|---|---|
| | IC | ERV | FVC | FEF$_{25-75}$ | PEFR | MVV | RV | TLC | D$_L$CO |
| 1 | 103 | 126 | 111 | 143 | 124 | 144 | 58 | 98 | 125 |
| 2 | 88 | 92 | 95 | 76 | 108 | 127 | 110 | 95 | 140 |
| 3 | 117 | 89 | 114 | 180 | 148 | 154 | 68 | 97 | 142 |
| 4 | 119 | 75 | 106 | 86 | 83 | 74 | 129 | 109 | 116 |
| 5 | 107 | 90 | 105 | 117 | 123 | 125 | 95 | 99 | 130 |
| 6 | 103 | 79 | 95 | 82 | 109 | 123 | 95 | 94 | 117 |
| 7 | 96 | 109 | 100 | 89 | 121 | 126 | 70 | 80 | 112 |
| 8 | 131 | 76 | 113 | 175 | 160 | 149 | 77 | 102 | 109 |
| 9 | 110 | 84 | 105 | 79 | 113 | 95 | 77 | 98 | 115 |
| 10 | 114 | 96 | 109 | 76 | 94 | 109 | 119 | 110 | 143 |
| M | 109 | 92 | 105 | 110 | 118 | 123 | 90 | 98 | 125 |
| ± SD | 11.7 | 15.0 | 6.5 | 39.2 | 21.8 | 23.5 | 22.5 | 7.9 | 12.4 |
| P* | ns | ns | ns | ns | 0.05 | 0.05 | ns | ns | 0.001 |

*Note.* See Table 2 for pulmonary function parameter abbreviation key.

*paired *t* test for significance of difference between means of actual (athlete) and predicted (sedentary) values.

lem, and Christie (1971) were used. A paired $t$ test assessed the significance of differences observed between the means for the athletes and predicted normal values. MVV and PEFR were significantly elevated among the elite athlete group ($p < .05$), and $D_LCO$ was also significantly higher ($p < .001$). All other pulmonary function means were within normal limits. Raven's (1977) study did not evaluate $D_LCO$, PEFR, and $FEF_{25-75}$. However, the athlete $FEF_{25-75}$ values appeared to fit into the two categories, with six lower than predicted (only 76-89%) and four higher (117-180%). Otherwise, among the variables studied by Raven's group and ours, there was no signficant difference between the elite athletes and predicted values for sedentary people.

A total of 33 treadmill tests were performed. Eight of the 10 athletes were tested more than once, following specifically different phases of training.

Thus, all tests were considered together instead of individual athlete mean values. $\dot{V}O_2$-AT averaged $70.0 \pm 7.1$ SD ml/min/kg, which was 88.2% of $\dot{V}O_2$-max. In 32 of 33 tests the $\dot{V}_E$-AT was at least 20% lower than the MVV. The mean $\dot{V}_E$-AT was $65.5 \pm 10.1$ SD percent of MVV. In 12 of these 32 test the Hr-AT was within 5 b/m of HR-max. For the single test where $V_E$-AT actually surpassed MVV (105%), the HR-AT was submaximal. No opportunity existed to repeat that particular MVV test. Thus, it was concluded that, at AT, ventilation limitation may have been a limiting factor to performance during only one test. Perfusion limitation, as judged by HR-AT approximating HR-max, occurred in 12 of 33 test (35%). The mean HR-AT was 178 $\pm$ 9.5 SD b/m.

$\dot{V}O_2$-max averaged $79.3 \pm 5.4$ SD ml/min/kg for all tests. At $VO_2$-max in ten test, all from three athletes, $V_E$ was $\geq 90\%$ of $M\dot{V}V$. In 22 tests from eight athletes $\dot{V}_E$ was $\geq 80\%$ of MVV. The mean $\dot{V}_E$ at $\dot{V}O_2$-max was 85.9 $\pm$ 11.5 SD percent of MVV. In all 33 tests HR-max was achieved before $\dot{V}O_2$-max. The mean HR-max was $189 \pm 5.4$ SD b/m. Thus, it was concluded that, at least among some athletes, maximum performance may be ventilation-limited, since their minute ventilation is closely approximating their voluntary ventilatory limits.

## Discussion

The response of breathing to steady-state exercise is generally considered as an efficient and adequate isocapnic hyperpnea achieved by optimizing frequency and tidal volume at a constant FRC. Flow-resistive work on the lung/chest is minimized, with optimal airflow achieved in terms of energy expended (Dempsey, Vidruk, & Mastenbrook, 1980). Typically, $\dot{V}_E$max is below MVV ($< 70\%$) in long-term or maximum short-term work (Dempsey, Hanson, Pegelow, Claremont, & Rankin, 1982). Thus the breathing response is well within pulmonary system limitations.

However, such studies have not emphasized highly trained elite runners with enormous performance capabilities. Our data indicate that in these people $\dot{V}_E$max may be considerably closer to MMV ($> 85\%$), and at this workload some of these athletes may be experiencing ventilation limitation. At AT, with

$\dot{V}_E$ averaging only 65.5% of MVV (76.8% of $\dot{V}_E$max), such limitation is unlikely. In view of the long near-maximal-intensity dash-to-the-finish kicks and sudden surges in pace to performance intensitites excess of AT during competitions, both of which often characterize today's top-level racing requirements athletes may need to perform their $\dot{V}O_2$max for a sizable time period. For those with $\dot{V}_E$ limitations, such efforts may not be sustainable very long.

Whether such pulmonary limitation is related more to diffusion (alveolar-to-capillary-to-arterial gas exchange) or to mechanical abilities of ventilation has not been elucidated. The significantly elevated $D_LCO$, MVV, and PEFR among the athletes studied here suggest that both mechanisms are enhanced. It is tempting to believe that their arduous training stimulates adaptive ventilatory performance changes in the diaphram, abdominal, and accessory muscles of breathing. No lung function data for these athletes are available prior to their beginning intense training; thus we do not know whether they were genetically endowed with such features, which in turn helped in their choice of distance running as a sport in which to excel. Whereas some had MVV and PEFR values lower than those observed in their respective normal comparison population, $D_LCO$ was consistently elevated.

It is well known that strength and endurance of the ventilatory muscles can be increased by specific muscle training (Bradley & Leith, 1978; Leith & Bradley, 1976), such as by daily repetition of an MVV test. It is also known that during tests where $\dot{V}_E$max is maintained for some minutes, it declines to a value not much above the exercise-measured $\dot{V}_E$ (Freedman, 1970) due to ventilatory muscle fatigue (Leith & Bradley, 1976; Roussos, Fixley, Gross, & Macklem, 1979). The subjects used for these studies were not highly trained athletes.

Inspiratory muscle training devices have also been used with considerable success among patients with chronic obstructive pulmonary disease (Sonne & Davis, 1982). Whether the increased respiratory muscle stimulation of intense endurnace training brings about comparable improved muscle performance in these groups needs further investigation.

If one rearranges the FEF25-75%, PEFR, and MVV data in Table 3, in order of highest-to-lowest values, one finds that those five athletes with the lowest FEF25-75% values are also the five athletes with the lowest PEFR values, with four of the five accounting for the lowest MVV values. Included in this group are the three athletes whose $\dot{V}_E$-max values were closest to their MVV. The variable of FEF25-75% is an excellent indicator of medium to small airway obstruction, and the ventilatory limitations at extreme workloads may be a clinical manifestation of such dysfunction. Bronchodilator spirometry was not performed as part of the routine pulmonary function workup to further investgate this relationship.

Dempsey et al. (1982) have suggested that pulmonary adaptations may not be relatively as great as the well-documented adaptations found in the cardiovascular system (elevated skeletal muscle blood flow, increased muscle capillary perfusion, shorter diffusion distances [Dempsey, Thomson, Forster, Cerny, Chosey, 1975]) and skeletal muscles (increases in mitochondrial density, myoglobin concentration, and Krebs cycle enzymes [Holloszy, 1976]). Their studies of elite endurance runners have identified a measurable arterial desaturation of $O_2$ from hemoglobin during intense work, suggesting that, during the time available for alveolar gas exchange, incomplete blood oxygenation occurs. We did not examine arterial blood $O_2$ status in our subjects.

The second observation concerns the relationship between $\dot{V}O_2$max and AT. Our data support the evidence of Pendergast, Cerretelli, and Rennie (1979) that trained subjects have high AT both absolute and when expressed as percent of $\dot{V}O_2$ max. Davis, Vodak, Wilmore, Nodak, and Kurtz (1976) as well as Rusko, Rahkila, and Karvinen (1980) go on to suggest that AT is correlated positively with $\dot{V}O_2$max. While this maybe partially true, with distance runners AT changes also (as does $\dot{V}O_2$max) with the particular type of training performed. Thus a 1500 m runner doing considerable anaerobic work in final preparation for a competitive season may raise his AT and either not change or possible decrease $\dot{V}O_2$ max in comparison to those values obtained during a pruely aerobic build up phase.

# References

Bates, D.V., Macklem, P.T., & Christie, R.V. (Eds.). (1971). *Respiratory function in disease* (2nd ed.), p. 93. Philadelphia: Saunders.

Behnke, A.R., & Wilmore, J.H. (1974). *Evaluation and regulation of body build and composition*. Englewood Cliffs, NJ: Prentice-Hall.

Bjure, J. (1971). Ergometry and physical training in pediatrics with special reference to pulmonary function. *Acta Paediatrica Scandinavica* (Supp. 217), 56-69.

Bradley, M.E., & Leith, D.E. (1978). Ventilatory muscle training and the oxygen cost of sustained hyperpnea. *Journal of Applied Physiology, 45*, 885-892.

Caiozzo, V.J., Davis, J.A., Ellis, J.F., Azus, J.L., Vandagriff, R., Prietto, C.A., & McMaster, W.C. (1982). A comparison of gas exchange indices used to detect the anaerobic threshold. *Journal of Applied Physiology, 53*, 1184-1189.

Cherniack, R.M., & Raber, M.B. (1972). Normal standards for ventilatory function using an automated wedge spirometer. *American Review of Respiratory Disease, 106*, 38-46.

Clausen, J.P. (1977). Effect of physical training on cardiovascular adjustments to exercise in man. *Physiological Reviews, 57*, 779-815.

Davis, J.A., Vodak, P., Wilmore, J.H., Vodak, J., & Kurtz, P. (1976). Anaerobic threshold and maximal aerobic power for three modes of exercise. *Journal of Applied Physiology, 41*, 554-560.

Dempsey, J., Hanson, P., Pegelow, D., Claremont, A., & Rankin, J. (1982). Limitations to exercise capacity and endurance: Pulmonary system. *Canadian Journal of Applied Sports Science, 7*(1), 4-13.

Dempsey, J.A., Thomson, J.M., Forster, H.V., Cerny, F.C., & Chosy, L.W. (1975). $HbO_2$ dissociation in man during prolonged work in chronic hypoxia. *Journal of Applied Physiology, 38*, 1022-1029.

Dempsey, J.A., Vidruk, E.M., & Mastenbrook, S.M. (1980). Pulmonary control systems in exercise. *Federation Proceedings, 39*, 1498-1505.

Dwyer, J., & Bybee, R. (1981). Cardiac indices of anaerobic threshold. *Medicine and Science in Sports and Exercise, 13*, 70.

Freedman, S. (1970). Sustained maximum voluntary ventilation. *Respiration Physiology, 8*, 230-244.

Holloszy, J.O. (1976). Adaptations of muscular tissue to training. *Progress in Cardiovascular Disease, 18*, 445-458.

Ivy, J.L., Withers, R.T., Van Handel, P.J., Elger, D.H., & Costill, D.L. (1980). Muscle respiratory capacity and fiber type as determinants of the lactate threshold. *Journal of Applied Physiology, 48*, 523-527.

Jackson, A.S., & Pollock, M.L. (1978). Generalized equations for predicting body density of men. *British Journal of Nutrition, 40*, 497-504.

Katch, V., Weltman, A., Sady, S., & Freedson, P. (1978). Validity of the relative percent concept for equating training intensity. *European Journal of Applied Physiology, 39*, 219-227.

Leith, D.E., & Bradley, M. (1976). Ventilatory muscle strength and endurance training. *Journal of Applied Physiology, 41*, 508-516.

McMiken, D.F., & Daniels, J.T. (1976). Aerobic requirements and maximal aerobic power in treadmill and track running. *Medicine and Science in Sports, 8*, 14-17.

Morris, J.F., Koski, A., & Johnson, L.C. (1971). Spirometric standards for healthy non-smoking adults. *American Review of Respiratory Disease, 103*, 57-67.

Naimark, A., Wasserman, K., & McIlroy, M. (1964). Continuous measurements of ventilatory exchange ratio during exercise. *Journal of Applied Physiology, 19*, 644-652.

Patton, R.W., Heffner, K., Baun, W., Ayres, J., Gettman, H., & Raven, P. (1979) Heart rate as a predictor of anaerobic threshold in runners and non-runners. *Medicine and Science in Sports, 12*, 94.

Pendergast, D., Cerretelli, P., & Rennie, D.W. (1979). Aerobic and glycolytic metabolism in arm exercise. *Journal of Applied Physiology, 47*, 754-760.

Pollock, M.L. (1977). Submaximal and maximal working capacity of elite distance runners. Part I: Cardiorespiratory aspects. *Annals of the New York Academy of Sciences, 301*, 310-322.

Raven, P.B. (1977). Pulmonary function of elite distance runners. *Annals of the New York Academy of Sciences, 301*, 371-380.

Reinhard, V., Muller, P.H., & Schmulling, R.M. (1979). Determination of anaerobic threshold by ventilation equivalent in normal individuals. *Respiration, 38*, 36-42.

Roussos, C., Fixley, M., Gross, D., & Macklem, P.T. (1979). Fatigue of inspiratory muscles and their synergic behavior. *Journal of Applied Physiology, 46*, 894-904.

Rusko, H., Rahkila, P., & Karvinen, E. (1980). Anaerobic threshold, skeletal muscle enzymes and fiber composition in young female cross-country skiers. *Acta Physiologica Scandinavica, 108*, 263-268.

Siri, W.E. (1961). Body composition from fluid spaces and density. In J. Brozek & A. Hanschel (Eds.), *Techniques for measuring body composition* (pp. 223-224). Washington: National Academy of Sciences.

Sonne, L.J. & Davis, J.A. (1982). Increased exercise performance in patients with severe COPD following inspiratory resistine loading. *Chest, 81*, 436-439

Volkov, N., Shirkavets, R., & Boulkevich, V. (1975). Assessment of aerobic and anaerobic capacity of athletes in treadmill running. *European Journal of Applied Physiology, 34*, 121-130.

Wasserman, K., & McIlroy, M.B. (1964). Detecting the threshold of anaerobic metabolism in cardiac patients during exercise. *American Journal of Cardiology, 14*, 844-852.

Wasserman, K., Whipp, B.J., Koyal, S.N., & Beaver, W.L. (1973). Anaerobic threshold and respiratory gas exchange during exercise. *Journal of Applied Physiology, 35*, 236-243.

Wilmore, J.H., & Costill, D.L. (1974). Semiautomated approach to the assessment of oxygen uptake during exercise. *Journal of Applied Physiology, 36*, 618-620.

Yoshida, T., Nagata, A., Maro, M., Takeuchi, N., & Sada, Y. (1981). The validity of anaerobic threshold determination by a Douglas bag method compared with arterial blood lactate concentration. *European Journal of Applied Physiology, 46*, 423-430.

# 14

# Physiological Characteristics of Elite Ice Hockey Players Over Two Consecutive Years

*David L. Montgomery and Jacques A. Dallaire*
MCGILL UNIVERSITY
MONTREAL, QUEBEC, CANADA

In recent years physiological profiles have been developed describing the characteristics of elite athletes in various sports. These profiles probably reflect the demands of the sport along with current training status. Coaches use the information to assess in-season and off-season conditioning programs as well as to compare the athletes' present and future potentials. Once strengths and weaknesses are identified, individualized training programs may be prescribed.

Several studies have described physiological profiles of ice hockey players. Reports on minor (Cunningham, Telford, & Swart, 1976; Dulac, Larivière, & Boulay, 1978; MacNab, 1979), recreational (Montgomery, 1979, 1981), university (Houston & Green, 1976; Léger, Seliger, & Brassard, 1979), junior (Gauthier, Cotton, Reed, & Hansen, 1979; Green & Houston, 1975; Houston & Green, 1976), national (Rusko, Hara, & Karvonen, 1978; Seliger, et al., 1972; Smith, Quinney, Steadward, Wenger, & Sexsmith, 1982; Vainikka, Rahkila, & Rusko, 1982), and professional (Minkoff, 1982; Reed, Cotton, Hansen, & Gauthier, 1979; Romet, et al., 1978) teams reveal the status of hockey players during a single season of play. However, little information is available on elite ice-hockey players over more than one playing year. The purpose of this paper is to describe the physiological characteristics of a professional hockey team over two consecutive years.

## Methods

The subjects in this study were professional hockey players under contract with the Montreal Canadians of the National Hockey League. Twenty-seven players were assessed during preseason training camp for the 1981-82 season, and 30 players were assessed for the 1982-83 season. Twenty-one players were common to both testing periods. Six players from this group participated in the 1981 Canada Cup, which is a tournament of the best teams in the world.

The hockey test battery included measures of body composition, flexibility, muscle strength and endurance, anaerobic endurance, and aerobic endurance. The testing for the 1981-82 season took place at the McGill University human performance laboratory and the 1982-83 testing occurred at the Montreal Forum ice arena. Each year a player completed all tests on a single day.

The physical characteristics of the players are reported in Table 1. The mean age of the subjects was 25 years. Percent body fat was estimated from the sum of six skinfolds—triceps, subscapular, umbilical, suprailiac, juxta nipple, and front thigh (Yuhaz, 1974). For the 21 players that were common to both years, the sum of six skinfolds decreased from 90 to 65 mm of fat. Since body weight did not change significantly, the players had increased their lean body masses. Comments from team officials suggested that the attitude toward off-season conditoning was changing during this period. Instead of players coming to training camp to "get-in-shape," the players were participating in a variety of off-ice training programs so that they arrived at camp "in-shape." Since several players had a clause in their contracts pertaining to body composition, there was a monetary incentive to arrive at playing weight.

The flexibility battery included three tests—a) a sit-and-reach test for trunk flexion; b) a back arch test for trunk extension; and c) a shoulder extension test. The test protocol has been previously described (Montgomery, 1981).

Dominant handgrip strength was determined using a Lafayette handgrip dynamometer with the score being the best of three trials. Upper body strength was assessed using the bench press. Maximal strength was the amount of weight that could be pressed once. The starting weight was selected at approximately 60% of the player's estimated maximum strength with weight added in 10 lb increments. About 3 min of recovery elapsed between lifts. Since four to six players were tested at one time, there was a feeling of competition among the group. When a lift was unsuccessful, the player was permitted two additional lifts. The bench press score is presented as an absolute score and relative to body weight.

Abdominal muscle endurance was assessed using a cadence sit-up test. The knees were flexed at 90° with the feet stabilized by the tester. Fingers were locked behind the neck. The sit-ups were performed at a rate of 25 per minute for a maximum of 4 min. Hence the maximum score was 100 sit-ups. Sit-ups performed to a cadence reduce the assistance from momentum that occurs in

**Table 1.** Physical characteristics of a professional hockey team ($M \pm SD$)

| Variable | 1981–82 ($n = 27$) | 1982–83 ($n = 30$) |
|---|---|---|
| Age (yr) | 25.0 ± 4.2 | 24.6 ± 3.7 |
| Weight (kg) | 85.9 ± 7.0 | 86.2 ± 8.0 |
| Sum of six skinfolds (mm) | 90.2 ± 19.8 | 62.4 ± 16.4 |
| Body fat (%) | 12.4 ± 1.9 | 9.7 ± 1.6 |

a speed sit-up test. When the cadence could not be maintained, the test was terminated.

Anaerobic power and capacity were measured during an "all-out" 30 s ride on a modified Monarch cycle ergometer. A resistance of 6 kg was selected for all players. This modification was made to the Wingate test so that feedback to the players could be provided. Data were presented to the players as revolutions completed and power output relative to body weight. Toe clips were added to the ergometer as well as dual microswitches which permitted pedal revolutions to be signaled each 0.5 revolutions to a recorder. Verbal encouragement was given throughout the trial. Pedaling rate was determined for each 5-s interval to calculate peak power and anaerobic capacity for 30 s. A fatigue index was computed as a percentage with the difference between the highest and lowest 5-s period compared to the highest output.

A treadmill was used for the aerobic endurance test in 1981-82. After a warm-up period to allow the player to become familiar with the treadmill, the grade was set at 10%. The initial velocity was 121 m/min (4.5 mph). Velocity was increased by 13.4 m/min (0.5 mph) every 2 min until volitional exhaustion. A Parkinson-Cowan gasometer was used to measure inspired ventilation. Expired gas samples were analyzed with Beckman oxygen and carbon dioxide analyzers in order to calculate $\dot{V}O_2$ max. Heart rate was continuously monitored using a Cardionics Cardiotachometer.

Since the testing for the 1982-83 season occurred at the ice arena, $\dot{V}O_2$ max was predicted using a cycle ergometer. Pedaling frequency was controlled at 60 rpm. The protocol used 120 watts as the initial power output. The resistance was increased by 30 watts every 2 min until volitional exhaustion. Heart rate was recorded at the end of each workload. $\dot{V}O_2$ max was predicted by the best-fitting line through the data points of heart rate and workload.

The data are presented as means and standard deviations. A paired $t$ test analyzed the differences between the two seasons for the 21 players common to both years.

## Results

The flexibility, muscle strength, and muscle endurance data are reported in Table 2. The flexibility scores were similar. A significant ($p < .05$) increase

**Table 2.** Flexibility, muscle strength, and muscle endurance characteristics of a professional hockey team ($M \pm SD$)

| Test | 1981–82 ($n = 27$) | | | 1982–83 ($n = 30$) | | |
|---|---|---|---|---|---|---|
| Sit-and-reach (cm) | 14.5 | ± | 5.5 | 16.5 | ± | 4.2 |
| Trunk extension (cm) | 44.5 | ± | 8.0 | 39.2 | ± | 7.7 |
| Shoulder extension (cm) | 39.2 | ± | 10.0 | 41.1 | ± | 10.1 |
| Hand grip (kg) | 66.6 | ± | 5.8 | 67.6 | ± | 7.8 |
| Bench press (kg) | 86.3 | ± | 17.1 | 98.1 | ± | 18.3 |
| Bench press/body weight | 1.00 | ± | 0.18 | 1.13 | ± | 0.18 |
| Cadence sit-ups (no.) | 54.2 | ± | 26.9 | 70.8 | ± | 22.5 |

existed in bench press strength and in cadence sit-ups. When expressed relative to body weight, strength improved 13%. Table 3 presents the flexibility, muscle strength, and muscle endurance data according to position for the sample of 21 players common to both seasons. Flexibility between forwards and defensemen did not differ. The goalies had a significantly greater range of motion on the trunk flexion and shoulder extension tests. The defensemen were significantly stronger than the forwards for the bench press test. This difference could be attributed to the larger mass of the defensemen; when the data were expressed relative to body weight, the scores were similar.

The anaerobic power, anaerobic capacity, and aerobic data are presented for the total group in Table 4. Comparison by position for the anaerobic meas-

**Table 3.** Flexibility, muscle strength, and muscle endurance by position for a professional hockey team ($M \pm SD$)

| Position | Goalies ($n = 3$) | Defensemen ($n = 6$) | Forwards ($n = 12$) |
|---|---|---|---|
| Sit-and-reach (cm) | | | |
| 1981-82 | 17.3 ± 3.3 | 15.8 ± 4.3 | 15.3 ± 5.5 |
| 1982-83 | 18.3 ± 1.5 | 14.8 ± 3.3 | 17.3 ± 4.4 |
| Trunk extension (cm) | | | |
| 1981-82 | 44.3 ± 7.6 | 46.7 ± 6.0 | 43.9 ± 6.6 |
| 1982-83 | 34.3 ± 10.5 | 41.5 ± 7.2 | 40.3 ± 8.4 |
| Shoulder extension (cm) | | | |
| 1981-82 | 46.3 ± 8.1 | 39.8 ± 8.6 | 38.7 + 12.0 |
| 1982-83 | 49.3 ± 12.9 | 36.8 ± 4.1 | 42.5 ± 12.8 |
| Hand grip (kg) | | | |
| 1981-82 | 63.3 ± 7.0 | 68.7 ± 8.3 | 66.2 ± 5.0 |
| 1982-83 | 61.0 ± 7.3 | 70.0 ± 7.3 | 64.3 ± 5.4 |
| Bench press (kg) | | | |
| 1981-82 | — | 96.6 ± 20.9 | 86.0 ± 11.9 |
| 1982-83 | — | 105.5 ± 24.7 | 93.2 ± 14.6 |
| Bench press/body weight | | | |
| 1981-82 | — | 1.05 ± 0.23 | 1.02 ± 0.15 |
| 1982-83 | — | 1.13 ± 0.28 | 1.10 ± 0.16 |
| Cadence sit-ups (no.) | | | |
| 1981-82 | 58.7 ± 35.6 | 64.8 ± 33.2 | 51.9 ± 19.2 |
| 1982-83 | 78.3 ± 20.2 | 72.0 ± 25.2 | 61.4 ± 20.7 |

**Table 4.** Anaerobic and aerobic characteristics of a professional hockey team ($M \pm SD$)

| Variable | 1981–82 ($n = 27$) | 1982–83 ($n = 30$) |
|---|---|---|
| Peak power (kpm/5s) | 434.0 ± 38.5 | 454.2 ± 42.5 |
| Peak power/wt | 5.06 ± 0.37 | 5.30 ± 0.56 |
| Anaerobic capacity (kpm/30s) | 2182 ± 201 | 2274 ± 197 |
| Anaerobic capacity/wt | 25.4 ± 1.5 | 26.5 ± 2.4 |
| Fatigue index (%) | 32.9 ± 9.1 | 34.2 ± 7.1 |
| $\dot{V}O_2$ max (ml/kg·min) | 55.6 ± 4.3 | 51.9 ± 5.3 |

ures is reported in Table 5. The defensemen had greater anaerobic power and capacity than the forwards only when the data were expressed as an absolute score.

Many studies have reported $\dot{V}O_2$ max (ml/kg•min) of elite hockey players. Table 6 summarizes these studies into three groups according to test methodology. The table lists 14 studies that have tested elite hockey players on a treadmill, 13 studies that have used a cycle ergometer, and 3 studies that have measured $\dot{V}O_2$ max while skating.

## Discussion

Time-motion analysis, heart rate telemetry, lactate analysis, and on-ice oxygen consumption studies have stressed the involvement of both aerobic and anaerobic energy systems for hockey players. While ice hockey is an intermittent game wth varying intensity and duration of activity and recovery, meaningful information can be obtained from aerobic and anaerobic laboratory tests when the data are compared over time. When sufficient data are collected over several years of testing elite players, strengths and weaknesses of a team and an individual may be evident. Test results can be used to individualize off-ice training programs.

The anaerobic test results suggested that the professional players were lower than the 1980 Canadian Olympic team (Smith et al., 1982). Since test metho-

**Table 5.** Mean anaerobic characteristics by position of a hockey team ($M \pm SD$)

| Variable | 1981–82 | 1982–83 |
|---|---|---|
| Peak power | | |
|   Goalies ($n = 3$) | 390 ± 21 | 426 ± 21 |
|   Defensemen ($n = 6$) | 456 ± 25 | 468 ± 32 |
|   Forwards ($n = 12$) | 437 ± 45 | 446 ± 49 |
| Peak power/body weight | | |
|   Goalies | 5.04 ± 0.41 | 5.43 ± 0.57 |
|   Defensemen | 4.93 ± 0.21 | 5.00 ± 0.20 |
|   Forwards | 5.16 ± 0.44 | 5.27 ± 0.49 |
| Anaerobic capacity | | |
|   Goalies | 1872 ± 157 | 2016 ± 136 |
|   Defensemen | 2325 ± 121 | 2337 ± 140 |
|   Forwards | 2211 ± 173 | 2240 ± 183 |
| Anaerobic capacity/body weight | | |
|   Goalies | 24.1 ± 1.1 | 25.6 ± 0.4 |
|   Defensemen | 25.1 ± 1.0 | 25.0 ± 1.0 |
|   Forwards | 26.1 ± 1.7 | 26.5 ± 2.0 |
| Percent fatigue | | |
|   Goalies | 36.3 ± 19.2 | 37.7 ± 11.1 |
|   Defensemen | 30.3 ± 3.6 | 35.2 ± 5.7 |
|   Forwards | 31.6 ± 8.8 | 32.9 ± 9.7 |

**Table 6.** Aerobic characteristics of various elite hockey teams

| Group | n | Wt (kg) | $\dot{V}O_2$ max (ml/kg·min) | Reference |
|---|---|---|---|---|
| **Treadmill** | | | | |
| University | 8 | 70.5 | 58.1 | Montpetit et al., 1979 |
| University | 10 | 72.8 | 61.4 | Léger et al., 1979 |
| Swedish National | 24 | 75.6 | 57.0 | Forsberg et al., 1974 |
| Junior | 18 | 77.1 | 56.4 | Green & Houston, 1975 |
| Finnish National | — | 77.3 | 61.5 | Rusko et al., 1978 |
| University | 8 | 77.4 | 61.3 | Green et al., 1978 |
| University | 19 | 77.6 | 58.9 | Green et al., 1979 |
| Junior | 9 | 78.7 | 59.1 | Green et al., 1979 |
| Junior | 48 | 78.8 | 55.4 | Houston & Green, 1976 |
| University | 11 | 79.5 | 56.4 | Montgomery, 1982 |
| University | 9 | 80.9 | 56.3 | Hutchinson et al., 1979 |
| Professional | 12 | 83.4 | 55.3 | Green et al., 1979 |
| Montreal Canadians 1981-82 | 27 | 85.9 | 55.6 | Present study |
| Professional | — | 86.4 | 53.6 | Wilmore, 1979 |
| **Cycle ergometer** | | | | |
| Quebec Nordiques 1972-73 | 12 | 75.9 | 54.1 | Bouchard et al., 1974 |
| University | 15 | 76.9 | 54.5 | Thoden & Jetté, 1972 |
| Junior | 24 | 77.0 | 58.4 | Bouchard et al., 1974 |
| University | 9 | 77.1 | 53.2 | Hermiston, 1972[a] |
| University | 18 | 78.1 | 55.2 | Romet et al., 1978 |
| Canadian National | 34 | 78.5 | 53.4 | Coyne, 1968[a] |
| Czechoslovakian National | 13 | 79.1 | 54.6 | Seliger et al., 1972 |
| University | 5 | 79.5 | 54.3 | Daub et al., 1983 |
| Canadian National | 23 | 81.1 | 54.0 | Smith et al., 1982 |
| Finnish National | — | 81.1 | 52.0 | Vainikka et al., 1982 |
| Junior | 9 | 82.4 | 52.6 | Green et al., 1979 |
| Professional | 38 | 82.3 | 43.5 | Romet et al., 1978 |
| Montreal Canadians | 29 | 86.8 | 51.9 | Present study |
| **Skating** | | | | |
| University | 17 | 73.7 | 55.0 | Ferguson et al., 1969 |
| University | 8 | 78.7 | 52.8 | Green, 1978 |
| University | 5 | 79.5 | 52.1 | Daub et al., 1983 |

[a]Cited in Marcotte & Hermiston, 1975.

dology differed, the results should not be compared. Smith et al. (1982) set the flywheel resistance according to a regression equation previously established by Evans and Quinney (1981). In this study, the flywheel resistance was set at a mean value of 6.0 kp. There is some evidence (LaVoie, Dallaire, Brayne, & Barrett, 1984) that a higher resistance would have produced a greater power output for the professional players.

The defensemen had greater absolute anaerobic power and capacity than the forwards. This could be attributed to their greater lean body mass. When the anaerobic results were divided by body mass, no significant differences existed between the forwards and the defensemen. The results were similar for both the 1981-82 and the 1982-83 seasons.

Although the $\dot{V}O_2$ max was assessed at the beginning of training camp, it is doubtful that the $\dot{V}O_2$ max would have increased by the midpoint or end of the competitive season. Previously, Green and Houston (1975) did not find any significant improvement in aerobic power over a season of hockey when two junior A teams were assessed with cycle ergometry. Recently, Daub, et al. (1983) reported no change in skating $\dot{V}O_2$ max over a season of ice-hockey training. While the $\dot{V}O_2$ max values reported here are not impressive when compared to cross-country skiers, cyclists, or distance runners, ice hockey is a skill-oriented game that requires substantial demands from the anaerobic energy system.

When the $\dot{V}O_2$ max was expressed in ml/kg•min, the forwards had significantly higher scores than the defensemen and goalies. Since the treadmill usually results in a higher $\dot{V}O_2$ max than the cycle ergometer, the data cannot be compared over the two seasons.

Although the players had been playing hockey at an elite level for an average of 8 years, the team $\dot{V}O_2$ max was only 55.6 ml/kg•min on the treadmill and 51.9 ml/kg•min on the bike. While these values are similar to other studies of elite players (Coyne, 1968, and Hermiston, 1972, cited in Marcotte & Hermiston, 1975; Thoden & Jetté, 1972), they are inferior to a few studies (Léger et al., 1979; Rusko et al., 1978; Smith et al., 1982; Wilson & Hedberg, 1975).

One explanation for the lower values may be the variation in the mean body weights of the players in these studies. The highest values reported were obtained by lighter players. In comparison, several studies that report lower values had players with a heavier mean weight (Table 6). In Table 6, 14 teams that have been evaluated on a treadmill are listed according to increasing body weight. The four studies that report a mean body weight in excess of 80 kg have $\dot{V}O_2$ max values ranging from 53.6 to 56.3 ml/kg•min. On the treadmill, there is a trend for $\dot{V}O_2$ max to decrease when body weight increases. The same trend is evident when the studies using the cycle ergometer are ranked according to body weight. Hence, a review of 30 groups tested in the laboratory or on-ice revealed that for hockey teams, the heavier the team, the lower the $\dot{V}O_2$ max will be.

Within a team, positional comparisons support this trend. Defensemen are usually taller and heavier than forwards, so it is not surprising that the defensemen had a lower $\dot{V}O_2$ max (ml/kg•min) than the forwards. Other invesigators (Green & Houston, 1975; Houston & Green, 1976; Smith et al., 1982) have reported similar findings.

In summary, professional hockey players spend about 9 months of the year actively involved in either daily on-ice practices or games, then spend 2 to 3 months preparing for the subsequent season. When encouraged to do more off-ice training, the players arrived at training camp carrying less body fat and more lean body mass. The greater muscle mass was evident in an increased maximum bench press and increased power output in the Wingate test. Due to the nature of ice hockey, it is unrealistic to expect the players to have an aerobic endurance comparable to marathon runners or an anaerobic endurance typical of sprinters. However, it appears that the energy delivery systems could be improved.

# References

Bouchard, C., Landry, F., Leblanc, C., & Mondor, J.C. (1974). Quelches-unes des caracteristiques physiques et physiologiques des joueurs de hockey et leurs relations avec la performance. *Mouvement*, **9**(1), 95–110.

Cunningham, D.A., Telford, P., & Swart, G.T. (1976). The cardiopulmonary capacities of young hockey players: age 10. *Medicine and Science in Sports*, **8**,(1), 23–25.

Daub, W.B., Green, H.J., Houston, M.E., Thompson, J.A., Fraser, I.G., & Ranney, D.A. (1983). Specificity of physiologic adaptations resulting from ice-hockey training. *Medicine and Science in Sports and Exercise*, **15**(4), 290–294.

Dulac, S., Larivière, G., & Boulay, M. (1978). Relations entre diverses mesures physiologiques et la performance à des tests de patinage. In the International Congress of Physical Activity Sciences, F. Landry & W.A.R. Orban (Eds.), *Ice hockey* (Vol. 10). Miami: Symposia Specialists.

Evans, J.A., & Quinney, H.A. (1981). Determination of resistance settings for anaerobic power testing. *Canadian Journal of Applied Sport Sciences*, **6**, 53–56.

Ferguson, R.J., Marcotte, G.G., & Montpetit, R.R. (1969). A maximal oxygen uptake test during ice skating. *Medicine and Science in Sports*, **1**(4), 207–211.

Forsberg, A., Hulten, B., Wilson, G., & Karlsson, J. (1974). Ishockey idrottsfysiologi ratport (Ice hockey: Sport physiology report no. 14) Stockholm: Trygg-hansa forlagsverksamheten.

Gauthier, R., Cotton, C., Reed, A., & Hansen, H. (1979). A comparison of upper body and leg strength between professional and major junior A ice hockey players. In J. Terauds & H.J. Gros (Eds.), *Science in skiing, skating & hockey*. Del Mar, CA: Academic Publishers.

Green, H.J. (1978). Glycogen depletion patterns during continuous and intermittent ice skating. *Medicine and Science in Sports*, **10**(3), 183–187.

Green, H.J., Daub, B.D., Painter, D.C., & Thomson, J.A. (1978). Glycogen depletion patterns during ice hockey performance. *Medicine and Science in Sports*, **10**(4), 289–293.

Green, H.J., & Houston, M.E. (1975). Effect of a season of ice hockey on energy capacities and associated functions. *Medicine and Science in Sports*, **7**(4), 299–303.

Green, H.J., Thomson, J.A., Daub, W.D., Houston, M.E., & Ranney, D.A. (1979). Fiber composition, fiber size and enzyme activities in vastus lateralis of elite athletes involved in high intensity exercise. *European Journal of Applied Physiology*, **41**(2), 109–117.

Houston, M.E., & Green, H.J. (1976). Physiological and anthropometric characteristics of elite Canadian ice hockey players. *Journal of Sports Medicine*, **16**, 123–128.

Hutchinson, W.W., Mass, G.M., & Murdoch, A.J. (1979). Effect of dry land training on aerobic capacity of college hockey players. *Journal of Sports Medicine*, **19**, 271–276.

LaVoie, N., Dallaire, J., Brayne, S., & Barrett, D. (1984). Anaerobic testing using the Wingate and Evans-Quinney Protocols with and without toe stirrups. *Canadian Journal of Applied Sport Sciences*, **9**(1), 1–5.

Léger, L., Seliger, V., & Brassard, L. (1979). Comparisons among $\dot{V}O_2$max values for hockey players and runners. *Canadian Journal of Applied Sport Sciences*, **4**(1), 18–21.

MacNab, R.B.J. (1979). A longitudinal study of ice hockey in boys aged 8–12. *Canadian Journal of Applied Sport Sciences*, **4**(1), 11–17.

Marcotte, G., & Hermiston, R. (1975). Ice hockey. In A.W. Taylor & F. Landry (Eds.), *The scientific aspects of sport training*, Springfield, IL: Charles C. Thomas.

Minkoff, J. (1982). Evaluating parameters of a professional hockey team. *The American Journal of Sports Medicine*, **10**(5), 285-292.

Montgomery, D.L. (1979). Characteristics of "old-timer" hockey play. *Canadain Journal of Applied Sport Sciences*, **4**(1), 39-42.

Montgomery, D.L. (1981). Hockey programs as a fitness vehicle for adult men. *CAHPER Journal*, **48**(2), 9–12.

Montgomery, D.L. (1982). The effect of added weight on ice hockey performance. *The Physician and Sportsmedicine*, **10**(11), 91–99.

Montpetit, R.R., Binette, P., & Taylor, A.W. (1979). Glycogen depletion in a game-simulated hockey task. *Canadian Journal of Applied Sport Sciences*, **4**(1), 43–45.

Reed, A.T., Cotton, C., Hansen, H., & Gauthier, R. (1979). Upper body strength and handedness—Shooting characteristics of junior and professional hockey players. In J. Terauds & H.J. Gros (Eds.), *Science in skiing, skating & hockey* (pp. 127–131). Del Mar, CA: Academic.

Romet, T.T., Goode, R.C., Watt, T., Allen, C., Schonberg, T., & Duffin, J. (1978). Possible discriminating factors between amateur and professional hockey players in Canada. In the International Congress of Physical Activity Sciences, F. Landry & W.A.R. Orban (Eds.), *Ice Hockey* (Vol. 10). Miami: Symposia Specialists.

Rusko, H., Hara, M., & Karvonen, E. (1978). Aerobic performance capacity in athletes. *European Journal of Applied Physiology*, **38**, 151—159.

Seliger, V., Kostka, V., Grusova, D., Kovac, J., Machovcova, J., Pauer, M., Pribylova, A., & Urbankova, R. (1972). Energy expenditure and physical fitness of ice-hockey players. *Internationale Zeitschrift Fur Angewandte Physiologie Einschliesslich Arbeitsthysiologie*, **30**, 283–291.

Smith, D.J., Quinney, H.A., Steadward, R.D., Wenger, H.A., & Sexsmith, J.R. (1982). Physiological profiles of the Canadian Olympic hockey team (1980). *Canadian Journal of Applied Sport Sciences*, **7**(2), 142–146.

Thoden, J.S., & Jetté, M. (1972). Laboratory measurements applied to the development and modification of training programs. In A.W. Taylor (Ed.), *Training—Scientific basis and application*. Springfield, IL: Thomas.

Vainikka, M., Rahkila, P., & Rusko, H. (1982). Physical performance characteristics of the Finnish national ice hockey team. In P.V. Komi (Ed.), *Exercise and sport biology*. Champaign, IL: Human Kinetics.

Wilmore, J.H. (1979). The application of science to sport: Physiological profiles of male and female athletes. *Journal of Applied Sport Sciences*, **4**(2), 103–115.

Wilson, G., & Hedberg, A. (1975). *Physiology of ice hockey*. Ottawa: Health and Welfare Canada, Fitness and Amateur Sport Branch.

Yuhaz, M.S. (1974). *Physical fitness and sports appraisal laboratory manual*. London, Ontario: University of Western Ontario Press.

# 15

# Comparison of Male and Female Olympic Speedskating Candidates

*Michael L. Pollock*
TEXAS HEART INSTITUTE
HOUSTON, TEXAS, USA

*Albert E. Pels III*
UNIVERSITY OF RHODE ISLAND
KINGSTON, RHODE ISLAND, USA

*Carl Foster*
MOUNT SINAI MEDICAL CENTER
MILWAUKEE, WISCONSIN, USA

*Dianne Holum*
1984 OLYMPIC SKATING TEAM
CHICAGO, ILLINOIS, USA

Previous reports have documented the aerobic capacity and body composition of male Olympic speedskating candidates (Maksud, Wiley, Hamilton, & Lockhardt, 1970; Maksud et al., 1982; Pollock et al., 1982). Data of female speedskaters are sparce (Saltin & Åstrand, 1967). Research has documented differences in aerobic capacity and body composition between males and females (Åstrand, 1967; Behnke & Wilmore, 1974; Drinkwater, 1973; Hermansen & Andersen, 1965; Saltin & Åstrand, 1967). These data show that males have a significantly higher maximal oxygen uptake ($\dot{V}O_2$ max) and lower body fat and higher lean body weight than females. Reviews by Wilmore (1975) and Wells and Plowman (1983) showed that these differences between sexes were significantly smaller when training between sexes was more similar. Little or no data exist comparing physiological variables of male and female athletes when training together for Olympic competition.

The purpose of this study was to evaluate and compare the cardiorespiratory response to maximum exercise and body composition of male and female speedskaters who were actively training for the 1984 Olympic speedskating team (USA).

## Method

The subjects of this investigation were 16 male and 15 female speedskaters. All subjects were volunteers. They were informed of the potential risks and benefits of the various testing protocols and signed an informed consent. Informed consent was signed by the parents of athletes who were under 18 years of age.

Subjects reported to the laboratory in the morning, prior to any training, and in a fasting state. Venous blood samples were drawn to determine hemoglobin and hematocrit values using standard procedures.

Body composition assessment included the measurement of standing and sitting height to the nearest 0.1 cm and body weight to the nearest 50g on an Acme Scale (model 4050M). Anthropometric determinations included seven skinfold fat measures. Next, skinfold fat was measured at the chest, axilla, triceps, subscapula, abdomen, suprailium, and front thigh using a Lange caliper. The caliper had a constant pressure of 10g/mm², and measures were taken on the right side. Skinfold fat data were measured and recorded to the nearest 0.5 mm. The location of the skinfold sites and method were described by Pollock, Wilmore, and Fox (1984).

Forced vital capacity (VC) was determined with the subjects seated using a rolling seal spirometer (Ohio Medical) according to the procedures outlined by Kory, Callahan, and Boren (1961). Residual volume (RV) was determined by the nitrogen washout technique described by Wilmore (1964) with a nitrogen analyzer (model 720, Ohio Medical). Although RV and underwater weighing determinations were administered separately, the same postural position (sitting) was used for both.

Underwater weighing was conducted in a 4 × 5 × 5 ft stainless steel tank in which a chair seat was suspended from a Chatillion 15 kg scale. The underwater weighing procedure was repeated 7 to 10 times and until three similar readings to the nearest 20 g were obtained (Katch, 1968). The three values were averaged. The technique for determining body density (BD) followed the method outlined by Goldman and Buskirk (1961); BD was calculated from the formula of Brozek, Grande, Anderson, and Keys (1963). The percent fat was calculated according to the formula of Siri (1961). The reliabilities of the skinfold fat, VC, RV, and BD measures have been published elsewhere (Pollock et al., 1976).

Maximal oxygen uptake was determined on a cycle ergometer (Biodyne, Schwinn/Excelsior Co.). The test was performed to maximum fatigue and included a continuous, multistage protocol. The test began at 50 watts for 2 min and was increased by 50 watt increments every 2 min until exhaustion. Heart rate and perceived exertion (RPE, Borg, 1962) were recorded at the end of each minute. Minute ventilation was calculated from inspired volumes measured during each minute of exercise using a Parkinson-Cowan gas meter (CD-4). Expired gas samples from a mixing chamber were analyzed as described by Wilmore, Allen, and Allen (1976) using Beckman $O_2$ and $CO_2$ analyzers (OM-11, LB-2). The gas analyzers were calibrated before and after each test using reference gases analyzed with the Haldane method.

The 3 months prior to testing (September, 1983) included an intense period of training 6 days per week for approximately 30 hr per week. Training was usually twice daily and included three to five long (2 hr) runs or bicycle rides per week, three to five tempo (interval) runs or bicycle rides per week, two to three endurance weightlifting sessions per week, and several sessions of dry-land skating drills and/or roller skating. Males and females trained together using similar methods. Six of 16 male skaters and 9 of 15 female skaters eventually competed for the USA in the Olympic Games or world championships (1984).

The statistical analysis included the calculation of means ($M$) and standard deviations (SD) for the total group and subgroups of Olympians and non-Olympians). A two-way analysis of variance was used to compare differences between sexes and skating groups (Olympians vs non-Olympians). A $p$-value $\leq .05$ was accepted as significant.

# Results

The physical characteristics and body composition values for male and female Olympic speedskaters and average young men and women are shown in Table 1. Data for the "average" groups were included for comparison purposes only; no statistical analyses were done. Male and female skaters differed significantly in all physical characteristics and body composition variables except age and the ratio of ht/sitting/ht. In comparison to the average groups, the skaters were similar in age, height, and the males in body weight. The female skaters were heavier than their nonathletic counterparts. Both male and female skaters were less fat and had greater amounts of fat-free weight (FFW) than the average groups.

Maximal cardiorespiratory and performance measures for male and female skaters are shown in Table 2. Maximum oxygen uptake expressed in L/min and ml/kg•min⁻¹ were significantly lower for female skaters in comparison to male skaters, but were similar when expressed in terms of ml/kg FFW•min⁻¹ (Figure 1). Performance time on the cycle ergometer was significantly greater for the male skaters when compared to the female skaters, while heart rate, respiratory exchange rate (R), and RPE were similar between groups.

Hemoglobin and hematocrit values were $15.5 \pm 0.8$ g/dl and $45.4 \pm 2.4\%$ for males compared to $13.7 \pm 0.7$ g/dl and $40.4 \pm 2.1\%$ ($p \leq 0.01$) for females.

When the speedskaters were dichotomized into Olympians and non-Olympians, no significant differences existed between male and female skaters, except the male Olympians were older than the male non-Olympians (Figures 2 to 4).

**Table 1.** Physical characteristics and body composition measures of male and female Olympic speedskating candidates

| | Speedskaters | | | | Average | | | |
| | Males (n = 16) | | Females (n = 15) | | Males[a] (n = 95) | | Females[b] (n = 83) | |
| Variable | M | SD | M | SD | M | SD | M | SD |
|---|---|---|---|---|---|---|---|---|
| Age (yr) | 22.2 | 4.1 | 19.7 | 3.0 | 19.7 | 1.5 | 20.2 | 1.2 |
| Ht (cm) | 178* | 7.1 | 165 | 6.0 | 180 | 6.4 | 166 | 5.9 |
| Sit ht (cm) | 93.8* | 3.6 | 87.4 | 2.8 | — | — | — | — |
| Ht/sit ht | 1.9 | 0.5 | 1.9 | 0.4 | — | — | — | — |
| Wt (kg) | 73.3* | 7.1 | 61.2 | 6.9 | 74.6 | 11 | 57.5 | 7.4 |
| BD (g/ml) | 1.081* | .005 | 1.061 | 0.009 | 1.068 | 0.010 | 1.043 | 0.014 |
| Fat (%) | 7.4* | 2.5 | 16.5 | 4.1 | 13.4 | 6.0 | 24.8 | 6.4 |
| Fat wt (kg) | 5.4* | 1.5 | 10.2 | 3.5 | 10.0 | 5.4 | 14.5 | 5.9 |
| FFW (kg) | 67.9* | 7.5 | 50.9 | 4.6 | 64.6 | 8.7 | 43.0 | 4.9 |
| Sum 7 skinfolds (mm) | 56.2* | 10 | 84.1 | 18 | 107 | 45 | 128 | 48 |
| VC (l) | 6.3* | 0.8 | 4.9 | 0.5 | — | — | 3.6 | 0.5 |

*Note.* BD = body density; FFW = fat-free weight; VC = vital capacity.
[a]Data compiled from Pollock et al., 1976.
[b]Data compiled from Pollock, Laughridge, Coleman, Linnerud, & Jackson, 1975.
*$p \leq .01$ between skating groups.

**Table 2.** Cardiorespiratory and performance measures of male and female Olympic speedskating candidates

| Variable | Speedskaters | | | | Average | | | |
| --- | --- | --- | --- | --- | --- | --- | --- | --- |
| | Males (n = 16) | | Females (n = 15) | | Males[a] (n = 48) | | Females[b] (n = 27) | |
| | M | SD | M | SD | M | SD | M | SD |
| $\dot{V}O_2$ max (L/min)$^{-1}$ | 4.39** | 0.4 | 3.17 | 0.3 | 3.20 | 0.5 | 2.29 | 0.2 |
| $\dot{V}O_2$ max (ml/kg·min$^{-1}$) | 59.3** | 4.4 | 52.2 | 4.5 | 43.6 | 5.1 | 38.4 | 4.7 |
| $\dot{V}O_2$ max (ml/kgFFW·min$^{-1}$) | 64.9 | 4.2 | 62.5 | 4.4 | — | — | — | — |
| HR max (beats/min) | 189* | 6.4 | 185 | 6.0 | 199 | 8.9 | 191 | 7.7 |
| R max | 1.23 | 0.4 | 1.22 | 0.6 | — | — | — | — |
| RPE max | 18.4 | 1.3 | 18.2 | 1.4 | — | — | — | — |
| Total time (min) | 9.8** | 1.0 | 7.4 | 0.8 | — | — | — | — |

*Note.* R = respiratory exchange rate; RPE = perceived exertion.
[a]Data compiled from Moffatt, Stamford, & Neill, 1977.
[b]Data compiled from Kearney, Stull, Ewing, & Strein, 1976.
*$p \leq .05$ between skating groups.
**$p \leq .01$ between skating groups.

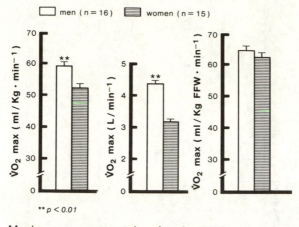

** p < 0.01

**Figure 1.** Maximum oxygen uptake of male and female speedskaters.

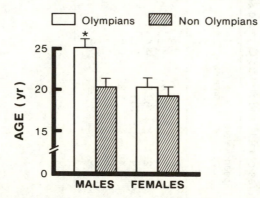

**Figure 2.** Comparison of age between Olympian and non-Olympian male and female speedskaters.

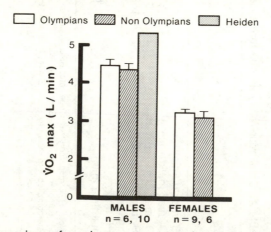

**Figure 3.** Comparison of maximum oxygen uptake, L/min⁻¹ among various speedskating groups.

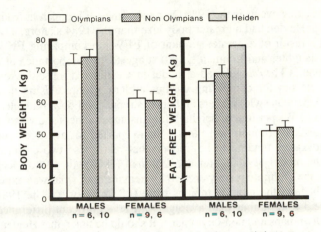

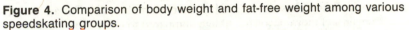

**Figure 4.** Comparison of body weight and fat-free weight among various speedskating groups.

## Discussion

In general, speedskaters training for Olympic competition have a high aerobic capacity and are low in body fat. Compared to other athletic groups, both male and female skaters would have lower $\dot{V}O_2$ max values than elite runners, cross-country skiers, and cyclists, but higher than nonendurance-type athletes (Åstrand & Rodahl, 1977; Pollock, 1977; Rusko, Havu, & Karvinen, 1978; Saltin & Åstrand, 1967). The male speedskaters' low body fat would be comparable to elite endurance athletes' (DeGaray, Levine, & Carter, 1974; Wells & Plowman, 1983; Wilmore, 1975), and the female skaters would not be as low as the 10-15% reported for elite endurance runners. The lower $\dot{V}O_2$ max of the speedskaters compared to other endurance athletes may partially be a result of the difference in the functional requirement needed for speedskating. Maksud et al. (1982, p. 220) summarized that speedskaters "tend to compete in a range of events from 500 m to 10,000 m, requiring 38 s to 15 min of effort. Thus, in contrast to the track athlete, the training specificity (of speedskaters) is reduced. The skater may be considered a hybrid between the pure sprinter and the distance runner" (p. ).

In comparison to the male skaters who were training for the 1980 Olympic Games, the present group was similar in body height and fat, but 3.5 kg heavier in FFW and 3.7 kg heavier in body weight. When these data were compared to the 1980 skaters who eventually made the Olympic team there was no differences between body weight and FFW (Pollock et al., 1982).

The $\dot{V}O_2$ max of the present skaters was 3.4 ml/kg•min$^{-1}$ lower than the combined group of male skaters reported by Maksud et al. (1982), but the skaters who eventually made the 1984 Olympic team had similar values as the 1980 Olympic team members. The difference in $\dot{V}O_2$ max of the 1984 skaters may partially be explained by the use of different modes of testing—the cycle ergometer in 1984 and the treadmill in 1980.

It is interesting to compare the values for $\dot{V}O_2$ max, L/min$^{-1}$, body weight, and FFW of the 1984 Olympic speedskaters with Eric Heiden, who won all five speedskating events in the 1980 Olympic games. It is apparent from Figures 3 and 4 that Heiden had a greater body size than the 1984 skaters. This difference was a result of a greater amount of FFW. In comparing FFW among athletes, Slaughter and Lohman (1980) suggested the importance of accounting for height. They developed a model that estimated musculoskeletal size and was relevant for comparing various athletic groups. Using this model, football (American style) players and other strength and power athletes showed the highest FFWs per unit of height, while distance runners showed the lowest. The elite distance runners were lower than reported for average young men, with speedskaters tending to be midway between these two extremes.

Using the model of Slaughter and Lohman (1980), the 1980 speedskaters who made the Olympic team were 1.8 kg heavier than what was expected for their height, and the non-Olympians were 0.8 kg heavier. The 1984 candidates were 3.8 kg higher than average with no significant difference shown between Olympians and non-Olympians. It should be noted that Heiden showed an excess of 8.3 kg. Thus the data of Heiden clearly shows a taller and physically stronger and more powerful athlete compared to other Olympians from both the 1980 and 1984 teams. The large $\dot{V}O_2$ max (L/min$^{-1}$) of Heiden shown in Figure 3 is a result of his greater FFW.

Successful speedskating includes a variety of factors including physiological characteristics, technical skills, and motivation. The differences found in physiological variables measured in this study between Olympians and non-Olympians were minimal or nonexistent. The data of Heiden suggest that certain body composition attributes, such as body height and FFW, may affect potential for highly successful speedskating performance. Also, as mentioned by Maksud et al. (1982), it may be more appropriate to express $\dot{V}O_2$ max in absolute terms since, in contrast to the runner, body weight/size are less related to air resistance than is frontal area (di Prampero, Cortili, Mognoni, & Saibene, 1976). Early studies showed differences in $\dot{V}O_2$ max between mature men and women of 20–30% even when $\dot{V}O_2$ max was expressed in terms of ml/kg•min$^{-1}$ of body weight (Åstrand, 1967; Drinkwater, 1973; Hermansen & Andersen, 1965; Saltin & Åstrand, 1967). Drinkwater (1973), Wilmore (1975), and Wells and Plowman (1983) have shown that these differences were much smaller between the sexes when expressed in term of ml/kg FFW•min$^{-1}$. This is in agreement with a meta-analysis of studies comparing $\dot{V}O_2$ max in men and women. In this analysis Sparling (1980) showed that the difference in $\dot{V}O_2$ max between sexes was only 12-15% when expressed in terms of FFW.

Drinkwater (1973) and Wilmore (1975) mentioned that much of the difference in $\dot{V}O_2$ max between men and women is a result of differences in exercise habits. Wilmore and Brown (1974) found that elite women distance runners were 15.9% lower in $\dot{V}O_2$ max than male elite runners (Costill & Winrow, 1970) when values were expressed in terms of body weight, but only 6.6% lower when expressed as FFW. Data from this study reflect the results of male and female speedskaters who were in intensive training to make the Olympic team. Both trained equally, side by side. The data from Table 1 and Figure 1 show an 11.9% difference between sexes when $\dot{V}O_2$ max was expressed in terms of body weight, but dropped to only 3.6% (nonsignificant) when calculated by FFW. Thus, results of the present study are in agreement with the notion that differences in physiological and performance values between males and females become less when groups train in a similar fashion. Even so, certain sex-specific differences related to relative hemoglobin content, and anthropometric and body composition will continue to affect differences in absolute performance.

In summary, this present study compared physical and physiological attributes of male and female speedskaters training for the 1984 Olympic team. Males were significantly greater in size, had less fat, and achieved a higher metabolic response during cycle ergometry than the females. These sex-related differences were less than those reported for nontrained individuals and for subjects that did not perform identical training programs. Additionally no difference existed between skaters that made the Olympic team and those that did not.

# References

Åstrand, I. (1967). Aerobic work capacity—Its relation to age, sex, and other factors. *Circulation Research*, **20**, (Suppl. I) 211–217.

Åstrand, P.O. Rodahl, K. (1977). *Textbook of work physiology*. New York: McGraw-Hill.

Behnke, A.R., & Wilmore, J.H. (1974). *Evaluation and regulation of body build and composition*. Englewood Cliffs, NJ: Prentice-Hall.

Borg, G. (1962). *Physical performance and perceived exertion*. Lund, Sweden: Gleerup.

Brozek, J., Grande, F., Anderson, J.T., & Keys, A. (1963). Densitometric analysis of body composition: Revision of some quantitative assumptions. *Annals of the New York Academy of Sciences*, **110**, 113–140.

Costill, D.L., & Winrow, E. (1970). Maximal oxygen intake among marathon runners. *Archives of Physical Medicine and Rehabilitation*, **51**, 317–320.

DeGaray, A.L., Levine, L., & Carter, J.E.L. (1974). Genetic and anthropological studies of Olympic athletes. New York: Academic Press.

di Prampero, P.E., Cortili, G., Mognoni, P., Saibene, F. (1976). Energy cost of speed skating and efficiency of work against air resistance. *Journal of Applied Physiology*, **40**, 584–591.

Drinkwater, B. (1973). Physiological responses of women to exercise. In Wilmore, J.H. (Ed.), *Exercise and sports sciences reviews* (Vol. 1). New York: Academic Press.

Goldman, R.N., & Buskirk, E.R. (1961). Body volume measurement by underwater weighing: Description of a method. In J. Brozek & A. Henschel A. (Eds.), *Techniques for measuring body composition* (pp. 223-244). Washington, DC: National Academy of Sciences National Research Council.

Hermansen, L., & Andersen, K.L. (1965). Aerobic work capacity in young Norwegian men and women. *Journal of Applied Physiology*, **20**, 425–431.

Katch, F.I. (1968). Apparent body density and variability during underwater weighing. *Research Quarterly*, **39**, 993–999.

Kearney, J.T., Stull, G.A., Ewing, J.L., & Strein, J.W. (1976). Cardiorespiratory responses of sedentary college women as a function of training intensity. *Journal of Applied Physiology*, **41**, 822–825.

Kory, R., Callahan, R., & Boren, H. (1961). The veterans administration-army cooperative study of pulmonary function. *American Journal of Medicine*, **30**, 243–258.

Maksud, M.G., Farrell, P., Foster, C., Pollock, M.L., Anholm, J., Hare, J., & Schmidt, D. (1982). Maximal $VO_2$, ventilation, and heart rate of Olympic speed skating candidates. *Journal of Sports Medicine and Physical Fitness*, **22**, 217–223.

Maksud, M.G., Wiley, R.L., Hamilton, L.H., & Lockhart, B. (1970). Maximal VO₂, ventilation and heart rate of Olympic speed skating candidates. *Journal of Applied Physiology*, **29**, 186-190.

Moffatt, R.J., Stamford, B.A., & Neill, R.D. (1977). Placement of tri-weekly training sessions: Importance regarding enhancement of aerobic capacity. *Research Quarterly*, **48**, 583-591.

Pollock, M.L. (1977). Submaximal and maximal working capacity of elite distance runners. Part I: Cardiorespiratory aspects. *Annals of the New York Academy of Sciences*, **301**, 310-322.

Pollock, M.L., Foster, C., Anholm, J., Hare, J., Farrell, P., Maksud, M.G., & Jackson, A. (1982). Body composition of Olympic speed skating candidates. *Research Quarterly for Exercise and Sport*, **53**, 150-155.

Pollock, M.L., Hickman, T., Kendrick, Z., Jackson, A., Linnerud, A.C., & Dawson, G. (1976). Prediction of body density in young and middle-aged men. *Journal of Applied Physiology*, **40**, 300-304.

Pollock, M.L., Laughridge, E., Coleman, E., Linnerud, A.C., & Jackson, A. (1975). Prediction of body density in young and middle-aged women. *Journal of Applied Physiology*, **38**, 745-749.

Pollock, M.L., Wilmore, J.H., & Fox, S.M. (1984). *Exercise in health and disease: Evaluation and prescription for prevention and rehabilitation*. Philadelphia: Saunders.

Rusko, H., Havu, M., & Karvinen, E. (1978). Aerobic performance capacity in athletes. *European Journal of Applied Physiology*, **38**, 151-159.

Saltin, B., & Åstrand, P.O. (1967). Maximal oxygen uptake in athletes. *Journal of Applied Physiology*, **23**, 353-358.

Siri, W.E. (1961). Body composition from fluid spaces and density. In J. Brozek & A. Henschel (Eds.), *Techniques for measuring body composition* (pp. 78-89). Washington, DC: National Academy of Sciences National Research Council.

Slaughter, M.H., & Lohman, T.G. (1980). An objective method for measurement of musculo-skeletal size to characterize body physique with application to the athletic population. *Medicine and Science in Sports and Exercise*, **12**, 170-174.

Sparling, P.B. (1980). A meta-analysis of studies comparing maximal oxygen uptake in men and women. *Research Quarterly for Exercise and Sport*, **52**, 542-552.

Wells, C.L., & Plowman, S.A. (1983). Sexual differences in athletic performance: Biological or behavioral? *Physician and Sports Medicine*, **11**, 52-63.

Wilmore, J.H. (1964). A simplified method for determination of residual lung volumes. *Journal of Applied Physiology*, **28**, 96-100.

Wilmore, J.H. (1975). Inferiority of the female athlete: Myth or reality. *Journal of Sports Medicine*, **3**, 1-6.

Wilmore, J.H., Allen, J.A. & Allen, A.C. (1976). An automated system for assessing metabolic and respiratory function during exercise, *Journal of Applied Physiology*, **40**, 619-624.

Wilmore, J.H., & Brown, C.H. (1974). Physiological profile of women distance runners. *Medicine and Science in Exercise*, **6**, 178-181.

# 16

# *The Study of Visuo-Manual Coordination in Rapid-Fire Pistol*

*Hubert Ripoll*
LABORATOIRE DE NEUROBIOLOGIE DES COMPORTEMENTS MOTEURS
PARIS, FRANCE

Although it seems obvious that vision plays an important role in the execution of pistol shooting, specialized technical publications consider it minimal. The only references to the rules of vision are purely subjective and the opinions are often contradictory. Thus, it is sometimes recommended that for speed shooting one should fix the gaze on the target and bring the weapon onto the direction of gaze (Raynaud & Prouzet, 1980). Others (Germont, 1973; Rouquier, 1978) recommend that one should fix the gaze on the target and visually assist the positioning of the gun for target shooting. The complexity of coordination between gaze and gun is again intensified in speed tests, particularly when the shooter must shoot several times at different targets. This particular speed test (i.e., rapid fire pistol event) is studied here. An investigation was carried out with experienced shooting instructors to determine the most practiced pedagogical principals. The instructors indicated that it is generally advisable to visually assist pistol transport from target to target by focusing the gaze on the "sight." The research objective is to identify the strategy of expert shooters so as to evaluate the relevance of this technical argument.

## Methods and Materials

A photo-oculographic gaze recorder, described by Papin, Hernandez, and Metges (1981), was used. The eye was illuminated by a point-shaped light source. The bright spot reflected by the cornea was video-recorded in the shape of a bright V. The V was coupled with the image delivered by a camera placed on the subject's observed visual field. The picture observed on the monitor showed the shifts and positions of the bright V as well as the various points of visual scanning within the observed visual field. A time basis superimposed on the image permitted an analysis of the time spent on the various visual fixations.

## Subjects

The behavior of five French international level shooters was studied. Each of these elite-level shooters had previously scored 585 points out of a maximum 600.

## Test Description

The shooter stood, arms alongside his body, at a 25 m distance from five targets. The shooter's task was to fire one shot at each of the five targets in either 8-, 6-, or 4-s runs.

Each round consisted of two runs taken at each speed. A two-round match had a maximum possible score of 600 points.

## Parameters Studied

The eye/hand coordination was studied in space and time during

- the vertical shift of the pistol from initial to final position on the first target and
- the horizontal shift of the gun from this first target toward the next ones.

The parameters retained related to the stabilization and transport of gaze and gun, the space/time organization of eye/hand coordination, and the rhythm of shots and precision.

## Data Compilation

A video analysis of the studied parameters was carried out to 20/100 s precision. The synchronization of different analyses was carried out by a microcomputer.

# Results

## Spatial Organization of the Attack

This maneuver consists of bringing the gun, held with a straight arm and pointed to the ground, up in line with the target so that gaze, gun, and target are aligned. Our recordings indicated that the initial gaze is always positioned on the target, either exactly on it (three shooters) or at the bottom of it (two shooters). In each case the eye/hand coordination involves a gap-reducing servo mechanism (Figure 1a). The target/gaze and gaze/gun gap gradually narrows until they coincide at target level. This gap-reducing coordination of different elements having to coincide cancels the necessity of pistol trajectory correction at the end of attack. It has previously been shown that this fault, evident in less expert shooters, can be caused by gaze focus on the gun (Figure 1b) (Ripoll, Papin, Guezennec, Verdy, & Philip, 1984). The principal effect of this technique involves the execution of visual microsaccades linked to gun displacements with a delayed final adjustment.

## Transition From Target to Target

In all shooters, gaze and gun shifting are independent. The mechanism consists of the execution of a visual saccade toward the target followed by a lifting of the weapon toward it (Figure 2a).

## Gaze Displacement

Gaze/target alignment provokes a single saccade which is space- and time-orientated, whatever the execution speed. Its average mean value is 20 100e s.

In a shooter less expert than the previous ones, although the functional independence between gaze and pistol continues, the eye/hand coordination involves a visual saccade of lesser amplitude followed by a last gaze alignment involving a slow, sliding movement. As the figure shows, the length of this adjustment is gradually reduced (a) during the same series, from 1st to

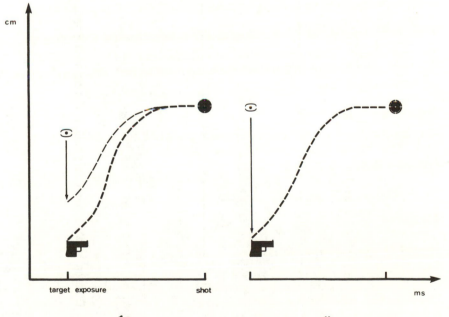

1a                                              1b

**Figure 1.** Eye/weapon coordination during attack.

5th target (Figure 2b) and (b) during different series with an increase in speed execution (8 s vs 6 s vs 4 s). Therefore, the more the speed increases, the more the behavior resembles that of expert shooters.

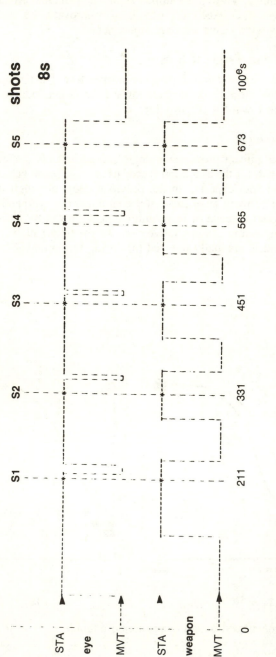

**Figure 2a.** Different eye/weapon coordinations during an 8 s series (mean durations, four shooters x two series each).

## Gun Displacement

Gun displacement was always continuous. Figure 2 shows that displacement always occurs after visual saccade execution. This asynchronous type of eye/hand commands can be the result of two consequences:

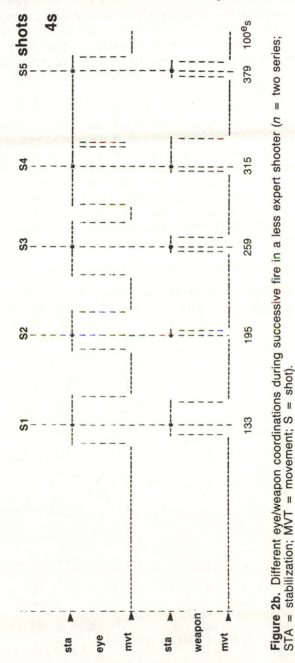

**Figure 2b.** Different eye/weapon coordinations during successive fire in a less expert shooter ($n$ = two series; STA = stabilization; MVT = movement; S = shot).

1. Mechanical: arm inertia which is superior to eye inertia involves a delay in execution.
2. Psychophysiological: the brachial command uses sensory messages consecutive to eye displacement. This provides the necessary direction and amplitude instructions to arm transport. Moreover, the fact that this displacement never presents correction shows that it results in a precise program controlled by visual calibration. The compared narrowing of eye/arm stabilization time at the moment of speed increase shows that eye/arm commands bring into play gradually differentiated command and control systems—positional for the gaze and dynamic for the arms.

## Precision

Considering the extreme rarity of precision errors, it is not possible to establish a correlation between precision and one of the studied factors, particularly the length of eye stabilization preceding the shot. However, the performance is systematically affected, attacking as well as shifting from target to target, when a correction saccade intervenes before the shot. In fact, the precision is a function of the initial visual calibration. The observed error of aim, which sets off a corrective saccade, is not enough to reorganize the arm displacement motor program. This point shows that the initial visual command and its influence on arm displacement are preprogrammed.

## Shot Frequency

The interval lengths decrease as speed increases; however, a perfect shot regularity exists no matter what the execution speed is (Figure 4). Different

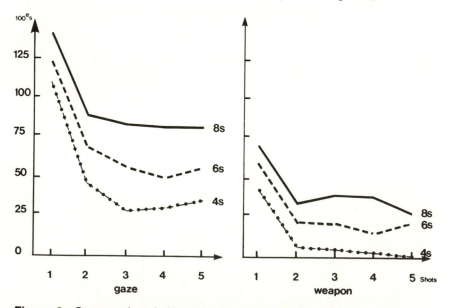

**Figure 3.** Compared evolution of gaze and weapon stabilization lengths before shooting (8 s, 6 s, 4 s [*M* durations]).

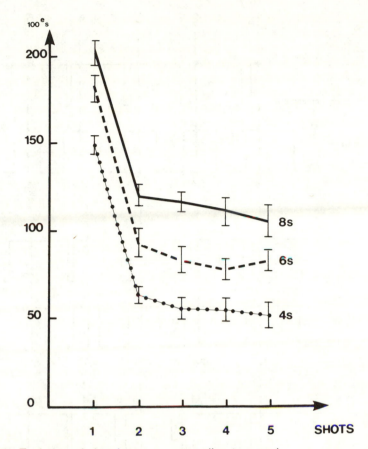

**Figure 4.** Evolution of shot frequency according to speed.

statistics between each interval length of the same series do not exist, except for the first interval whose length is superior due to mechanical restraints on arm displacement. This result justifies a preprogramming of shot rhythm.

### Relation Between Different Speeds

A relation exists between the temporal interval in two successive shots in a series (I) and the series duration (D) (i.e., temporal interval between 1st and 5th shots). This fraction I/D is stable whatever the shot speed. Therefore, there is a planning of the shot sequence. The interval duration is always a constant by-product of the series to which it belongs (Figure 5). The fraction is 24.97 % ($\sigma \pm 2.21$). The minimal variability of the fraction I/D corresponds to the maximum gap interval which is respectively about 12.3 ms, 11.4 ms, and 10.2 ms in 8 s, 6 s, and 4 s.

This demonstrates that before the target appears, the shooter has already estimated the adequate fraction I/D with a precision of 2.21 % of the sequence length. This capacity shows that highly elaborate planning mechanisms of

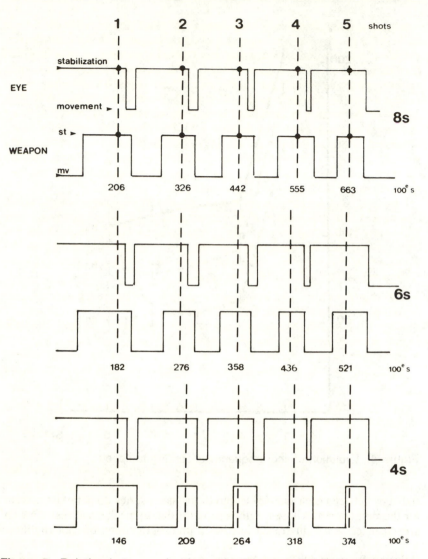

**Figure 5.** Relation between shot interval and sequence length according to speed (*M* durations, five shooters × two series at each speed—8 s, 6 s, 4 s).

space/time parameters exist. The invariant development would permit an effective cooperation between ocular and brachial coordination mechanisms.

## Discussion

The description of visual-manual command in expert shooters shows a functional independence between visual and manual commands. This gap-reducing mechanism is simultaneously used during the attack phase and is used when shifting from target to target. It consists of a gaze alignment on the aimed target, preparatory to the gun calibration on this reference position. A hypothesis on the functional role of this mechanism may be suggested. The gaze functioning on the target could provide the shooter with a "self-centered" reference system centered on the shooter's body (Paillard & Beaubaton, 1978). With this reference the target's position could be evaluated relative to the body, using the optical centering formed by the gaze axis. This reference-searching system, illustrated by current research in neurology (Paillard & Beaubaton, 1978), might provide, through a series of successive calibrations, eye in the head, head on the trunk, and arms relative to body proprioceptive messages which could subsequently ensure precise weapon positioning.

The remaining puzzling question concerns the reasons why shooters chose this pattern of behavior since no instructive guidance had been given and their shots were carried out instinctively. It can be assumed that this behavior is most compatible with speed and precision restraints inherent in the task. Its development relies on the controlling of a certain number of psychophysiological control procedures with the capacity to

- Calibrate the target with a peripheral vision which permits a saccade gaze transport adjusted in direction and distance,
- Align the arm with the eye, programming its transport on the basis of visual movement information treated in peripheral vision, and
- Position the arm on the basis of proprioceptive information which is complementary to visual information and intended to "feel the arm on eye position."

Sensory feedback produced by saccade eye displacement is effective inasmuch as it would respond to a preprogrammed mechanism of high-level precision.

## Pedagogical Considerations

These results show that eye/hand coordination, contrary to conventional opinions, does not respond to a synergy mechanism transporting gun and gaze, but to a differentiated command. Eye saccade and gaze alignment on the target will therefore play an important role in shot precision. The acquisition of the coordination and the pedagogical means of improving it may then be suggested. Eye/hand coordination, reducing the gap, can only be mastered if a thorough proprioceptive education of the body/arm positioning is considered. This concerns education of the proprioceptive sensation of the arm position compared to the eye/head/body axis. The arm is referred to the parameters provided by visual anchorage on the target owing to retina coordinate transformation allowing a reference system transfer centered on the environment in a self-centered system referred to the body. This education is only effective if it uses exercises capable of orientating the student's attention to identify relevant proprioceptive signals.

Recommended procedures include the following:

- Learning to execute large eye saccades, bringing the gaze focus onto distinct targets
- Aligning the index finger or the gun on a visually located target after visual saccade, and particularly varying the displacement speeds

- Executing the shot with partial or complete occultation of arm and weapon
- Executing the shot in total obscurity with only the target visible

# References

Germont, J.R. (1973). Pistolet: Comment faire un 10 [How to make a 10]. *Les cahiers du pistolier et du carabinier, 2*, 3-7.

Paillard, J., & Beaubaton, D. (1978). De la coordination visuomotrice à l'organisation de la saisie manuelle [From visuomotor coordination to organization of reaching]. In H. Hecaen & M. Jeannerod (Eds.), *Du contrôle moteur à l'organisation du geste* (pp. 225-260). Paris: Masson.

Papin, J.P., Hernandez, P., & Metges, C. (1981). L'exploration visuelle de radiographies du thorax [Visual scanning of thorax radiographs]. Rapport C.E.R.M.A. 81 12 LCBA.

Raynaud, C., & Prouzet, Y. (1980). Le champion Olympique 1980. Corneliu Ion répond aux questions de C. Raynaud [The 1980 Olympic champion Corneliu Ion answers questions from C. Raynaud]. *Les cahiers du pistolier et du carabinier, 53*, 35-42.

Ripoll, H., Papin, J.P., Guezennec, J.Y., Verdy, J.P., & Philip, M. (1984). Analysis of visual scanning patterns of pistol shooters—Duelling pistol. Manuscript submitted for publication.

Rouquier, A. (1978). Une méthode de tir aux armes de poing [A learning method of pistol shooting]. *Cahiers du pistolier et du carabinier*. Spécial tiré à part, 13-22.

# 17

# Self-Instructional Training: A Cognitive-Behavioral Approach to Psychological Preparation of Elite Gymnasts

*Claude Sarrazin and Madeleine Hallé*
UNIVERSITY OF MONTREAL
MONTREAL, QUEBEC, CANADA

The use of therapeutic cognitive-behavioral procedures in interventions with athletes (Ravizza & Rotella, 1982; Smith, 1980) results in certain problems encountered in sport psychology, predominantly in the areas of methodology and theoretical rationale. The most frequent methodological problems encountered stem from the research design and the definition of variables.

The first aspect to be considered in methodology relates to the choice of research design imposed by the nature of the questions raised by psychological consultants. Since interest has been centered principally on intrapersonal variations as well as on the process of change which promotes athletic excellence, the category of designs for single case studies seems the most appropriate.

The second aspect of the methodological questions relates to the definition of variables and their measurements. Certain factors relative to the independent variable are recognized as being capable of influencing the therapeutic effectiveness of psychological intervention (Bergin & Lambert, 1978). The quantity, duration, and frequency of appointments, the sex and experience of the psychologist, as well as the location and number of participants per session are among those of weighted importance for psychological intervention in sport. In fact, these very factors constitute the modalities for adaptation in each athletic milieu, thus determining an aspect essential to all therapy—the specificity of the independent variable (Bergin & Lambert, 1978).

This research was supported by funds from F.C.A.C., Gouvernement du Québec, grant # EQ 2035.

In conjunction with the effectiveness of therapy, the conceptual and functional definition of dependent variables is another methodological consideration of primary concern. In order to evaluate which levels have been most influenced by treatment, Bergin and Lambert (1978) have outlined the need to measure the changes in an individual according to the emotional, cognitive, and physiological components of human behavior. This holistic approach toward the individual allows for a better comprehension of the process of change and, in addition, promotes a more specific follow-up, which may in turn prevent relapses (Marlatt & Gordon, 1980).

With regard to the theoretical rationale used to explain the psychological dimension of athletic excellence, the intervention sector of sport psychology has up to now been based on the theoretical models and tools of clinical psychology; hence, it has allied itself closely with a curative-medical approach, which has as a goal the return of the individual to a state of normal function. Sport psychology seeks, therefore, as its ultimate objective the maximization of human potential, thereby implicating the facets of development and perfection of psychological capacities, as well as the prevention of problems likely to interfere with the attainment of this goal.

In order to better reply to the specific objectives of sport psychology and, at the same time, the requirements of the athletic milieu, the first goal of this study is to show that a psychological intervention, which is primarily preventative in nature, can improve the output of young athletes in training. The second aim consists of fine-tuning a methodological approach, thereby providing solutions for the methodological problems mentioned earlier.

# Method

## Subjects

This study was conducted with six female gymnasts, aged 11 to 15 years, during their training with Club Gymnix Inc., Montreal. They have had from 3 to 5 years of competitive experience at the national level.

## Psychological Intervention

Meichenbaum's (1977) Self-Instructional Training (SIT) was the psychological intervention employed for this study. The treatment had as its goal the modification of personal cognitions in order to develop an individual capacity for self-instruction that would subsequently provoke adapted behavioral responses to the various problem-causing situations encountered.

Meichenbaum ties together the theoretical bases of both cognitive and behavioral approaches and suggests as an explanatory model that the occurence of adapted behavior is the result of a sequence that corresponds to the three stages of treatment. These are respectively the awareness of behavior and maladapted cognitions, the understanding and acceptance of paradigmatic stimulus→cognitions→behavior, and the learning of adapted cognitions and behavioral patterns.

The experimentation was carried out over two semesters, each beginning with a baseline period, followed by eight sessions from September to December of 1982 and 20 sessions from January to May of 1983. Each appointment was held in an isolated corner of the palestra, with five gymnasts in the group, prior to or during training. The meetings with the female psychologist were scheduled 1 day in advance and varied from 5 to 20 min in duration.

## Levels of Measurement

Two levels of measurement were employed in order to verify the effectiveness of the SIT application. The first level measured the active ingredient of treatment, that is, the use of adapted verbalizations in anxiety-causing situations; additionally this includes five measurements representing modified responses according to the physiological, emotional, and cognitive components of anxiety. The measurements recorded pertained to behavioral patterns of relaxation, organization of material, ideo-motor activity, problem-solving, and a subjective evaluation of anxiety.

The second level measured the efficiency of training through the percentage of active work/event and the number of repetitions of the anxiety-causing movement.

## Research Design

The formula design for the single-case study, based on the withdrawal of treatment (Ladouceur & Bégin, 1980), was the experimental protocol employed. The basic ABAB format was maintained for the younger gymnasts, while the older girls followed a modified format, A $B_1$ $B_2$. In the latter case, the baseline of the second semester was omitted for ethical considerations. It seemed inappropriate to interrupt psychological preparation during a period of time corresponding to an important national competition (Canada Games).

## Methods of Analysis

The variables were analyzed according to the techniques of analysis for chronological series, as defined by Gottman and Glass (1978). This technique is more specifically known as Generalized Least Squares Estimates for cross-sectionally correlated and time-wise autoregressive model with heterocedasticity across equations (Berk, Hoffman, Maki, Rouma, & Wong, 1979).

# Results

### Subjects 1, 2, and 3

Subjects 1, 2, and 3 were older gymnasts demonstrating similar behavioral patterns; however, in the case of Subject 2, who was observed on the bars, this was delayed. Table 1 illustrates the averages and reveals a significant reduction ($p < .01$) in patterns of relaxation and problem-solving from the first phase of treatment, $B_1$, for Subjects 1 and 3, who were observed on the balance beam.

It is only in phase 2 of treatment, $B_2$, that Subject 2 showed this reduction ($p < .05$).

Subject 3 significantly reduced ($p < .01$) her patterns of material organization in $B_1$ and $B_2$, while Subject 2 did so only in $B_2$ ($p < .01$). Only subject 3 showed a decrease in ideo-motor activities ($p < .05$), this occurring exclusively in phase $B_1$. Although a statistical analysis could not be carried out on the evaluation of anxiety because of an insufficient number of points, we can still note an apparent decrease of anxiety in phases $B_1$ and $B_2$ for subjects 1 and 3, while that of Subject 2 increases in $B_1$ and diminished again in $B_2$.

On the second level of measurement, which reflects training efficiency, different results were found. Thus in $B_1$ Subject 2 reduced her percentage of work ($p < .05$), while for Subject 1 it showed an increase in $B_2$ ($p < .01$) because of work being done on compulsory exercises. None of the subjects showed a significant variation in the number of repetitions of the anxiety-causing movement.

**Table 1.** Averages of behavioral pattern as used in the analysis of data for the three older subjects and for each stage of the experimental protocol

| Behavioral patterns | Subject no. | A | Stage $B_1$ | $B_2$ |
|---|---|---|---|---|
| Relaxation | 1 | 3.24 | 1.25 | 1.28 |
| | 2 | 0.17 | 0.79 | 0.43 |
| | 3 | 1.60 | 0.33 | 0.23 |
| Ideo-motor activity | 1 | 7.62 | 3.63 | 3.49 |
| | 2 | 0.67 | 1.00 | 0.17 |
| | 3 | 5.60 | 2.72 | 0.88 |
| Equipment | 1 | 1.67 | 1.18 | 1.82 |
| | 2 | 3.83 | 4.29 | 2.93 |
| | 3 | 2.07 | 1.17 | 1.23 |
| Problem-solving | 1 | 3.90 | 2.25 | 2.44 |
| | 2 | 4.17 | 9.63 | 6.39 |
| | 3 | 4.00 | 2.17 | 0.84 |
| Anxiety-causing movements | 1 | 9.10 | 4.88 | 8.13 |
| | 2 | 7.00 | 4.08 | 3.02 |
| | 3 | 3.67 | 5.94 | 6.72 |
| Percentage of work | 1 | 24.33 | 24.06 | 32.56 |
| | 2 | 13.17 | 10.96 | 9.61 |
| | 3 | 26.07 | 25.28 | 30.86 |
| Anxiety[a] | 1 | 6.07 | 5.45 | 4.73 |
| | 2 | 1.80 | 3.31 | 0.11 |
| | 3 | 1.60 | 0.14 | 0.02 |

*Note.* The unit of measurement for the first five behavioral patterns is the average of exhibitions of such behavior per training. Anxiety is evaluated subjectively on a scale of 1-10.
[a]There is no statistical analysis of anxiety because of an insufficient number of points.

## Subjects 4, 5, and 6

The results obtained from the younger gymnasts are presented in Table 2. They are, for the most part, isolated and for this reason do not permit the establishment of behavior, such as illustrated by the older group.

Two significant results surfaced in the first level of measurement. First, in Subject 5 on the balance beam an increase ($p < .01$) in ideo-motor activities in $B_1$ and $B_2$ was noted. For her part, Subject 4, who was observed on the bars, showed a reduction in her patterns of relaxation in $B_1$ and $B_2$. The evaluation of anxiety varied for all three subjects. In the case of Subject 4 anxiety decreased in $B_1$ but increased again in $B_2$; in Subject 5 it showed a progressive reduction in $B_1$ and $B_2$; and in Subject 6 the level of anxiety grew in $B_1$ and diminished in $B_2$.

On the second level, measurements obtained were characterized by a significant reduction in work ($p < .01$) for Subject 4 in phase $B_1$, as well as a decrease in the number of repetitions of the anxiety-causing movement ($p < .05$) in $B_2$ in the case of Subject 6.

**Table 2.** Averages of behavioral patterns as used in the analysis of data for the three younger subjects and for each stage of the experimental protocol

| Behavioral patterns | Subject no. | A | B | A | B |
|---|---|---|---|---|---|
| Relaxation | 4 | 0.50 | 0 | 0.50 | 0 |
| | 5 | 0.29 | 0.07 | 0.25 | 0.07 |
| | 6 | 0.36 | 0 | 0 | 0.24 |
| Ideo-motor activity | 4 | 1.50 | 2.72 | 1.93 | 2.29 |
| | 5 | 4.29 | 13.44 | 12.25 | 10.93 |
| | 6 | 5.18 | 8.69 | 8.83 | 6.82 |
| Equipment | 4 | 4.50 | 1.36 | 1.07 | 2.04 |
| | 5 | 0.71 | 0.71 | 1.50 | 0.73 |
| | 6 | 0.91 | 1.23 | 0.67 | 1.29 |
| Problem-solving | 4 | 8.90 | 4.36 | 3.43 | 2.08 |
| | 5 | 3.86 | 5.86 | 1.56 | 1.67 |
| | 6 | 6.64 | 6.15 | 3.44 | 3.65 |
| Anxiety-causing movements | 4 | 1.40 | 2.09 | 4.00 | 3.08 |
| | 5 | 0.36 | 4.36 | 5.44 | 6.00 |
| | 6 | 5.64 | 5.85 | 9.61 | 9.12 |
| Percentage of work | 4 | 15.40 | 7.36 | 7.50 | 7.58 |
| | 5 | 22.36 | 19.00 | 22.50 | 20.67 |
| | 6 | 13.82 | 19.54 | 27.94 | 22.06 |
| Anxiety[a] | 4 | 2.25 | 2.00 | 1.38 | 1.87 |
| | 5 | 8.00 | 4.80 | 5.42 | 4.16 |
| | 6 | 3.12 | 3.30 | 3.60 | 1.76 |

Note. The unit of measurement for the first five behavioral patterns is the average of exhibitions of such behavior for training. Anxiety is evaluated subjectively on a scale of 1-10.
[a]There is no statistical analysis of anxiety because of an insufficient number of points.

## Discussion

According to Meichenbaum (1977), Self-Instructional Training leads the individual, confronted by a problem-causing situation, to reduce unadapted cognitions and to increase cognitions that are self-instructional. This change in cognitions promotes appropriate behavior patterns.

In this research project, the aspect of anxiety in gymnastics was manifested right from the baseline period, as the subjective evaluation of anxiety. During this period the exhibition of certain behavioral patterns, coping skills, was also observed. Hence, for Subjects 1 and 3, there was a reduction in subjective evaluation of anxiety from the first stage of treatment which dealt with the detection of unadapted cognitions. This reduction from the beginning to the end of treatment was also accompanied by a reduction in coping skills.

These results supported the belief that two of the older gymnasts had been able to develop, through age and/or experience, certain coping skills when confronted with certain anxiety-causing situations. The treatment, however, based on the detection of maladapted cognitions could lead to an emotional change, thereby reducing the gymnasts' recourse to modified behavioral patterns.

In addition to this, because these adapted behavioral patterns do not habitually make up part of that repertoire valued in the athletic milieu and are not systematically incorporated and reinforced by the coach in the training process, it is highly unlikely for such patterns to be exhibited in a situation which is no longer emotionally disturbing. The cognitions spontaneously exhibited by the gymnasts during training and sessions definitely support this assumption.

The isolated results, obtained in the first level of measurement with the younger gymnasts, underline the importance of long-term follow-up in order to ensure complete acquisition of the new mode of function. In addition, this reflection indicates the major influence of coaching style as well as the values current in the athletic environment.

The divergence in their evaluations of anxiety illustrates well the inconsistency in the attitudes of the young gymnasts toward problem-causing situations.

With regard to efficiency of training, the obtained results point to the overpowering influence of environmental demands. In fact, improved adaptation, as manifested in the first level of measurement by the older subjects, did not result in significant modifications to the number of repetitions of the anxiety-causing movement (Subjects 1, 2, and 3) or to the percentage of work (Subject 3). In the younger gymnasts no consistent connection can be made. Therefore, it seems that no direct link exists between the psychological intervention carried out in this study and the efficiency of training.

In conclusion, the results of this study illustrate that Meichenbaum's Self-Instructional Training, when incorporated directly into the regular training of female gymnasts, provokes certain behavioral patterns which can be interpreted as improved adaptative responses to anxiety-causing situations caused by fear when confronted with a specific movement or by the stress of competition. These results are more obvious in the 12-16 year age group than in the group of 11-year-olds.

In addition, this study shows that the theoretical and methodological considerations raised in sport psychology can be resolved through the use of a psychological procedure with a preventative perspective, through the systematic definition of variables, as well as through the use of a research protocol and an appropriate statistical analysis.

# References

Bergin, A.E., & Lambert, M.J. (1978). The evaluation of therapeutic outcome. In S.L. Garfield & A.E. Bergin (Eds.), *Handbook of psychotherapy and behavior change: An empirical analysis* (2nd ed.) (pp. 139-190). New York: Wiley.

Berk, R.A., Hoffman, D.M., Maki, J.E., Rouma, D., & Wong, H. (1979). Estimation procedures for pooled cross-sectional and time series data. *Evaluation Quarterly, 3*, 385-410.

Gottman, J.M., & Glass, G.V. (1978). Analysis of interrupted time-series experiments. In T.R. Kratochwill (Ed.), *Single subject research (pp. 197-237)*. New York: Academic Press.

Ladouceur, R., & Bégin, G. (1980). *Protocole de recherche en sciences appliquées et fondamentales* [Research protocol for applied and fundamental sciences]. Québec: Edisem.

Marlatt, G.A., & Gordon, J.R. (1980). Determinants of relapse: Implications for the maintenance of behavior changes. In P.O. Davidson & S.M. Davidson (Eds.), *Behavioral medicine: Changing health lifestyles*. New York: Brunner Mazel.

Meichenbaum, D. (1977) *Cognitive-behavior modification: An integrative approach.* New York: Plenum.

Ravizza, K., & Rotella, R. (1982). Cognitive somatic behavioral interventions in gymnastics. In L.D. Zaichowsky & N.T. Sime (Eds.), *Stress management for sport* (pp 25-36). Reston, VA: AAHPERD Publications.

Smith, R.E. (1980). A cognitive-affective approach to stress management training for athletes. In C. Nadeau (Ed.), *Psychology of behavior in sport*. Champaign, IL: Human Kinetics.

# 18

# A Comparison of the Grab Start and Track Start as Utilized by Competitive Swimmers

*In-Sik Shin and Jack L. Groppel*
UNIVERSITY OF ILLINOIS AT URBANA-CHAMPAIGN
URBANA, ILLINOIS, USA

Various swimming start techniques have been studied by coaches and researchers. The results of these studies were equivocal, stating that various starting techniques were the fastest. As a consequence of this, the starting technique thought to be fastest per individual was used most often in competitive swimming.

Until the early 1970s, the conventional arm swing style was believed to be the best starting technique. Several techniques were first suggested for the arm swing style, which included the use of a straight back swing, a circular back swing, and a forward swing only. In the early 1970s, the conventional arm swing start style lost its popularity to the grab start, which is performed by gripping the front edge of the starting block while in the set position. During that period, the track start (which is similar to the grab start except for the separation of the feet, front, and back) was also introduced as a possible superior starting technique. Although conflicting results existed concerning the speed of the different starting techniques, most researchers (Bower & Cavanagh, 1975; Disch, Hosler, & Bloom, 1979; Hanauer, 1972; Roffer & Nelson, 1972) agreed that the grab start was faster than the conventional start.

After Fitzgerald (1973) introduced two modified track starts (the bunch and track starts) as possible swimming start techniques, the track start was compared to the grab start with respect to several temporal variables by Ayalon, Van Gheluwe, and Kanitz (1975), Zatsiosky, Bulgakova, and Chaplinsky (1979), and LaRue (1983). Fitzgerald (1973), Ayalon et al., (1975), and LaRue

(1983) found that the time to water entry was less for the track start then the grab start based on the studies using visual comparison (Fitzgerald, 1973), a timing device system (Ayalon et al., 1975), and cinematographic technique (LaRue, 1983). LaRue also reported that the completion time to a certain specified distance were faster with the track start than the grab start for 18 collegiate women swimmers. Conversely, Zatsiosky et al., (1979) found that the track start was slower than the grab start for 45 highly skilled men to reach the 5.5 m mark.

The purpose of this study was to compare the kinematic aspects of the grab start and track start in competitive swimming with regard to selected temporal and kinematic components. Specifically, the dependent variables investigated were take-off time, water entry time, and the time to reach the 11 m mark. Displacement of the hip joint from starting block to head touch of the water surface was compared (Figure 1). Mean horizontal velocity was defined as the mean horizontal velocity of the hip joint during flight.

Projection and water entry angles were defined as the absolute acute angles between the line connecting the hip joints over two frames and an imaginary horizontal line at take-off and just before water entry (Figure 1). At the take-off and water entry positions the angles between horizontal and the line passing through the ankle and hip or hip and shoulder joints were calculated as ankle-hip angle at take-off and hip-shoulder angle at water entry, respectively. When the subject performed the track start, the front leg was used to measure the ankle-hip angle.

## Method

For the investigaton, 11 subjects (6 women and 5 men) were selected from the University of Illinois varsity swimming teams. All of the subjects had more

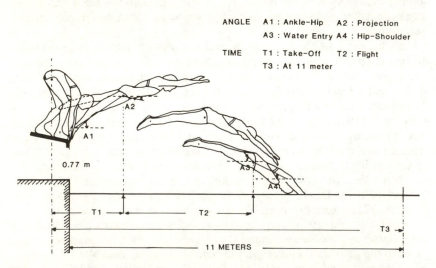

**Figure 1.** Graphical expression of the definitions of the variables.

than 4 weeks of training for both swimming start styles during their regular training hours. A 16 mm motor-driven Locam camera was operated at 80 frames per second to record each trial. The camera was set on a tripod 9 m away from the swimming direction.

The testing was conducted at the University of Illinois indoor swimming pool during December 1983. Testing conditions attempted to simulate race start as closely as possible. Each subject performed both starts followed by freestyle swimming at highest speed past the 11 m mark.

When the coach gave a preliminary verbal signal the camera was turned on. If the swimmer was in a steady state, the gun was fired. When the subject completely submerged in the water the camera was turned off. The time at the 11 m mark was measured with a stopwatch by an assistant coach. During each trial the subject, coach, and assistant coach evaluated the subject's performance with respect to the speed and appropriateness of the start and the smoothness and speed of the swimming. If one of the three gave a negative evaluation, the trial was repeated until all three judges were satisfied with the trial.

To reduce data from the film a Vanguard projector and a Numonics digitizer were used. A low-pass digital filter program was used to smooth the data. The value of the most appropriate start of each style was used as input to a dependent $t$ test at $p < .05$.

## Results and Discussion

The track start and grab start were compared with respect to the temporal variables which included take-off time, water entry time, and 11 m completion time. The results of the temporal variables are shown in Table 1. Among the tested temporal variables, the mean take-off times of .73 s for the track start and .77 s for the grab start were significantly different. The result of a faster take-off with the track start than the grab start was consistent with the results of the study by Ayalon et al., (1975). However, exact numeric data of the track start were not available from the former study. The mean times of water entry and 11 m completion were not significantly different between the track start and grab start. The effects of several factors might affect the time measurement at 11 m which would contribute to the large variability in completion time.

The mean horizontal displacements of the hip joint for the track start and grab start were 2.67 m and 2.73 m, respectively, which were significantly different at the .05 level. The difference of the mean horizontal velocities of the hip joint were also significant ($p < .05$) for the two starting styles.

Among the angles tested in this study, only the means of the ankle-hip angles at takeoff were significantly different. The ankle-hip angles at take-off were 29.4° and 33.3° for the grab and track starts, respectively.

When the subjects used the track start they tended to jump a little earlier with a higher leg angle (or ankle-hip angle), compared to when they used the grab start. This might produce the differences in the horizontal displacement and velocity of the hip joint.

**Table 1.** Means and standard deviations (in parentheses) of temporal and kinematic variables for the grab and track starts over 11 subjects

| Variables | Grab | | Track | | $t$-value |
|---|---|---|---|---|---|
| Temporal (s) | | | | | |
| Takeoff time | 0.77 | | 0.73 | | 4.2* |
| Water entry time | 1.21 | (0.049) | 1.18 | (0.059) | 1.601 |
| 11 m completion time | 4.91 | (0.44) | 4.86 | (0.39) | 1.03 |
| Displacement (m) | | | | | |
| Starting block to the hip joint | 2.73 | (0.20) | 2.67 | (0.23) | 3.196* |
| Velocity (m/s) | | | | | |
| Horizontal velocity of the hip joint | 4.22 | (0.30) | 4.05 | (0.24) | 2.457* |
| Angles (degree) | | | | | |
| Projection angle at takeoff of the hip joint | 7.3 | (4.86) | 8.5 | (6.75) | 0.559 |
| Water entry angle of the hip joint | 46.0 | (5.02) | 48.1 | (5.94) | 1.186 |
| Ankle-hip joint angle at takeoff | 29.4 | (4.01) | 33.3 | (4.15) | 3.178* |
| Hip-shoulder joint angle at water entry | 35.2 | (7.4) | 36.2 | (7.0) | 0.238 |

*$p < .05$.

## Conclusion

Within the limitations of this study, it is concluded that the track start provides a faster take-off time than the grab start. However, despite a slower take-off time with the grab start, the start itself covers a longer flight distance than the track start. Since the completion times at 11 m were not noticeably different, both swimming start styles could be used. Although the decision on which technique to use should be made on a individual basis, further study is necessary to find the effect of two different starting styles on the transient phase from gliding to swimming.

## References

Ayalon, A., Van Gheluwe, B., & Kanitz, M. (1975). A comparison of four styles of racing start in swimming. *International series on sport science* II (pp. 232-240). Baltimore: University Park Press.

Bower, J.E., & Cavanagh, P.R. (1975). A biomechanical comparison of the grab start and conventional starts in competitive swimming. *International series on sport science* II (pp. 225-232). Baltimore: University Park Press.

Disch, J.G., Hosler, W.W., & Bloom, J.A. (1979). Effects of weight, height, and reach on the performance of the conventional and grab starts in swimming. *International series on sport science* VIII (pp. 215-221). Champaign, IL: Human Kinetics.

Fitzgerald, J. (1973). The track start in swimming. *Swimming Technique*, **10**(3), 89-94.

Hanauer, E.S. (1972). Grab start faster than conventional start. *Swimming World.* **13**, 8-9, 54-55.

LaRue, R.J. (1983). A biomechanical comparison of the grab start and track start in competitive swimming. *AAHPERD Convention Abstracts,* Reston, VA: AAHPERD.

Roffer, B.J., & Nelson, R.C. (1972). The grab start is faster. *Swimming Technique,* **8**, 102-103.

Zatsiosky, V.M., Bulgakova, N. Zh., & Chaplinsky, N.M. (1979). Biomechanical analysis of starting techniques in swimming. *International series on sport science* VIII (pp.199-206). Champaign, IL: Human Kinetics.

# 19

# Physiological Profile of Elite Athletes to Maximal Effort

*Savvas P. Tokmakidis, Alexander Tsopanakis, Eleftherios Tsarouchas, and Vassilis Klissouras*
HELLENIC SPORTS RESEARCH INSTITUTE
ATHENS, GREECE

The purpose of this study is to present physiological characteristics of Greek elite athletes in different Olympic sports during maximal effort and provide norms for selected physiological variables, such as maximal aerobic power $\dot{V}O_2$ max), maximal anaerobic capacity (LA max), maximal muscular strength (F max), maximal explosive strength (h max), and maximal muscular frequency contraction (f max). Several studies have been conducted in this respect for ($\dot{V}O_2$ max), lactate, and other variables, such as those by Costill (1967, 1970) and his associates, Saltin (for ref. see Milvy, 1977), Gollnick and his associates (Gollnick & Hermansen, 1973), and others (Skinner & McLellan, 1980). In addition, other investigators have examined the muscular strength of athletes (Bührle & Schmidtbleicher, 1981); the athletic profile of professional football players (Wilmore, Parr, Haskell, Costill, Milburn, & Kerlan, 1976), the cardiovascular function in women's basketball (Sinning, 1973); the functional capacity in top weightlifters, swimmers, runners, and skiers (Ŝprynarová & Parîzková, 1971); and the working capacity of young competitive swimmers (Cunningham & Eynon, 1973).

This study is a modest contribution toward the formulation of the biological profile of elite athletes and the identification of those characteristics which are considered to determine outstanding athletic performance.

## Methods

A total of 590 elite athletes (476 males and 114 females), members of the Greek national teams in 19 different Olympic sports, were tested in our Institute from 1979-1983 (Table 1).

**Table 1.** Sex, age, weight, and height of Greek elite athletes in various Olympic sports

| Sport | Sex | n | Age (yr) | | | Weight (kg) | | | Height (cm) | | |
|-------|-----|---|------|---|-----|------|---|------|-------|---|------|
| Long-distance | | | | | | | | | | | |
| running | M | 18 | 21.5 | ± | 3.2 | 64 | ± | 4.1 | 173.8 | ± | 4.2 |
| | F | 9 | 18.5 | ± | 1.0 | 50.7 | ± | 4.9 | 159.3 | ± | 6.3 |
| Cycling | M | 14 | 23.1 | ± | 4.7 | 68 | ± | 3.7 | 176.2 | ± | 5.5 |
| Pentathlon | | | | | | | | | | | |
| modern | M | 8 | 21.2 | ± | 3.6 | 65.3 | ± | 5.5 | 173 | ± | 4.8 |
| Boxing | M | 33 | 20.6 | ± | 3.4 | 67.8 | ± | 11 | 171.1 | ± | 7.3 |
| Swimming | M | 74 | 14.2 | ± | 2.4 | 59.5 | ± | 11.8 | 167.5 | ± | 10 |
| | F | 78 | 13.7 | ± | 2.1 | 54 | ± | 9.7 | 161.5 | ± | 6.6 |
| Soccer | M | 59 | 25.3 | ± | 3.1 | 76.4 | ± | 5.4 | 178.2 | ± | 4.8 |
| | M | 9 | 16.3 | ± | 2.7 | 60.4 | ± | 9.4 | 171.9 | ± | 9.6 |
| | F | 5 | 15.6 | ± | 1.5 | 60.1 | ± | 5.8 | 164.4 | ± | 4.4 |
| Handball | M | 24 | 19.3 | ± | 1.3 | 75.6 | ± | 8 | 180.6 | ± | 5 |
| Rowing | M | 25 | 19.9 | ± | 3 | 83.7 | ± | 5.5 | 184 | ± | 4.9 |
| Wrestling | M | 23 | 21.6 | ± | 3.5 | 73 | ± | 13 | 169.7 | ± | 7.1 |
| Water polo | M | 48 | 21.5 | ± | 4.4 | 78.2 | ± | 8.5 | 178.2 | ± | 7.2 |
| Basketball | M | 32 | 20.3 | ± | 4.1 | 87.5 | ± | 9.5 | 191.3 | ± | 32.6 |
| | F | 14 | 19.8 | ± | 1.7 | 66 | ± | 10.2 | 174.5 | ± | 6 |
| Gymnastics | M | 4 | 19.5 | ± | 1.3 | 70.1 | ± | 5.6 | 178.7 | ± | 5.6 |
| Volleyball | M | 19 | 20.5 | ± | 4.3 | 77.4 | ± | 6.7 | 188.4 | ± | 6.3 |
| Fencing | M | 6 | 21.7 | ± | 6 | 71.5 | ± | 7.4 | 180.5 | ± | 7.3 |
| Judo | M | 15 | 19.9 | ± | 3.2 | 69.3 | ± | 8.2 | 172 | ± | 8.3 |
| Sailing | M | 19 | 27 | ± | 5 | 80.7 | ± | 8.8 | 178.1 | ± | 5.6 |
| Weight lifting | M | 17 | 22.7 | ± | 3.2 | 89.2 | ± | 18.7 | 172 | ± | 7.7 |
| Shooting | M | 29 | 31.2 | ± | 10.6 | 76.7 | ± | 12.8 | 172.7 | ± | 7.2 |
| | F | 8 | 24.1 | ± | 6.8 | 59.8 | ± | 9.3 | 166 | ± | 7.5 |

The physical performance capacity of all subjects was evaluated by continuously monitoring their gas exchange and heart rate while they ran on a treadmill with increasing intensity (Beckman MMC system and an ECG telemetry system, simultaneously operating with a Phillips electrocardiograph). The exercise consisted of an initial familiarization period of walking and running, followed by a run at zero elevation for 5 min at a speed of 8 kmh $^{-1}$ for females and 10 kmh$^{-1}$ for males, which increased to 12 kmh $^{-1}$ and 15 kmh$^{-1}$, respectively for a further 3 min. Thereafter, speed remained unchanged, while elevation was progressively increased at 2.5% grade every minute until the subject was unable to continue the effort.

The cyclists performed maximal exercise on a mechanically braked bicycle ergometer with 60 rpm with load increments of 360 kpm/min applied every 2 min.

Maximal anaerobic capacity was assessed from lactate production. For this purpose a blood sample (50-100$\mu$l) was taken from an arterialized fingertip exactly after the 4th minute of maximal effort and lactic acid concentration was determined on an automatic lactate analyzer (LA-640, Kontron-Roche) using a method modified in our Institute (Tsarouchas, Tsopanakis, & Klissouras, 1983).

Tachodynamic properties of the lower extremities were measured as follows: Maximal muscular strength (F max) was measured by an electronic strain gauge at a fixed knee joint angle of 90°. An electronic barotachometer was used for the assessment of vertical jump, that is, the explosive strength (h max), which was performed without initial motion, with a 0.30 m acceleration distance. Maximal cycling frequency contraction (f max) was estimated using an electronic frequency meter, while the subject reached maximal pedaling frequency on a bicycle erogmoter without load.

## Results and Discussion

The average ($\dot{V}O_2$ max) values of male athletes in the different sports are graphically presented in Figure 1. It can be seen that distance runners and cyclists had the highest values while shooters and weightlifters had the lowest.

In general, athletes engaged in sports with high aerobic demands tend to demonstrate a high ($\dot{V}O_2$ max), which is in good agreement with the literature (Costill, 1970; Wilmore et al., 1976).

The difference in ($\dot{V}O_2$ max between the wrestlers, weightlifters, and swimmers, and those tested by other researchers is small (Costill, 1967, Cunningham & Eynon, 1973; Shephard, Godin & Campbell, 1974; Sinning, 1973). The gymnasts and cyclists in this study had substantially lower values than those reported by others (Conger & Macnab, 1967; Gollnick et al., 1972).

Figure 2 shows the results for female athletes who follow a similar trend to male athletes. The difference between males and females in different sports range from 9% (basketball) to 24% (distance running).

With respect to the maximal anaerobic capacity, as is noted in Figure 3, athletes of modern pentathlon produced the highest blood lactate, while high values were also observed for soccer players, rowers, and runners. Judo and weightlifting athletes produced the lowest values.

Comparing these results with those for female athletes, no significant difference was found in swimming, while long-distance runners had 18% lower values. It is interesting to note that our soccer players produced the same amounts of lactate during maximal effort as the German soccer national team (Nowacki & De Castro, 1984).

With respect to the tachodynamic properties (Table 2), there is a tendency for both male and female athletes who engage in speed events to have higher maximal muscular strength and power than those who engage in endurance events. This observation is also in agreement with existing theories. International comparisons are difficult to make for tachodynamic properties, because there are wide differences and approaches in their assessments.

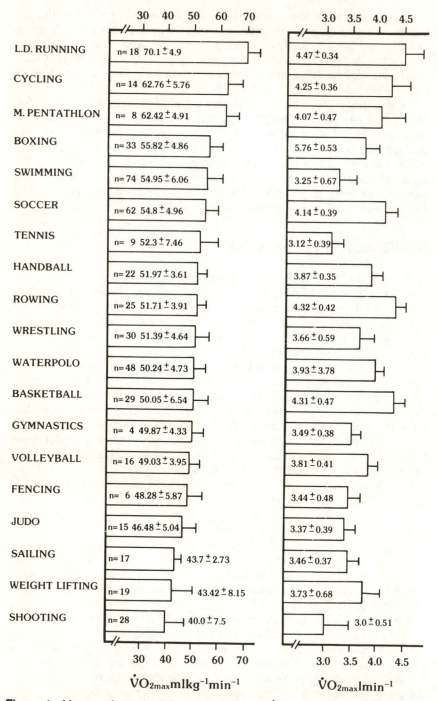

Figure 1. Mean and standard deviation values of ($\dot{V}O_2$ max) obtained from male Greek elite athletes in various Olympic sports. ($\dot{V}O_2$) = maximal oxygen uptake.

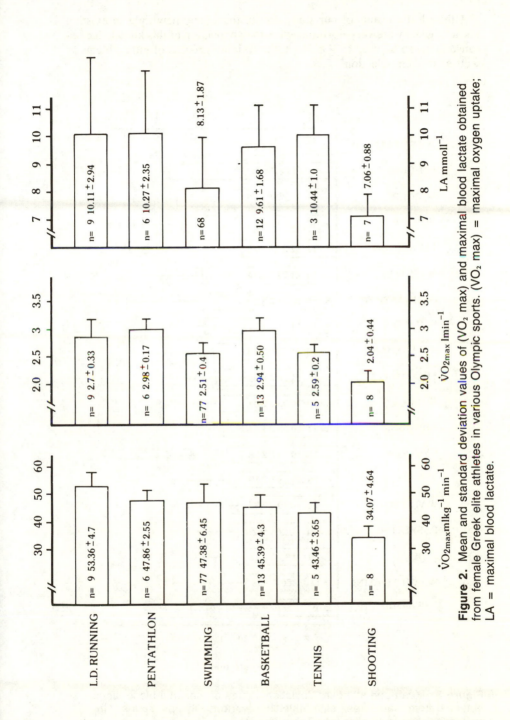

**Figure 2.** Mean and standard deviation values of ($\dot{V}O_2$ max) and maximal blood lactate obtained from female Greek elite athletes in various Olympic sports. ($\dot{V}O_2$ max) = maximal oxygen uptake; LA = maximal blood lactate.

Although the results of our study do not throw any new light in existing knowledge they are very instrumental in the application of this knowledge because they can be used as a guide in the training process of elite athletes as well as in their selection.

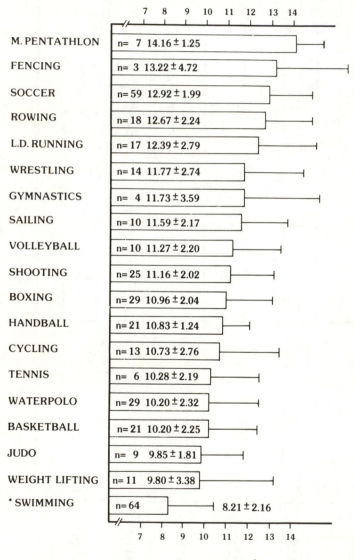

**Figure 3.** Mean and standard deviation values of maximal blood lactate obtained from male Greek elite athletes in various Olympic sports. *In swimming, age is smaller (see Table 1).

**Table 2.** Tachodynamic properties (*M ± SD*) of male and female Greek elite athletes in various Olympic sports: maximal muscular strength (Fmax), maximal explosive strength (hmax) and maximal cycling frequency (fmax)

| Sport | Sex | n | hmax(m) | n | fmax (Hertz) | n | Fmax/BW |
|---|---|---|---|---|---|---|---|
| Long-distance running | M | 14 | 0.343 ± 0.047 | 15 | 3.42 ± 0.30 | 15 | 2.71 ± 0.47 |
|  | F | 4 | 0.297 ± 0.04 | 4 | 3.08 ± 0.36 | 4 | 2.26 ± 0.22 |
| Cycling | M | 14 | 0.329 ± 0.064 | 9 | 3.80 ± 0.29 | 9 | 2.66 ± 0.45 |
| Modern pentathlon | M | 8 | 0.367 ± 0.039 | 8 | 3.85 ± 0.2 | 8 | 2.65 ± 0.37 |
|  | F | 4 | 0.367 ± 0.04 | 4 | 3.51 ± 0.04 | 4 | 2.56 ± 0.20 |
| Boxing | M | 9 | 0.360 ± 0.048 | 9 | 3.48 ± 0.12 | 9 | 3.02 ± 0.47 |
| Swimming | M | 21 | 0.334 ± 0.047 | 25 | 3.31 ± 0.27 | 26 | 2.27 ± 0.32 |
|  | F | 24 | 0.285 ± 0.029 | 25 | 2.77 ± 0.27 | 28 | 2.04 ± 0.26 |
| Soccer | M | 55 | 0.419 ± 0.040 | 55 | 3.53 ± 0.25 | 55 | 3.13 + 0.42 |
| Tennis | M | 5 | 0.306 ± 0.064 | 2 | 3.52 ± 0.19 | 5 | 2.16 ± 0.26 |
| Handball | M | 23 | 0.345 ± 0.046 | 23 | 3.60 ± 0.29 | 23 | 2.85 ± 0.5 |
| Rowing | M | 18 | 0.377 ± 0.043 | 12 | 3.67 ± 0.19 | 18 | 2.67 ± 0.42 |
| Wrestling | M | 14 | 0.385 ± 0.060 | 13 | 3.71 ± 0.31 | 14 | 3.24 ± 0.48 |
| Basketball | M | 23 | 0.410 ± 0.030 | 25 | 3.45 ± 0.27 | 24 | 2.51 ± 0.34 |
|  | F | 12 | 0.357 ± 0.027 | 14 | 3.18 ± 0.4 | 13 | 2.45 ± 0.35 |
| Volleyball | M | 9 | 0.478 ± 0.056 | 9 | 3.50 ± 0.32 | 8 | 2.81 ± 0.56 |
| Fencing | M | 3 | 0.433 ± 0.029 | 3 | 3.49 ± 0.10 | 3 | 3.14 ± 0.20 |
| Judo | M | 10 | 0.394 ± 0.039 | 8 | 3.67 ± 0.28 | 10 | 2.98 ± 0.52 |
| Sailing | M | 5 | 0.380 ± 0.030 | 5 | 3.61 ± 0.32 | 5 | 2.86 ± 0.10 |
| Weight lifting | M | 12 | 0.423 ± 0.053 | 12 | 3.61 ± 0.28 | 12 | 3.93 ± 0.78 |
| Shooting | M | 14 | 0.323 ± 0.065 | 14 | 3.29 ± 0.28 | 10 | 2.07 ± 0.29 |

# References

Bührle, M., & Schmidtbleicher, D. (1981). Komponenten der maximal-und schnellkraft. In H. Schorndorf (Ed.), *Sportwissenschaft,* 11 Jahrgang, 1.

Conger, P.R., & Macnab, R.B.J. (1967). Strength, body composition and work capacity of participants and nonparticipants in women's intercollegiate sports. *Research Quarterly,* 38, 184-192.

Costill, D.L. (1967). The relationship between selected physiological variables and distance running performance. *Journal of Sports Medicine,* 7, 61-66.

Costill, D.L. (1970). Metabolic responses during distance running. *Journal of Applied Physiology,* 28, 251-255.

Cunningham, D.A., & Eynon, R.B. (1973). The working capacity of young competitive swimmers, 10-16 years of age. *Medical Science in Sports,* 5, 227-231.

Gollnick, P.D. (1973). Biochemical adaptations to exercise: Anaerobic metabolism. In J.H. Wilmore (Ed.), *Exercise and Sport Sciences Reviews* (Vol. 1). New York: Academic Press.

Gollnick, P.D., Armstrong, R.B., Saubert, C.W. IV, Piehl, K., & Saltin, B. (1972). Enzyme activity and fiber composition in skeletal muscle of untrained and trained men. *Journal of Applied Physiology,* 33, 312-319.

Milvy, P. (Ed.). (1977). The marathon: Physiological, medical, epidemiological and psychological studies. *Annals of the New York Academy of Sciences,* 301.

Nowacki, P.E., & De Castro, P. (1984). Development of the biological performance of German National Football Teams. In N. Bachl, L. Prokop, & R. Suckert (Eds.), *Current topics in sports medicine* (pp. 560-575). Wien-Baltimore: Urban & Schwarzenberg.

Shephard, R.J., Godin, G., & Campbell, R. (1974). Characteristics of sprint, medium and long-distance swimmers. *European Journal of Applied Physiology,* 32, 99-116.

Sinning, W.E. (1973). Body composition, cardiovascular function, and rule changes in women's basketball. *Research Quarterly,* 44, 313-321.

Skinner, J.S., & McLellan, T.H. (1980). The transition from aerobic to anaerobic metabolism. *Research Quarterly for Exercise and Sport,* 51, 234-248.

Šprynarová, S., & Parîzková, J. (1971). Functional capacity and body compostion in top weight-lifters, swimmers, runners, and skiers. *International Zeitschrift Angew Physiology,* 29, 184-194.

Tsarouchas, E., Tsopanakis, A.D., & Klissouras, V. (1983). In H. Melerowicz & W. Franz (Eds.), *Standardisierung Kalibrierung und Methodic in der Ergometrie.* Berlin: Fachubach-Verlagsgesellschaft.

Wilmore, J.H., Parr, R.B., Haskell, W.L., Costill, D.L., Milburn, L.J., & Kerlan, R.K. (1976). Athletic profile of professional football players. *The Physician and Sportsmedicine* 4, 45-54.

# 20

# *Assessing the Motivations of Athletes: Further Tests of Butt's Theory*

*Craig A. Wrisberg, Thomas J. Donovan, Susan E. Britton, and Samuel J. Ewing*
THE UNIVERSITY OF TENNESSEE
KNOXVILLE, TENNESSEE, USA

Although the topic of athletic motivation has traditionally stimulated much interest among coaches, performers, and sport scientists, systematic theorizing on the subject has been minimal. Such a state of affairs may be due in some part to a general dearth of theory formulation and testing in experimental sport psychology (see Landers, 1983, for a more complete discussion). However, the topic of sport motivation appears to be even less developed theoretically than the other areas of inquiry in the psychological study of sport (e.g., arousal-performance theory, attribution theory , leadership theory, social facilitation theory).

The complexity of the concept of motivation (see Alderman, 1974; Atkinson, 1968; Lawther, 1978; Singer, 1980; Youngblood & Suinn, 1980, for more thorough discussions of this topic) has likely discouraged theorizing by sport scientists to some degree. Alderman's (1974) interpretation of the concept typifies the broad approach taken by most scholars. According to Alderman (1974, p. 186), motivation should be viewed in reference to the "tendency for the direction and selectivity of behavior to be controlled by its connections to consequences, and the tendency of this behavior to persist until a goal is achieved." From this perspective the emphasis is clearly on the purposive characteristics of a person's actions. In keeping with this view, one approach to the study of sport motivation has been to identify the motives that influence the pursuits of elite athletes.

In her theory of sport motivation, Butt (1973, 1976) has proposed a variety of motivations that might affect the behavior of performers. The primary fo-

185

cus of the theory is on relationships predicted between various types of psychological and social motivations. While low to moderate relationships are proposed between aggression (psychological) and cooperation (social), conflict (psychological) and cooperation (social), and competence (psychological) and competition (social), the psychological motivations of aggression and conflict are predicted to be strongly related to the social motivation of competition, while the psychological motivation of competence is expected to have strong association with the social motivation of cooperation.

Butt's (1976) theory appears to be well-conceived. Most importantly it is testable, containing a number of clear-cut predictions and offering an instrument that may be used to assess the strength and direction of relationships among proposed psychological and social motivations that have the potential to influence the sporting behavior of athletes. Surprisingly, there have been few tests of Butt's theory. To our knowledge, the only published reports of research findings have taken the form of summary statements of investigations (e.g., Butt, 1979a) with, in some cases, suggested applications for sport practitioners (e.g., Butt, 1980). To date, the only detailed research conducted to test predictions of the theory was performed to determine the reliability and stability of items included in the *Short Scales* (Butt, 1979b). In this experiment 67 males and 121 females were tested. Of the total sample surveyed, 115 subjects were university students involved in various sporting and leisure activities (e.g., jogging, tennis, skiing, and ice-hockey). The remainder of the subjects were members of a competitive swimming club. The results suggested some support for the relationships between psychological and social motivations predicted by Butt (1976). For females, significant ($p < .005$) relationships were found between the motivations of aggression and competition, conflict and competition, and competence and cooperation. Except for a lower level of significance obtained for the aggression-competition relationship ($p < .05$), the same pattern of results was obtained for males. The only finding that did not support Butt's predictions was a significant ($p < .005$) correlation between aggression and cooperation for females.

In short, the available literature dealing with Butt's theory of sport motivation represents insufficient evidence to suggest generalization of the predicted relationships among psychological and social motivations to athletes of different ages and/or sports. While the simplicity of the theory has definite appeal, it remains to be determined whether its predictions can account for substantial sources of variation in the motivations of athletes. The purpose of the present study, then, was to determine the generalizability of the relationships between psychological and social motivations predicted by Butt to elite athletes of various ages and representing a variety of competitive sports.

## Methods

### Subjects

The data for the study were collected between the summer of 1982 and the spring of 1983. A total of 370 subjects (243 females and 127 males) completed Butt's (1979b) *Short Scales for the Measurement of Sport Motivations* and a sport-specific questionnaire. The subjects were divided into the following categories: 185 female age-group gymnasts; 36 female junior-elite gymnasts; 12 female Division I university varsity swimmers; 10 female age-group swimmers; 17 male age-group swimmers; and 110 male professional baseball players. The subjects' ages ranged from 10-28 years, consisent with those reported by Butt (1979b). Informed consent statements were obtained from all subjects.

## Procedures

Most testing was completed during the noncompetitive season. The age-group gymnasts were involved with gymnastics exhibitions given during the 1982 World's Fair in Knoxville, TN. The junior-elite gymnasts were tested during a preseason training camp. The college and age-group swimmers were tested shortly after the completion of their competitive seasons. The professional baseball players were assessed during an instructional league experience in Florida or during their AA competitive season.

An attempt was made to maintain consistent testing conditions for all groups. The testing protocol included (a) the distribution of consent forms and explanation of testing procedures (b) the distribution and completion of the sport-specific questionnaire (each sport had a unique sport-related questionnaire that was used to obtain basic demographic information and sport background data, e.g., length of time involved in the sport, number of years of formal competition, favorite or best event/position), (c) the distribution and completion of Martens's (1977) *Sport Competition Anxiety Test* (administered as part of another study, the results are not included in the present paper) and, (d) the distribution and completion of the Short Scales. The tests were distributed, and the administrator answered any questions raised by the subjects. The subjects were instructed to answer all statements or as many as were applicable to their sports.

The Short Scales instrument includes 25 statements that probe the subject's feelings about sport participation. An estimate of the strength of each of the five motivational components (aggression, conflict, competence, competition, cooperation) was obtained from subjects' responses to questions assessing that component. Subjects responded by marking "yes" or "no" to each question, with a "yes" scored as a "1" and a "no" as a zero. Five questions were designated to assess the strength of each of the five motivational components. Thus, scores estimating the strength of each component for each subject varied from zero (i.e., low) to 5 (i.e., high).

## Results

The means, standard deviations, and split-half reliability estimates of aggression, conflict, competence, competition, and cooperation items were computed for each group of athletes. In addition, Pearson product-moment correlations were calculated to determine the strength and direction of relationship between the various psychological and social motivations proposed by Butt (1976).

The means, standard deviations, and split-half reliabilities for questions on the Short Scales for each motivational component for each group are presented in Table 1.

For comparative purposes descriptive statistics from Butt's (1979b) study on young competitive swimmers and recreationally active university students are also included. Butt's finding of an unusually low competition score for females was not replicated by the scores of females tested in this study. Except for the lower conflict scores of the female junior-elite gymnasts, the mean values for each of the motivational components were generally higher than those obtained by Butt. Of particular note were the high conflict and competition scores of the female collegiate swimmers and the high cooperation scores for all groups tested.

Split-half reliabilities fluctuated considerably more than those reported by Butt. Coefficients were uniformly lower for the aggression items than for those estimating the other components, ranging from .10 for female age-group gymnasts to .42 for female age-group swimmers. With the exception of the female collegiate swimmers, reliabilities were higher and more consistent (range = .53 - .71) for conflict items. Questions assessing the remaining motivational components were characterized by uneven correlations across groups. In each case, reliability coefficients for most of the groups were uniformly high, but those of one or two groups were extremely low. For competence items the low-reliability groups were the female age-group gymnasts and the male professional baseball players. For competition questions and cooperation items the reliability coefficients of female junior-elite gymnasts and male professional baseball players were atypically low.

In order to test the strength of the interrelationships predicted in Butt's model, product-moment correlations were computed. Responses for items measuring each of the three psychological motivations (aggression, conflict, and competence) were correlated with those estimating levels of each of the two social motivations (competition and cooperation). The resulting correlations for each of the sport groups in the present study along with those reported by Butt (1979b) are presented in Table 2.

## Aggression and Competition

Butt's prediction that aggression is strongly related to competition received mild support from the present correlational data. Correlations obtained for the groups with large sample sizes (i.e., female age-group gymnasts and male professional baseball players) were similar (in size and level of significance) to those she found. However, the only other group for which the aggression-competition correlation approached significance was male age-group swimmers. Coefficients for the remaining groups were low, and three of the four were negative.

## Aggression and Cooperation

According to Butt, the motivational components of aggression and cooperation should not be strongly (positively) related. However, she reported a significant correlation for these components for females. A similar finding was obtained for female collegiate swimmers in the present study. The only other

**Table 1.** Means, standard deviations, and split-half reliability coefficients for questions measuring each motivational component

| Group | Aggression | | | Conflict | | | Motivational Component Competence | | | Competition | | | Cooperation | | |
|---|---|---|---|---|---|---|---|---|---|---|---|---|---|---|---|
| | M | SD | $r_{tt}$ | M | SD | $r_{tt}$ | M | SD | $r_{tt}$ | M | SD | $r_{tt}$ | M | SD | $r_{tt}$ |
| Butt (1979b) | | | | | | | | | | | | | | | |
| Males (n = 67) | 2.7 | 1.4 | .51 | 2.4 | 1.4 | .60 | 2.3 | 1.4 | .56 | 2.7 | 1.6 | .72 | 3.8 | 1.4 | .68 |
| Females (n = 121) | 2.4 | 1.3 | .43 | 2.3 | 1.5 | .57 | 2.2 | 1.5 | .59 | 1.7 | 1.7 | .75 | 3.3 | 1.5 | .66 |
| Age-group gymnasts | | | | | | | | | | | | | | | |
| Females (n = 185) | 3.0[a] | 1.1[a] | .10[a] | 2.9 | 1.4 | .58 | 3.9 | 1.1 | .30 | 3.2 | 1.4 | .63 | 4.6 | 0.8 | .49 |
| Junior-elite gymnasts | | | | | | | | | | | | | | | |
| Females (n = 36) | 2.7 | 1.0 | .14 | 2.2 | 1.6 | .71 | 3.8 | 1.4 | .70 | 2.5 | 1.0 | .10 | 4.4 | 0.7 | .03 |
| Collegiate Swimmers | | | | | | | | | | | | | | | |
| Females (n = 12) | 3.1[b] | 1.3[b] | .13[b] | 4.6 | 0.8 | .25 | 2.8 | 1.9 | .74 | 4.1[b] | 1.3[b] | .68[b] | 4.2 | 1.5 | .92 |
| Age-group swimmers | | | | | | | | | | | | | | | |
| Males (n = 17) | 3.1 | 1.5 | .24 | 2.5 | 1.5 | .56 | 2.8 | 1.4 | .54 | 3.1[c] | 1.6[c] | .74[c] | 4.1[c] | 1.4 | .75 |
| Females (n = 10) | 2.9 | 1.6 | .42 | 3.3 | 1.5 | .68 | 2.7 | 1.3 | .53 | 2.8 | 1.0 | .77 | 3.8[d] | 1.4[d] | .94[d] |
| Professional baseball players | | | | | | | | | | | | | | | |
| Males (n = 110) | 3.2 | 1.3 | .36 | 2.9 | 1.4 | .53 | 3.6 | 1.0 | .16 | 3.5 | 0.9 | .04 | 4.7 | 0.7 | .27 |

[a] n = 179. [b] n = 11. [c] n = 15. [d] n = 16.

**Table 2.** Correlations of each of the three psychological motivations (aggression, conflict, and competence) with each of the two social motivations (competition and cooperation)

| Group | Aggression | | Conflict | | Competence | |
|---|---|---|---|---|---|---|
| | Comp | Coop | Comp | Coop | Comp | Coop |
| Butt (1979b) | | | | | | |
|   Males ($n = 67$) | .25* | .03 | .44*** | .04 | .06 | .35*** |
|   Females ($n = 121$) | .43*** | .26*** | .42*** | .13 | .12 | .33*** |
| Age-group gymnasts | | | | | | |
|   Females ($n = 181$) | .29*** | − .20*** | .40*** | − .04 | .13 | .09 |
| Junior-elite gymnasts | | | | | | |
|   Females ($n = 36$) | − .08 | .30 | .12 | .04 | − .03 | − .01 |
| Collegiate swimmers | | | | | | |
|   Females ($n = 12$) | − .23 | .56* | .42 | − .36 | − .57* | .45 |
| Age-group swimmers | | | | | | |
|   Males ($n = 17$) | .40[a] | − .03[b] | .36[a] | .04[b] | .04[b] | .25[b] |
|   Females ($n = 10$) | − .42 | .09 | .19 | − .07 | .27 | − .04 |
| Professional baseball players | | | | | | |
|   Males ($n = 110$) | .32** | .15 | .33** | .05 | .19* | .31** |

*Note.* Comp = competition; Coop = cooperation.
[a]$n = 15$.  [b]$n = 16$.  *$p < .05$.  **$p < .01$.  ***$p < .005$.

significant relationship was negative, occurring for the group of female age-group gymnasts. The latter correlation, as well as the low and nonsignificant coefficients obtained for the other groups, offered more impressive support for Butt's prediction.

## Conflict and Competition

The strong relationship between conflict and competition components predicted by Butt was again found only for the large-sample groups. The correlations for both female age-group gymnasts and male professional baseball players revealed a significant association between these two motivational components. Such results are consistent with those reported by Butt. For the remainder of the groups correlations were mildly positive, but none were statistically significant.

## Conflict and Cooperation

The strongest support for the various motivational relationsips predicted by Butt was the "nonfinding" of a significant correlation between conflict and cooperation for any of the groups. This was accompanied by very little variation in the size of the coefficients across groups.

## Competence and Competition

For the most part the correlations between competence and competition were low and nonsignificant, as predicted by Butt. A significant negative correlation found for female university swimmers also suggested support for Butt's prediction. The only significant positive correlation was obtained for male professional baseball players.

## Competence and Cooperation

In her model of sport motivation, Butt predicts that athletes who are motivated by competence at the psychological level will be motivated by cooperation at the social level. Results she has reported support this prediction. The data of the present study, however, suggested a weaker association between these two components. For most groups, correlations were low and positive with the only significant association obtained for male professional baseball players.

# Discussion

The results of the present study appear to offer modest support for Butt's theory of sport motivation. Regarding those components which she predicts should be strongly related, several significant correlations were obtained. However, in all cases statistical significance was found only for those groups represented by large (i.e., $n > 50$) sample sizes. Thus, given the modest size of these correlations (range of significant $r$'s = .29 - .40) it might be speculated that increased sample size was an important determinant of statistical significance (Steel & Torrie, 1960).

Perhaps more compelling for Butt's model was the finding of consistently lower correlations between the motivational variables which are predicted to be weakly associated according to the theory. Most impressive was the uniformly low and nonsignificant relationship between conflict and cooperation obtained for all groups. Similar correlational patterns were found for the relationships between aggression and cooperation and between competence and competition. In the case of the aggression-cooperation coefficients only those obtained for female intercollegiate swimmers deviated from the patterns of nonsignificant correlations. Similarly, a significant association between competence and competition was obtained only for the group of male professional baseball players. Of additional interest in the analysis of relationship between aggression and cooperation and between competence and competition was the finding of one significant negative correlation in each case. For female age-group gymnasts aggression was negatively related to cooperation and for female intercollegiate swimmers competence was negatively associated with competition. Both findings suggest that the motivational combination of aggression and cooperation as well as that of competence and competition may at times be incompatible.

In light of the split-half reliability coefficients obtained for questionnaire items representing the various motivational components, the correlational data from the present study must be viewed with some caution. Of particular note were the consistently low reliability values found for the group of items representing the motivational component of aggression. Subjective reports from subjects revealed a lack of comprehension of the exact intent of certain aggression statements, particularly those depicted by one word (e.g., "impulsive" and "powerful"). During administration of the Short Scales, clarification of such terms was often necessary, particularly for younger subjects. One step toward increasing the clarity of questions might be to expand single word descriptions of aggression into more explicit statements. Of perhaps more fundamental concern for Butt's theory is the fact that the present findings as well as the results of other studies on sport motivation have revealed that aggression lacks strength as a motive for performers in both individual sports and in physical contact sports (see Alderman, 1978, for discussion). Thus, the status of aggression as a sport motivation remains somewhat equivocal.

One other aspect of the pattern of reliabilities obtained for the clusters of questions representing the various motivational components involved the larger range in the size of coefficients among the various groups. For example, the coefficient for competition items obtained for female age-group swimmers was .77 while that found for male professional baseball players was .04. Such a discrepancy suggests that performers of different ages, genders, and/or those who participate in different sports may interpret the meaning of question differently. Moreover, it is possible that questions which have relevance for an athlete from one sport (e.g., gymnastics) may be inappropriate for a performer from another sport (e.g., baseball). For example, the question "Did you ever feel determined to come in first?" may have special meaning for a gymnast who performs on the balance beam, but have an uncertain connotation for a shortstop in baseball. In a similar vein several subjects indicated that their responses to questions would have been different if "participating" had been interpreted as "training" rather than as "competing"; yet the preliminary statement on the Short Scales questionnaire includes *both* training and competing in the initial instructions to subjects. It reads "During the last month while participating (training or competing) in (fill in *one* sport) did you ever feel _____?" Thus, it appears that additional testing is needed to assess the connotations of various questions for different categories of performers.

In spite of the fact that sport motivation is a multivariate phenomenon, evidence suggests that some delimitation of the important motivational factors influencing involvement in an activity is possible. Of the three psychological and two social components of sport motivation proposed by Butt, several have been implicated in the research of other investigators. The factor of competence is particularly pervasive in the literature on motivation. Deci (1975) has suggested that intrinsically motivated behavior stems from a person's need to feel competent in his or her environment. That sport settings represent an environment in which competence may be expressed is suggested in the results of research by Roberts, Kleiber, and Duda (1981). They found that fourth- and fifth-grade males and females who were participants in organized sports had higher levels of perceived competence than did nonparticipants. In a similar investigation involving a large sample of eighth- and ninth-grade females Nicholson (1979) found that regular sport participants expressed more concern about playing well in athletic contests than did nonparticipants. Taken together these findings suggest that an important motivation for sport involvement stems from the perception that athletics affords one with an opportunity to demonstrate competence.

Further research in sport motivation must be characterized by a sensitivity to the needs of athletes which might be met in sport settings. In this regard the theoretical efforts of Birch and Veroff (1966) warrant serious consideration. They have proposed seven major incentive systems that purportedly account for the goal-directed behavior all people engage in. The assumption underlying this proposal is that the needs of people are reflected in their resulting behaviors or actions. The choice of any particular action is presumed to be associated with specific incentives that are attractive (i.e., those to which value is attached) to the person *at the moment*. Research that has been conducted to determine the incentive systems that characterize athletic populations has revealed that the systems of "excellence" (i.e., achievement) and "affiliation" are consistently the strongest (Alderman, 1978; Alderman & Wood, 1976). In discussing achievement as an incentive, Alderman (1976, p. 213) suggested that "in our culture this is probably the master incentive system working in sport as we know it." From the standpoint of Butt's model it should also be noted that competence is often highly related to the motive to achieve. Of perhaps some concern to Butt's theory is her omission of the incentive of affiliation. It is of course possible that some underlying commonality exists between the concept of affiliation and Butt's social component of cooperation. However, Alderman (1976) has pointed out that the two most powerful affiliation incentives are both negative; specifically, the fear of rejection and the fear of social isolation. Given the positive connotation usually associated with the term "cooperation," it is possible that some revision of this motivational component may be necessary.

In summary, the results of the present study offer some encouragement for the future of research testing Butt's model of sport motivation. However, some revision of the theoretical notions underlying the five motivational components proposed by Butt may be necessary to provide a more complete picture of the patterns of motivation which shape the decisions and behaviors of athletes. It is suggested that Birch and Veroff's (1966) thinking on incentive systems might be profitably utilized to modify the motivational constructs proposed by Butt. Of primary importance is the identification of those motivational components or incentive systems which have potential salience for sport performers at any given moment. Only then will determination of the level of motivational consistencies across performers of various ages, genders, sports, and skill levels be possible.

# References

Alderman, R.B. (1974). *Psychological behavior in sport*. Philadelphia: W.B. Saunders.

Alderman, R.B. (1976). Incentive motivation in sport: An interpretive speculation of research opportunities. In A.C. Fisher (Ed.), *Psychology of sport* (pp. 205-221). Palo Alto, CA: Mayfield.

Alderman, R.B. (1978). Strategies for motivating young athletes. In W.F. Straub (Ed.), *Sport psychology: An analysis of athlete behavior* (pp. 49-61). Ithaca, NY: Mouvement Publications.

Alderman, R.B., & Wood, N.L. (1976). An analysis of incentive motivation in young Canadian athletes. *Canadian Journal of Applied Sport Sciences*, **1**, 169-176.

Atkinson, J.W. (1968). *Motives in fantasy, action, and society*. Princeton, NJ: Van Nostrand.

Birch, D., & Veroff, J. (1966). *Motivation: A study of action*. Belmont, CA: Brooks-Cole.

Butt, D.S. (1973). Aggression, neuroticism, and competence: Theoretical models for the study of sports motivation. *International Journal of Sport Psychology*, **4**, 3-15.

Butt, D.S. (1976). *Psychology of sport: The behavior, motivation, personality, and performance of athletes*. New York: Van Nostrand Reinhold.

Butt, D.S. (1979a). The psychologist's contribution to sport organization and the athlete: An example. In P. Klavora & J. V. Daniel (Eds.), *Coach, athlete, and the sport psychologist* (pp. 74-81). Champaign, IL: Human Kinetics.

Butt, D.S. (1979b). Short scales for the measurement of sport motivations. *International Journal of Sport Psychology*, **10**, 203-216.

Butt, D.S. (1980). What can psychology offer to the athlete and the coach? In R.M. Suinn (Ed.), *Psychology in sports: Methods and applications* (pp. 78-85). Minneapolis, MN: Burgess.

Deci, E.L. (1975). *Intrinsic motivation*. New York: Plenum Press.

Landers, D.M. (1983). What ever happened to theory testing in sport psychology? *Journal of Sport Psychology*, **5**, 135-151.

Lawther, J.D. (1978). Developmental stages for motivation in sport. In W.F. Straub (Ed.), *Sport psychology: An analysis of athlete behavior* (pp. 86-95). Ithaca, NY: Mouvement Publications.

Martens, R. (1977). *The Sport Competition Anxiety Test*. Champaign, IL: Human Kinetics.

Nicholson, C.S. (1979). Some attitudes associated with sport participation among junior high school females. *Research Quarterly*, **50**, 661-667.

Roberts, G.C., Kleiber, D.A., & Duda, J.L. (1981). An analysis of motivation in children's sport: The role of perceived competence in participation. *Journal of Sport Psychology*, **3**, 206-216.

Singer, R.N. (1980). Motivation in sport. In R.M. Suinn (Ed.), *Psychology in sports: Methods and applications* (pp. 40-55). Minneapolis, MN: Burgess.

Steel, R.G., & Torrie, J.H. (1960). *Principles and procedures of statistics*. New York: McGraw-Hill.

Youngblood, D., & Suinn, R.M. (1980). A behavioral assessment of motivation. In R.M. Suinn (Ed.), *Psychology in sports: Methods and applications* (pp. 73-77). Minneapolis, MN: Burgess.